Blessed Bi Spirit

Blessed Bi Spirit

Bisexual People of Faith

Edited
by
DEBRA R. KOLODNY

Continuum
New York London

2000

The Continuum International Publishing Group Inc
370 Lexington Avenue, New York, NY 10017

The Continuum International Publishing Group Inc
Wellington House, 125 Strand, London WC2R 0BB

Printed in the United States of America

Library of Congress Cataloging-in-Publication Data

Blessed bi spirit : bisexual people of faith / edited by Debra R. Kolodny.
p. cm.
Includes bibliographical references.
ISBN 0-8264-1231-9 (pbk.)
1. Bisexuals—Religious life. I. Kolodny, Debra R.

BL625.9.B57 B54 2000
291.1'783765—dc21

99-057312

Contents

Acknowledgments

SHEPHERDING THIS WORK has been a blessing. I have learned much from each contributor, delightful and courageous people all, and I have learned much about myself and my relationship with God. It was not always easy. I obviously do not share all of the opinions of all of the authors, nor do I share a practice or theology with most. Through it all I strove to ensure the authenticity of each author's voice, to accurately depict and differentiate personal experience from long-standing tradition or practice, and to honor difference. I appreciate the willingness of each author to engage in this challenging work as I endeavored to create a cogent and respectful whole. Thank you.

Being offered the stewardship of this project was itself a tremendous gift. Thank you to Amanda Udis-Kessler, who conceived of this work and conducted initial calls for submissions, only to decide that she could not continue. Words are not sufficient to express my gratitude for the opportunity to deepen my path with this project.

To my friends and family who supported me in the long gestation process, to my Rosh Chodesh group who conducted ritual with me, to my partner, Ken, who was my in-house computer guru and technical support, and to all of those who journey with me on my path . . . you are an inspiration to me one and all.

Baruch HaShem. Blessed be the Name.

Foreword: Conjectures of a Supportive Bi-Stander

MARY E. HUNT

LET ME JUST ADMIT IT UP FRONT. I used to joke that being bisexual meant having sex twice a year, or, less creatively, that bi-sexuals were people who bought sex. Such jokes were a way for righteous, if beleaguered, lesbian and gay people to express a certain disdain for people whom we thought had not quite arrived, were hedging their bets, or saving their skins in a violently homo-hating environment. It was assumed that they were not helping "the cause" and might even have been hurting it some by not clearing up the ambiguity of their sexuality. Transgendered people did not enter our consciousness in those days, and if they did I can only imagine the jokes we would have conjured. "Queer" was still used derisively, not yet reclaimed as an umbrella term for all sexual outlaws who refuse to conform to rigid roles, and it certainly did not, in those unenlightened days, include bisexuals.

Fortunately, I have learned the error of my ways, namely, that such jokes only display the fears and ignorance of the jokester and show a profound disrespect for other peoples' lives. Such jokes are horizontal violence of the worst order, and the act of telling them is an example of oppressed people copying their oppressors. Now I know a little more about why I and so many committed lesbian and gay activists, including religious people who should have known better, joked about bisexuality and failed to take it with the seriousness it deserved in the past two decades. I would like to mend my ways and encourage a more mature, respectful conversation with those who will forgive the indiscretions.

As a lesbian, I am honored to join the bisexual people who are offering their reflections in this volume so that all religious communities might benefit from their wisdom. I do so as a white feminist theologian from the Catholic tradition with a preferential option for those who are marginalized. Today that includes bisexual people, who have been left aside both by heterosexuals who wrote them off as queer and by lesbian and gay people who wrote them off as undecided. Theirs is too much wisdom to waste.

Trappist monk Thomas Merton wrote a popular book entitled *Conjectures of a Guilty Bystander,* in which he claimed (in language I have updated to reflect current usage), "I do not have clear answers to current questions. I do have questions, and as a matter of fact, I think one is known better by her/his questions than by her/his answers. To make known one's questions is, no doubt, to come out in the open oneself."[1] I am not sure that he meant "come out" as we do today. Nonetheless, I have gratefully adapted his title to frame my own thinking about how the religious insights of bisexual people must be added to the mix of those who seek spiritual and political justice. It is precisely the injustice to bisexual people that I and others committed by trivializing their experiences and negating their claims to selfhood that needs to change. Religion is a good place to start. Theology, like sexuality, is complicated and contested territory.

Out of the Theological Void

Theology and spirituality articulated from the perspective of bisexual persons are long overdue. Yet virtually all bi theological reflection to date has been derivative, with "bisexual" a category tacked on reflexively to "lesbian/gay." For me and for other lesbian and gay theologians to "add bisexual and stir," as if doing so discharges our obligation to include more people and is therefore enough, is to miss the importance of being changed by every new insight. Now we too need to stop, listen and act differently because our bi friends speak.

What better reason could there be to build a new branch of theological reflection and spirituality, given that theology, understood in feminist liberation terms, begins with experience? And, what does the experience of bisexuals represent? As far as I can tell, there is no common agreement on the various and sundry categories of sex and gender, much less any consensus on what constitutes a bisexual. Even our most basic categories,

[1] Thomas Merton, *Conjectures of a Guilty Bystander* (Garden City, N.Y.: Doubleday, 1968), 5.

such as male and female, man and woman, are no longer fixed. Cross-gender or transgender people raise new, important questions. Thus, even such long-standing terms as lesbian and gay are less than clear. It could be that a male friend today will be a female friend tomorrow, causing cataclysmic conceptual shifts for the people in the relationships, mixing up what were once thought to be fixed categories. This is the fruit of tremendous work in both sexology and biology that is still only in its infancy. Attempts to dismantle "the apartheid of sex" that has so limited all of us are important justice struggles.[2]

While such long-used terms as "man" and "woman" are in flux, so too is "bisexual." In using this term, I add the proviso that we are all talking about something that is changing quickly, as science, culture, and our children's children grow. Most religions teach that the human person is finally much more than the sum of her/his parts, a useful resource for living with this profound ambiguity that characterizes contemporary knowledge about sexuality. In my tradition, when things get this complicated at least we can dig into our texts and claim, "in all things, charity." Other traditions have similar options, proving what Daniel C. Maguire calls "the renewable moral energy of religion."[3]

Theology, from a feminist liberation perspective, is the way in which religious people share insights, stories, and reflections on issues of ultimate meaning and value. It is more an art than a science, more a process than a product, more an invitation than a dictum. Although every tradition does not have one, theologies are ways we talk about what is important to us, assuming that the divine is part of the equation. Into this light we need to bring bisexual peoples' ways of believing, acting, and hoping so that the whole global community may learn something new. That is why bisexual theologies and spiritualities will, I predict, take their rightful place next to lesbian, gay, queer, and transgendered approaches.

Several Supportive Conjectures

I offer the following conjectures as food for thought in this larger theological conversation. I intend them as supportive affirmations that might be useful in moving the conversation toward deeper insights.

[2] For a provocative example of this literature, see Martine Rothblatt, *The Apartheid of Sex: A Manifesto on the Freedom of Gender* (New York: Crown, 1995).

[3] Daniel C. Maguire, "Population-Consumption-Ecology: The Triple Problematic," in

Bisexual people must speak for themselves

The history of theology is replete with instances of people speaking for others with dreadful consequences. The most obvious example is men who spoke for women for millennia in Judaism and Christianity until finally, quite recently, we women began to name our own questions and offer our own answers. Likewise, heterosexual hegemony meant that lesbian/gay people never were permitted voice (much less vote, in most instances) on religious policies and principles, directives and ethical pronouncements that pertained to us. Now that we are beginning to make some progress, including the welcome words of queer Muslims and Buddhists, queer pagans and witches, it would be a contradiction to restrict bisexual people from full expression, even if what they say calls into question and/or contradicts lesbian/gay experiences. Theology is not a game to win but a process in which to participate faithfully.

It is not that bisexual experiences as such are so unique. Issues of race, gender, economic access, physical ability, nationality, and age all shape different points of view, as does sexuality. But openness to learning from bisexual experiences is one more acknowledgment of the importance of particularity. It points out the critical need for categories to expand as people increasingly speak for themselves.

Hesitation by some lesbian/gay religious activists to hear bisexual people on their own terms likely stems from the same fear of change with which heterosexual people greeted our early efforts. If indeed one could be lesbian/gay and Christian, for example, perhaps even an ordained minister in that faith, then it seemed that certain taboos and teachings had to go by the wayside. This proposition continues to wreak havoc in many denominations and religious groups. Heterosexual people found it threatening to think that they could be lesbian/gay. Likewise, if being bisexual is acceptable, what does that mean for homosexual people? Could they also be bisexual? Surely some lesbian and gay people find asking such questions to be more than they want to explore, an understandable reaction given how difficult it has been to get this far. But it is still no excuse to abort an important conversation.

Rather than welcoming such insights as part of the unfolding mysteries of creation, many people simply add "bisexual" to a kind of laundry list of "l/g/b/t" people for whom they struggle without ever hearing the

---

Christianity and Ecology, ed. Mary Evelyn Tucker and John Grim (Cambridge, Mass.: Harvard University Press, forthcoming).

particularity of bi experiences on their own terms. I have done this in my work, erring on the side of a kind of inclusion that is really a subtle way to exclude. This is a liberal trap to be named and avoided.

The alternative is no more attractive, namely, leaving out bi until and unless bisexual people speak up, the theory being that advocacy for oneself is important. But the pernicious nature of our current situation is that we are damned if we do and damned if we don't, for which the only way out is for bisexual people to lead the way. This will take some doing since it will mean leaving aside the unspoken competition in queer communities for the prize as "most oppressed." It will involve tossing overboard the mistaken notion that bisexual people are more privileged than lesbian/gay people. And it will require adopting the mind-set that while there is plenty of oppression to go around, there is an infinite amount of love and justice that can be put to the service of social change. Religious teachings as simple as "love your bi neighbor" can't hurt.

Bisexuality reminds us that "either/or" questions and answers are largely unhelpful in religions as in daily life

Once bisexual people join the conversation as full partners, it is harder to see the world in binary categories—heterosexual/homosexual; out/closeted; ally/enemy. The world no longer breaks down into hierarchically dualistic categories, with one of the binaries always positive or good, the other negative or bad. In fact, the binaries are no longer operative because something has come along to break their spell. Enter bisexuality, a third option among, perhaps, many.

Such a change in a whole way of thinking is extremely upsetting—in the most helpful way possible! Think of it in terms of how we have been taught to see the world: God/world; human/animal; male/female; white/black; heterosexual/homosexual, with the first of the pair always valued more highly than the second. Bisexual people contradict this dynamic because they are living proof that it is an inadequate way to think. It excludes their reality entirely.

The lesson for theology and ethics is clear: a primary way of thinking that has been foundational for whole religious traditions is no longer adequate. Ethics based on right/wrong, true/untrue, good/bad that ignore the context in which something is done, the circumstances that shape it, are not nuanced enough to deal with twenty-first century life. I do not mean to suggest that bisexuality is a cure-all, but symbolically and epistemologically it is a giant step forward. For religious people it means that we can enter into the fullness of our traditions and let the mysteries unravel a little more easily because of the contribution of bisexual people.

Bisexuality may increase in frequency now that it is more acceptable on its own terms, prompting the need for new religious reflection

Theology and ethics are imaginative activity because none of us has ever lived in a fully just and loving world. We can only imagine. In the case of bisexuality, the number of people who self-define as bisexual may increase, including some now lesbian/gay-identified people, not to mention some heretofore heterosexuals, because their imaginations have been enlarged, their possibilities multiplied. This comes as a threat all around—to conservative heterosexuals who do not want to lose any more ground than they have "lost" already in what they call the sex wars, and to some progressive queers who think that pushing the envelope means we have to clone ourselves in order to make headway.

The former dynamic is beyond my ken, as I cannot imagine how one holds back the tides of change other than engaging in the repressive tactics of the religious right, which I abhor. But the latter dynamic intrigues me because I think the temptation to adhere to categories and thus, as in all hierarchical dualism, for bisexuality to continue to be put down results from a serious lack of imagination on the part of some of my lesbian and gay colleagues.

I prefer to learn from women and men who describe experiences I have not had, and then try to imagine the theological and spiritual consequences. For example, Jan Clausen, a longtime lesbian who left her woman partner for a man, now describes herself as a "floating" woman.[4] What does this mean religiously? Who else is floating and where might she or he be headed? Does this mean that the rest of us are, by contrast, standing still? Is it time for us to examine our experiences, to see if we are stuck rather than simply clear?

Taking bisexual people seriously, realizing that if they can be who they are I must reexamine myself in their light, prompts such questions. It does not mean that I will necessarily become bisexual. In my case that seems highly unlikely unto impossible, given my relational history and current commitments. But the impetus to "never say never," the screen against saying "I'm not a bisexual but . . . ," comes from an honest if rigorous

[4] Jan Clausen, *Apples and Oranges: My Journey Through Sexual Identity* (Boston: Houghton Mifflin, 1999).

engagement with this new, growing reality on its own terms. Only then can we ask what it means in a particular faith tradition, and what it means for us. That is the stuff of serious reflection. There is plenty of work to do.

Bisexuality points toward theological fullness

A good place to start such theological reflection is to ask what the reality of bisexuality says about the divine. Do bisexual people have new insights into the nature of the divine? If so, what might they be, given the move beyond "either/or" and the increase in imaginative possibilities? What about ethics? Bi people help to clarify the need for more nuanced ethical reflection. What about matters of fidelity and family that arise so often when relationships are in the balance?

To most questions about religion and bisexuality the only adequate answer now is "we don't know yet." We do not know what new insights will emerge, what new claims on human freedom and what new contributions to human community will bubble forth as more people are able to live in the fullness of who they are. And as they are part of creation, they reflect a fuller sense of that divine–human cooperation, therefore revealing more and more of the divine itself. It may be premature to say so, and not for me to do as a supportive bi-stander, but I think this will be the next step as the conversation deepens. I await it eagerly and cheer it on in the meanwhile.

Conclusion

What it is for me to say is how we who are lesbian and gay can be supportive bi-standers. Implicit, of course, is that we encourage our bi friends to speak out, not in relation to our issues but on the compelling basis of their own. Second, we can begin to jettison our "either/or" approaches to religious reflection, not waiting for them to name the ambiguity but to embrace it ourselves. Third, we can make clear in our own thinking and writing that when we include bi, we do so because we have been attentive to bi people, not simply because it is politically correct to be rhetorically inclusive. Finally, we can stay alert to the religious insights to come from bisexual people, allowing them to permeate our sometimes rigid, if ever so hard-won, perceptions. That way we honor the divine, who is surely as bi as she is anything else.

Introduction

Blessed Bi Spirit

THE CHALLENGE OF FINDING A TITLE for this work was considerable. What words could reflect the spectrum of spiritual tradition practiced and described by a group as large and diverse as the one represented in this anthology? Some authors argued that shortening the word bisexual to "bi" stripped us of our humanity, of our sexuality, and should therefore be avoided. In a work that seeks to honor the sexual *as* spiritual, we certainly didn't want to perpetuate this dualism. Others resisted the pun in using the word "bi" as a stand-in for the word "by." Puns are for books on humor, not for serious works, they said. While we didn't want to diminish the value of the content by making light of it, many felt that lightheartedness was an essential element of a spiritual path. Perhaps you have heard the one about angels flying because they take themselves lightly?

After much dialogue and searching, *Blessed Bi Spirit* emerged as the phrase best capable of holding all of the intentions of this collection. *Blessed,* read as an adjective with the accent on the first syllable, invites the reader to ponder what particular blessings an embodied bisexual spirit might be living or offering. *Blessed,* read as a verb in the past tense and pronounced "Blest," invites the reader to "hear" the word "Bi" as "by" and to think about the spiritual blessings bestowed upon bisexuals, unique to our particular way of living and loving.

And, in choosing this title, we express an essential bisexual spiritual truth. Regardless of the structure, rituals, and principles of our path, or of the divine name to whom we offer our prayers, bisexual people of faith live consciously and continually in the place where the twain meet. Taking action and being acted upon, offering blessings and receiving them, dwelling in our immanence as we remember and yearn for and experience transcendence. We **are** *blessed bi spirit.*

Blessed and Yet under Attack

Many of us have heard that there are three things we are *not* supposed to talk about in "polite" company: sex, religion, and politics. Because we might offend someone when we articulate a view so disparate from theirs that the ensuing conflict takes on a life of its own, we are told to keep our views on these matters to ourselves.

We are about to break the rules. Politely.

Merely breaking this rule is not noteworthy. Others have talked about the intersection of spirit and sex in very positive ways. For example, in the past twenty years there has been a proliferation of texts and workshops on tantric sex, the Eastern spiritual practice that is explicitly sexual.[1] Access to the sexual principles and practices contained in Jewish kabbalistic texts such as the *Zohar,* once limited to those who could read Hebrew, is now available to a wider audience as more English-writing authors speak of them.[2] Body Electric workshops held around the United States integrate a variety of spiritual paths with sexual experiential exercises, inviting participants to specifically integrate spirit and body through sexuality. Certain pagan practices have long connected sex and spirit. This is true in many rituals, and it reaches its most powerful intersection in the rarely practiced Great Rite, where two people channel the energies of God and Goddess, literally becoming divine beings incarnate.[3] Many have also focused on sexual orientation and religion. Congregations that intentionally welcome gay, lesbian, bisexual, and transgender (GLBT) members are on the rise. GLBT-specific denominations are expanding their ministries.

[1] See, for example, June Campbell, *Traveller in Space: In Search of Female Identity in Tibetan Buddhism* (New York: George Braziller, 1996).

[2] See, for example, Arthur Waskow, *Down to Earth Judaism: Food, Money, Sex and the Rest of Life* (New York: Quill, William Morrow, 1995), 296, 304–6, 311, 370.

[3] Margot Adler, *Drawing Down the Moon: Witches, Druids, Goddess Worshippers, and Other Pagans in America Today* (Boston: Beacon Press, 1986), 110.

Heterosexual and GLBT faith leaders are speaking out publicly regarding the spiritual wholeness of people, regardless of sexual orientation.[4]

Discussion of the intertwining of sex and politics was brought to new heights in the late 1990s when White House sex scandals dominated media attention and almost brought down a sitting president. During this same period, the political arena was flooded with extraordinarily negative rhetoric condemning naturally occurring, loving, and respectful sexuality on religious grounds. The vituperative opposition of the Christian Radical Right to same-sex marriage, adoption by same-sex parents, rescission of sodomy laws, passage of hate crimes legislation, and ending workplace discrimination based on sexual orientation has further intermingled sex, politics, and religion in public discourse. This hate was personalized in 1999, when a print and television advertising campaign sought to convince homosexual and bisexual peoples that they could and should convert to heterosexuality.[5]

This personalization, fueled by specious scriptural or faith-based arguments, has instigated a rise in hate crimes against GLBT peoples. And, in its most profane manifestation, we see small angry bands of "believers" screaming "GOD HATES FAGS" at the funerals of gay men killed because they were gay.

So much for politeness.

Destiny

It is in this climate, and at this time, when hearing the voices of an all too frequently invisible population is so critical. Why, though, is a conversation particular to the bisexual spiritual experience so important, and also unique?

Individuals blessed with the possibility of a love that transcends the artificial, socially constructed boundary of gender identity (masculine/feminine) as well as the biologically constructed boundary of sex (male/

[4] The Religious Leadership Roundtable, established in July 1998 in order to amplify the voice of pro-GLBT faith organizations in pubic discourse, promote understanding and respect for GLBT people, and promote understanding of and respect for a variety of faith paths and for religious liberty within GLBT communities is a good example of the growing positive faith focus on sexual orientation diversity.

[5] This was created and funded by groups such as the Family Research Council, the Christian Coalition, the Center for Reclaiming America for Christ, Concerned Women for America, and the American Family Association.

female) can speak to several theological principles as no one else can. Qualities or aspirations such as those of balance (yin/yang), of integration, oneness or wholeness (the inner marriage of male and female deities in polytheistic traditions; the inner marriage of immanence and transcendence in any tradition), of loving that of God within every person (a Quaker ideal, and a principle in many traditions), of the special relationship of the outsider or the outcast and God (a theme deeply ingrained in Christian theology), or of the special relationship of one chosen to perform a specific role (an often controversial theme embedded in Judaism and in many indigenous traditions) take on new meaning and possibility for us.

Indeed, contemporary bisexuals are not the first to ponder whether we have a specific spiritual inheritance. Indigenous traditions have long identified a role of the highest spiritual order for the person who loves someone of the same gender. Called gatekeepers by the Dagara of West Africa and *berdache,* or Two Spirit by many Native Americans, these people, often shamans, are born into a very special destiny.[6] In this volume, authors from a variety of traditions further explore the inherent blessing of loving beyond the bounds of gender.

Whether Buddhist, Hindu, Twelve-Step, pagan, indigenous, Christian, or Jew, who is better equipped than the bisexual or transgender individual to create rituals that honor boundless love and the sacredness of spirit embodied in *both* men and women and those who fall between and outside of those categories? Who else can look at sacred sexual traditions, all of which hold specific relevance to the biological sex of the people involved, and live out those practices with partners of both sexes, either in the flesh or in the mind, allowing for a richness and complexity of experience and consciousness not afforded those who limit their partners to those of only one sex?

And finally, who is better situated to help our dialogue move beyond the false rhetoric of, "You're ok if you're born that way, but if you choose, you're going to lose"? Bisexuals are heralded as the weak link in the GLBT struggle for equal rights by those who demonize same-sex love because of our seeming ability to choose the sex of our partner(s). The argument goes something like this: "If bisexuals can choose, so can all of you

[6] See, for example, Will Roscoe, *The Zuni Man-Woman* (Albuquerque: University of New Mexico Press, 1991); and Malidoma Patrice Somé, *Of Water and Spirit: Ritual, Magic, and Initiation in the Life of an African Shaman* (New York: Putnam, 1994).

homosexuals and God ordains that you choose to be heterosexual." Rather than address the complexities of a bisexual orientation and the sacredness of all love, most of our allies have strategically and/or fearfully adopted the battle cry: "It's biological!"

Whether or not choice exists for us any more than anyone else, bisexuals have been cast into the middle of this fray. We therefore have a special role to play in revealing the intellectual emptiness of this posture. The truth is that for us, as for people of all orientations, serendipity, hormones, environment, genetics, emotion, and spirit interact in a wildly unpredictable dance that results in attraction, courtship, and partnering. Exactly how they interact cannot be scientifically deduced—at least not today. But more pertinent to the work of this anthology, stories of the devotion and of the faith- and love-based contributions of bisexual people expose the lie of our detractors—the lie that says that the exercise of choice or free will is a legitimate reason for denouncing love. The truth is that whether by choice or genetic imperative, love is holy. That truth remains whether we love women or men or both. To extrapolate from that truth, social acceptance and legal rights should never depend on our being unable to exercise free will. Ironically, if people of faith really believed that a biological mandate was an essential precondition for legitimacy, then no convert would ever be allowed into the fold—after all—they weren't "born" that way!

When one understands bisexuality as the sum total of all of the implications of loving others at the level of the SOUL, and not merely at the level of the physical BODY, one understands that this capacity is indeed our most fortunate destiny, and a state of exquisite grace.

Speaking to Destiny

The formidable task of giving voice to this inheritance is taken up by thirty-one authors, coming from a variety of traditions and speaking from a broad range of practice. Great effort was made to include representatives from every major faith tradition, but unfortunately we are missing a Muslim voice. And, with only thirty-some authors, it was impossible to represent every denomination, stream, and faith tradition. Even with this limitation, an intriguing byproduct of the commitment to represent a broad variety of traditions is the appearance of theological overlap among different paths. Perhaps a lesson here is that, as the Buddha says, we are all the same in different ways. I look forward to hearing all of the unrepresented voices in the near future. This volume is only the beginning of what promises to be an enduring conversation.

Authors engage with the question of spirit and bisexuality from three directions. In "By Our Lives, Be We Spirit: Holy Identity," they explore how the essence of their bisexual being has holy purpose and/or divine intention.[7] This is manifested in many ways: in acts of social justice, as personal bridges, in healing or in channeling a unique manifestation of God energy in the world.

In "Communion with Spirit: Wholeness is Holy," authors speak more directly to the theological principles or specific teachings, practice, and ritual that are informed by, expanded by, or made manifest through their bisexual orientation.

In "Wrestling with Spirit: Who Defines Holiness," several writers explore their struggles within or separation from paths that did not embrace their bisexuality. They describe their journeys toward spiritual wholeness or acceptance within that tradition, or through the finding or creation of new traditions. Others look for and find principles within their path that support their bisexuality without struggle.

Though many authors in this volume quote scripture, and some directly address the homophobic and biphobic dogma flowing from certain interpretations of biblical text, this anthology is not an attempt to refute, point by point, the arguments used to say that bisexuals are "unnatural" or, worse yet, "hated" by God. These voices pour forth from souls who are deeply connected with their own sense of grace. Each story affirms and proclaims the inherent holiness of its author.

Blessed bi spirit. Blessed be. Ameyn.

[7] "By Our Lives, Be We Spirit" is a lyric from a Ferron song, "Testimony," from the album of the same name. *Testimony,* Lucy Records, Nemesis Publishing, Vancouver, B.C., 1980.

PART 1

By Our Lives Be We Spirit: Holy Identity

Sacre Coeur

Greta Ehrig

In the space of two
lightly touching hands

Rodin saw tenderness, prayer,
a form of holiness he called

Cathedral. What is after all
the architecture of God?

If our Creator's house is constructed
cruciform, if Spirit only enters

the clean, curved coolness
of mosque or synagogue,

what about the high-vaulted
moss-strewn corridor of trees

which leads me
not into temptation but

the redemption of river
and leaves? Hail, my own

mucky body, regaled
by the scintillant light.

Tell me.
Who to love. When.

I can not hear for the multitude
singing, and in the vast and intimate

chambers of my heart,
whether Love comes as a man

or a woman, singular or
plural, is of no concern

to the soul flown open
as a window to God.

The Holy Leper and the Bisexual Christian

AMANDA UDIS-KESSLER

> *There is no longer Jew or Greek, there is no longer slave or free, there is no longer male and female; for all of you are one in Christ Jesus.*
>
> —Galatians 3:28

> *If Jesus is holy, then clearly holiness is not about separation.*
>
> —Mike Riddell[1]

JESUS' LIFE CALLS TO ME IN MANY WAYS, inviting me to love God, myself, and my neighbors, to trust God utterly and to relinquish my fear, to give myself in service and to strive for a justice that would do justice to God's mercy. Jesus offers me a model of what it means to be a teacher, a healer, a servant, a prophet, a martyr. I could spend the rest of my days trying to learn from him and striving to follow him in the particularities of my own life circumstances.

One lesson I draw from Jesus' life is that God meets us where we are and welcomes us into abundance. God does not invite us by demanding that we abandon our deepest selves. Instead, the kingdom is offered to us at precisely those most sad and joyous, most broken and healing, most vulnerable places. If I am to take this lesson seriously, I must ask what Jesus has to say to me as a bisexual person, capable of emotionally and sexually loving both women and men, often mistrusted and sometimes rejected by both heterosexuals and lesbian/gay people. If I am to find God in the life of this Rabbi from Nazareth, what word of hope is there that my sexual identity can draw me closer to God, through Jesus, in some way?

[1] Mike Riddell, *Third Way* (December 1996): 31, as quoted in *The Other Side* (May/June 1997): 57.

The Gospels, of course, do not record any sayings of Jesus on homosexuality, let alone bisexuality, and it is impossible to know from the available biblical scholarship whether he was attracted to women, men, both or neither (though I would tend to doubt the last possibility). Yet, there is another level of inquiry for me, which draws upon plentiful Gospel material and beyond, into mystery and silence. Jesus was not merely a teacher, preacher, healer, and prophet; he was also, at his core, a shatterer of boundaries, destroyer of margins, and dismantler of statuses in the name of God's boundless, all-inclusive love. It is this facet of Jesus' work that most threatened the authorities of his time and brought him to the cross, and it is in this legacy that I find my own potential for loving beyond at least certain boundaries, welcomed and sanctified.

Biblical scholar Marcus Borg, among others, has detailed the status-driven politics of holiness and purity which had become manifest among Jews in Jesus' culture.[2] Social inequality in Jesus' time depended on hierarchical dualisms, as do today's commonly recognized forms of social inequality—racism, sexism, class inequality, heterosexism, ageism, ableism, and the like. Hierarchical dualisms are value systems in which two opposite social categories are defined, one of which is valued (white, male, rich, heterosexual, adult, able-bodied) and one of which is devalued (person of color, female, poor, lesbian/gay, very young or very old, disabled).

Borg's account of the politics of holiness, on which I rely below, has certain limitations which bear mentioning before exploring his explanation of hierarchical dualism. First, it is but one of a number of analyses of this period and has not by any means received scholarly consensus. Second, for the purposes of this essay, I am not focusing on the ways in which Jewish law was frequently grounded in deep concerns for social justice and in caring for the stranger and the poor, for example, the tradition of *tikkun olam,* the repair of the world. While this tradition may not have received primary attention under the circumstances faced by Jews in that era, it was not absent. In fact, it can be helpful to understand Jesus (as Borg does) not as the founder of a new non-Jewish religion but as the leader of a Jewish revitalization movement attempting to refocus Jews on this very issue. Finally, no account of Jewish life in this period is complete without recalling that the Jews lived under Roman occupation and faced aspects of oppression ranging from unjust taxation and imposition of Roman religious practices to arrest and death for any activity that could be seen as a threat or challenge to the Romans.

[2] See Marcus Borg, *Jesus, A New Vision: Spirit, Culture and the Life of Discipleship* (New York: HarperCollins, 1987); idem, *Meeting Jesus Again for the First Time: The Historical Jesus and the Heart of Contemporary Faith* (New York: HarperCollins, 1994).

Having thus provided a context for Borg's perspective, let me turn to the core of what Borg calls the politics of holiness: the question of whether a given individual was pure or impure, clean or unclean. Borg claims that the answer to this question meant the difference between social welcome and social disapproval, even ostracism—which, in such an honor-and-shame-based culture, could amount to social death. On the pure/clean/valued side of the equation Borg locates rich (or at least economically solvent) Jewish men in good health and in a position to count themselves among the righteous by following the extensive Jewish laws in their entirety. Among the impure, unclean, and devalued, Borg finds the poor, Gentiles, women, the sick, and those Jews considered sinners for not being able to keep the laws (usually by virtue of being poor, women, sick or some combination of all three). Jesus' frequent references to whores and tax collectors should be understood in this context, argues Borg; whores (unchaperoned women, some of whom were actually prostitutes) and tax collectors (seen as shills for the occupying Roman empire, forced to handle "profane" money, generally trusted about as much as young African-American men are trusted by security guards in stores today) were thought of as among the biggest "sinners" in the purity system. It is not a coincidence that Jesus welcomed them over and over again, told stories in which God's love for them was clear, and told the purveyors of the purity system that tax collectors and prostitutes were getting into the kingdom of God before the so-called righteous.

Jesus could offer this welcome to outcasts because of his own experience of God's love and welcome, which Jesus translated into a call to be compassionate as God is compassionate (Luke 6:36)—that is, beyond boundaries. He spoke of a gracious Father who sends rain on the just and unjust, urged his followers to love not just neighbor but enemy as well, and instituted a new social structure for eating, a table fellowship in which rich and poor, righteous and sinner, men and women were at the same table in total violation of the purity rules (e.g., Matt. 9:10; Mark 14:3–9; Luke 11:37–38; 14:1; 19:1–10). He treated women, Gentiles, the poor and the sick with dignity and respect (with one interesting exception, Matt. 15:21–28, in which he came around at the end), and he welcomed children, considered nobodies in his culture (e.g., Matt. 18:1–6, 10; 19:13–14; Luke 9:46–48; 10:38–42; 21:1–4; John 4:5–42; 8:1–11). He challenged his culture's hierarchical family structure in ways that would horrify today's "family values" crowd if they paid attention to it (e.g., Matt. 8:21–22; 10:34–37; 12:48–50; 23:9; Luke 11:27–28; 14:26), and he skewered wealth (Matt. 6:19–21, 24; 19:21–24; Luke 4:13–14; 6:20, 24, 30, 34–35; 12:15–21; 14:33; 16:19–25), piety, and prestige (Matt. 6:1–6, 16–18; Mark

9:35; 12:38–39; Luke 14:7–11; 18:10–14) as marks of status. He also engaged in what AIDS activists would call a direct action against Purity Central (the temple, heart of the politics of holiness). Jesus apparently saw God's graciousness as shattering boundaries and understood the appropriate human response as right relationship with God, others, and self, which likewise required boundary shattering. Jesus offered us/called us to liberation from legalisms into love, from class into compassion, from status into solidarity. (My best understanding of the kingdom of God today is that it is simply life in love, compassion, and solidarity with self, others, and the Holy.)

Perhaps Jesus' most awesome boundary crossing took place in his healing work. Sickness was a mark of uncleanness, and many of the people he healed were doubly unclean, such as Gentiles (Matt. 8:5–13; 15:21–28; Luke 17:1–19), or the woman with a "bleeding problem" (Matt. 9:20–22; Jewish law defined menstrual blood as an unclean substance). Jesus also healed on the Sabbath, breaking the temporal boundary between sacred and profane (Matt. 12:10–13; Luke 13:10–17). While the story about the demoniac in the graveyard (Mark 5:1–17) is probably not historically accurate, it fits what we know of Jesus that he would enter a graveyard (unclean) inhabited by a man with unclean spirits (worse) and send the spirits into a herd of nearby pigs (the most unclean animal, according to Jewish law). Crossing the barriers between healthy and sick people allowed Jesus to offer people with little hope a chance to cross back into the world of the well, but he was only able to do this by himself crossing into the world of the sick and, therefore, the world of the unclean.

Most of the time, when Jesus healed those with eczema or psoriasis, what is commonly mistranslated today as leprosy, he touched them (e.g., Matt. 8:2–4; Luke 7:22). Touching a leper meant that Jesus took on leprosy himself, both in the sense of risking exposure to the condition, and in the sense of socially becoming a leper for all intents and purposes. Jesus, beloved of God, accepted this "uncleanness" in order to offer healing, and rather than becoming a leper, he sanctified leprosy. Lepers in Jesus' culture lost their status as clean when their condition became public. Yet Jesus appears to have interacted with lepers without losing his "clean" status, perhaps because of his healing ability or the authority with which he taught. At the very least, there is no evidence that he either behaved as an unclean person was supposed to, or that he was treated as unclean by those around him (with one exception, Mark 3:30). Thus, Jesus became what we might call a holy leper or a God-filled outcast; he was somehow simultaneously clean and unclean, an impossibility in the face of the dualism at the heart of the politics of holiness. His impossible status did what no political protest of the time could have done: it collapsed the core of the dualism undergirding the politics of holiness. In other words, by becoming a holy leper, Jesus demolished the categories of "holy" and "leper" as hierarchical opposites, freeing lepers to be holy and enabling those people defined as pure (e.g., the Pharisees) to encounter their own "uncleanness," their full humanity.

This perspective on uncleanness is, I suspect, a somewhat uncommon way to think about Jesus' gift to humanity. Christians are more likely to focus on Jesus' bridging of the gap between humanity and divinity, to celebrate his conquest of death for all time by the way he died, or to argue (as René Girard did in *Violence and the Sacred*) that Jesus, in taking on the role of scapegoat, rid the world of its need for scapegoats.[3] However much these characterizations of Jesus' work may speak to me, I am most awed and humbled by his willingness to become unclean and his resulting conquest over uncleanness and the pure/impure dichotomy that has fueled so many hierarchical dualisms. This work of Jesus offers me hope that my bisexuality, far from being a sin, disease, or case of confusion, might be God's way of working gracefully in me against exclusivism and categorization, on behalf of God's joyful and inclusive kingdom.

Different people, of course, have different gifts, challenges, and life missions, and I don't mean to suggest that being bisexual is in any way better than the alternatives, or that everyone must become bisexual in order for the kingdom to come. That would require a miracle beyond any we see in the scriptures! It does seem to me, though, that Jesus, the holy leper, is well situated to welcome Amanda, the "neither gay nor straight/ both gay and straight," to challenge me and to reassure me.

Jesus the holy leper speaks to my bisexuality by offering me a model for life outside the boundaries of destructive hierarchical dualisms. Jesus does not appear to have spent much energy worrying about the impossibility of his status, since there was too much kingdom work to do and since his experience was that nothing was impossible with God.

If I am to follow Jesus in this way, I can and must relinquish my concerns and anger about people who deny the existence of bisexuality. Let them believe what they believe. In the meantime, I'd rather work on bringing the kingdom a little closer than wrangle over the "truth" of my sexual identity. If bisexuality really is a threat to the gay/straight dichotomy, if it

[3] René Girard, *Violence and the Sacred,* trans. Patrick Gregory (Baltimore, Md.: Johns Hopkins University Press, 1979).

challenges people overly invested in the status quo on both sides of the equation, perhaps that's because it is supposed to do so. In the meantime, says Jesus, I'm free to stop worrying about rejection and to offer such healing as is mine to give by crossing boundaries in love. He challenges me to do this work in remembrance of him, and if the boundaries I cross are somewhat different from the boundaries he crossed, so be it (though the people defined as unclean today include sexual minorities of all stripes).

I suspect that, in addition to my being called to feed the hungry, attend to the sick, visit the prisoner, and house the homeless as much as anyone else on the planet, I'm also called to find ways to use my bisexuality, my form of "holy leprosy," in the service of inclusivity and welcome. I can, for example, strive to make God's love manifest in all of my relationships, sexual and nonsexual, regardless of the genders involved. I can refuse to behave as though men were superior to women (traditional sexist values) or as though women were superior to men (a common response to sexism, but not, I think, the ultimate word about who we can be as human beings). I can offer particular encouragement to others who cross boundaries of gender, sexuality, race, and class, by word and by example, and I can try to be alert to the unique, wonderful, and surprising gifts of individuals without either disregarding or idolizing their gender identities or sexual orientations. These kinds of work are not limited to bisexual people, of course, but my bisexuality can help me carry them out. Undoubtedly, there are more tasks ahead which I cannot envision now, but for which my bisexuality will also be a gift.

Finally, then, Jesus does offer a word of hope for my sexual identity. Jesus' example, if "translated" as I have tried to do here, reassures me that if I live my bisexuality with such kingdom values as love, compassion, honesty, integrity, and forgiveness, my sexual identity can and will be used in the service of the kingdom and will be part of the solution rather than part of the problem (as the street evangelists would have it). The "symptom of sin and alienation" so derided by biblical literalists can actually be a gift of grace to draw me closer to God the Great Lover, as I seek the kingdom through my bisexuality and offer that bisexuality back to the kingdom again. I pray in Jesus' spirit that this work may give shape to my days, I offer thanks for a God who won't let mere human boundaries stop love, and I praise the Rabbi whose love took him beyond all such boundaries in God's service. Amen.

God Is a Divine Androgen

SOROR OCHO

In the Beginning

I REMEMBER LOOKING IN THE MIRROR when I was five years old and wondering, "Am I a girl that looks like a boy, or a boy in a little girl's body?" This question posed no problems, but was an acute observation on the nature of my essential self. Androgyny has always felt balanced to me, like the two aspects of myself coming together and uniting, yet retaining their unique essence. I remember reading Walt Whitman's beautiful erotic poetry in *Leaves of Grass* as a teenager and experiencing a profound kinship with his insight and acceptance of his androgyny and bisexuality.

Since my earliest recollection I have been androgynous and bisexual. My early experimentation with childhood sex play involved both boys and girls and this felt perfectly natural to me. As I grew up, like most children I began to assimilate the more traditional gender identification roles. By my fifteenth birthday I was preoccupied with looking feminine, being pretty, wearing makeup, and having a boyfriend. When I officially went "steady" at fifteen, I became MISS HETEROSEXUAL. I dated and fell in love with a handsome, popular musician and lost my virginity to him. But, despite my focus on femininity, I maintained what could be called more masculine qualities. I identified more with my mind and reasoning abilities than my emotions, loved science and exploration, was fiercely independent, self-reliant, and stronger than most girls I knew. I could wallop a powerful punch that caused boys older than I to treat me with respect. I was fearless, never running away from a confrontation. My attachment to heterosexuality lasted until my twentieth birthday, when my familiar interest in females became rekindled by a sweet and sensual girl friend who expressed sexual interest in me. This reawakened my bisexuality and reconnected me to my androgynous whole.

I attended Catholic school until I was sixteen, when a change in my family's economic situation caused my sister and me to be placed in public school. I was born into an upper-middle-class home in Havana, Cuba. My grandfather was a physician and my father an electrical engineer. We moved to the United States in 1961, like many Cubans seeking political freedom. My mother and grandmother maintained very traditional Roman Catholic beliefs and values, which felt foreign to me. My grandfather and father were both scientists who encouraged me to analyze and use my reasoning abilities to understand myself and the world around me.

I searched for a spiritual philosophy that was at peace with the body, the temple of the soul, and with the very essence of our being, "the life force," a philosophy which recognized that the life force ultimately leads us to unity with the universe, god, and to transcendence. Uncomfortable with the Catholic indoctrination of my youth, I sought answers to spiritual and philosophical questions in the theory of reincarnation, spirituality, metaphysics, science, philosophy, mysticism, world religions, psychology, and nature.

My search for truth awakened me to the discovery that God/Goddess is a Divine Androgen and that our souls are bisexual. I realized that I had intuitively understood this as a child: we all contained a bisexual potential which ultimately evolved into the androgynous image of our creator. God was half male and half female, the yin and the yang within the circle of life in constant becoming. I found support for this realization within alchemical teachings.

Alchemy was the ancient practice of turning base metals into "gold" by utilizing laboratory methods of distillation, coagulation, and dispersion. But this was only an outer symbol for the "true work" of the alchemist, which did not occur in the laboratory and was spiritual in nature. The "true work" focused on the laws of spiritual transformation and the cycles of growth and refinement that all things in the universe are subject to. Contained within this alchemical lore were the teachings of the Divine Androgen. Alchemy taught that "gold" was a metaphor for the spiritually evolved human being which was born when each individual consciously united its male and female aspects within itself. The mystical process of integrating the male and female halves was known to alchemists as the "Alchemical Marriage," the image of the Divine Androgen.

My understanding was reinforced when I read *The Secret Doctrine of the*

Rosicrucians. Within that text, by an anonymous author, is the following paragraph:

> The One became Two. The Neuter became Bi-sexual. Male and Female—the Two in One—evolved from the Neuter. And the work of generation began. The First Manifestation as the Eternal Parent, as a Bi-sexual Universal Being, combining within itself the elements and principles of both Masculinity and Femininity, is known in Rosicrucian Teachings as "The Universal Hermaphrodite" and the "Universal Androgen." . . . The conception of the Bi-Sexuality in the Universal Manifestation, or Universal Being, is one met with on all sides in the ancient esoteric and occult philosophies in all lands. In ancient Greece, in Ancient India, and in Ancient Atlantis, Persia, and Chaldea the doctrine formed an important part of the Inner Teachings. In its highest forms, this teaching lay at the very heart of the Ancient Mysteries, and resulted in the very highest and noblest conception of the divinity and worthiness of Sex.

I learned of the mystical order of the Knights of Templars, a holy secret society during the Middle Ages in Europe that safeguarded the secrets of the Divine Androgen in the image and icon of "Baphomet." Baphomet is represented in the Fifteenth Major Arcana card of the Tarot cards, which bears the image of a being that has the head of a goat and a body that is half-man and half-woman. Symbolically this card depicts the mysteries of our androgynous bisexual nature and is indicative of spiritual initiation.

Interestingly, Jungian psychology supported my understanding. According to Jung, one of the primary aspects of psychological integration occurs when the man marries his inner woman and the woman marries her inner man. This creates an androgynous being that is whole and complete. Eventually, we will all resemble the Divine or Universal Being, a Divine Hermaphrodite, bisexual androgen, beyond polarity, yin and yang, having transcended duality.

Today I believe that humanity as a whole is awakening spiritually. As we do so, we become aware of our bisexual potential and of our divine androgynous nature. So many people are now openly exploring the trans- or pan-gender frontier of our human sexuality. The traditional roles of male and female have become blurred. Men have discovered that they too are nurturing, intuitive, and emotional. Women have emerged as skilled workers in what were traditionally male jobs. More and more people are exploring the depths of human sexuality through sexual play and an eroticism that has taken on a new innocence. Growing in popularity is the ancient spiritual practice of tantric yoga, based on Indian and Persian mystical teachings that acknowledge that the goddess and god live in each of us and find all forms of sexual expression right, meaningful, and healing.

I see bisexuality as a natural step in the development of our androgyny. God is both male and female, active and passive, containing and reconciling all things. This oneness is expressed as love, harmony, and desire for union. I am grateful for having been born an androgynous, bisexual female; it makes me feel closer to my creator and more compassionate toward all of life. Our greatest gift is our freedom of choice. There exist infinite possibilities in the expression of love, sexuality, and spirituality. I believe that in the new millennium many more will share the bisexual experience as one of the many avenues available to us in creating joy, freedom, love, and beauty in our spiritual and sexual expressions.

Bi God: Rediscovering an Ancient Self

MARCIA DEIHL

Different Drummer

I BEGAN MY DEVIANT SPIRITUAL PATH when I was three years old, as a family audio tape reveals. A sleepy little southern-accented voice blesses my family, my froggy, and all my dolls, and then, at the end, piously adds, "Ahhhh-George." What? Where did this "George" thing come from? My parents' guess was that I confused the Holy Ghost with a character from one of my favorite childhood stories called *Georgie the Ghost.* I am sure that I wasn't yet a budding feminist, objecting to the "men" fragment of the word "*Amen.*" My folks were more amused than upset, even though my father was a Presbyterian minister. Although we prayed at bedtime and before every meal, we weren't pious, invoking the Lord in every sentence or anything like that. Presbyterians are, above all, *tasteful.*

Although I wasn't consciously rebellious at three, as I grew up I somehow kept straying from the faith practice of my parents. Naturally, I went to church as a toddler—the cute little minister's daughter with the Dutch-boy haircut, pretty yellow dress, and black patent leather shoes. I spent the long hour of my father's weekly service next to the loving pillow lap of my grandmother, drawing on a piece of paper and asking her for gum or mints. All was well until one day, in the middle of the service, I said—more like yelled—my first sentence, "Let's get out of here!" My mother claims that everyone looked around, but no one suspected such a tiny thing was capable of such a loud, clear voice.

As I grew older, native nihilism turned to thoughtfulness. At eight or nine, I started wondering about those stories of our wonderful Presbyterian missionaries who valiantly brought "the Good News" to the "savages" overseas. I didn't see why we thought our guy, Jesus, was the only one to make or break eternal life. The teachers seemed to think it was very important to save these poor foreign people by telling them the Truth and baptizing them; otherwise, they might go to hell. That seemed unfair, even laughable, and from that time on I treated the whole religion thing as a joke. Although I pulled the usual teenage tricks of passive-aggression (substituting the names of boys I liked for "Jesus" during the hymns), I dutifully kept attending Sunday school, church, and evening youth fellowship—after all, Dad was the minister, and he paid my allowance. Although I was a "good girl" on the surface, I deeply resented having to put on such a corny act.

At least I had school, where I relaxed and excelled. But that wasn't perfect either. I didn't understand social life. All I wanted, I noted in my senior year diary, was "to have a spiritual vision." Only my high school French teacher, Mr. Mezinsky, saw my confusion. His words saved me: "It's not you; it's this small town. Just hold on until college."

Mr. Mezinsky was right, and I burst onto the college scene at Boston University. Although I studied hard, I got sidetracked by the year 1968. In the spring of my freshman year, the assassination of Dr. Martin Luther King Jr., the escalation of the war against the Vietnamese, and the death of Robert Kennedy all intruded upon my academic obsessions. By the time I got my B.A. in music history and education, I had become so radicalized that I refused to participate in my own Phi Beta Kappa meeting. I wanted to "serve the people."

For two years after college ended, I worked as a secretary and lived in Cambridge in various communal households of hippies, Marxists, and crashers. Before the harsher late-1970s splits of hippie-versus-politico set in, everyone was gloriously mushed together, and although I thought of myself as a leftist, I sampled the free Thursday night yoga classes in a Harvard Square church basement and the women's center-sponsored Tai Chi lessons. I thought nothing of spending Sunday afternoons sitting in meditation at the Ananda Marga Society's communal house on Wendall Street, Tuesday evenings in Marxist/Leninist organizing discussions, and Wednesday evenings studying astrology at the Hippocrates Health Institute in Boston.

When I did meditate, I was not consciously seeking a connection with any kind of personal God. I used it strategically, much like the military, to clear my mind and to focus, but most importantly, to stop my binge eating. Although I didn't believe in God, I did believe in a common light, a shared unity, and an active ethics of fairness and kindness.

In the early 1970s, I entered a feminist studies graduate program at Cambridge-Goddard Graduate School for Social Change and joined what was then called the Rounder Records Collective. Within a year or so, I'd earned a masters degree, lost my virginity, and written my spiritual "coming out" letter in the *Boston Phoenix,* an alternative weekly. My letter was a search for other "Wheelie/Feelies"—seekers who desired both an activist and a spiritual life. Replies ranged from prisoners to SDS cofounder Carl Oglesby, and eight of us met for a while, talking leftist politics, Carlos Casteneda books, and whether Rennie Davis had sold out when he started following some boy guru. Soon Carl and I started playing recorders together in Harvard Square at night, and after he told me he was tired of politics and just wanted to play music and hang out, the group eventually dissipated.

A year later, I left Rounder and spent the remainder of my twenties trying out several other jobs, lovers, and roommates. But I never stopped exploring the spiritual dimension. I tried grunting and slam dancing with orange-clad Sri Rajneesh disciples, learning relaxation response meditation through my health plan, taking classes in bioenergetics (in this case, naked group dips in somebody's Brookline basement hot tub), sitting quietly at Quaker meetings, celebrating diversity at Unitarian church services, and worshiping the moon at Goddess rituals. But my life was always split in two, even within the women's community. Most of my friends called themselves either socialist feminists, who put class division as first priority, or "cultural feminists" (also called "radical feminists"), who maintained that the male/female power imbalance was the "primary contradiction." I didn't dare share my explorations into "the opiate of the people" with my anarchist Rounder comrades or my Marxist study groups. And I had to agree with my New Age friends that some radicals thrived more on self-righteous tantrums than on helping the people.

But my own search would not be squelched, even if spirituality was too intimate to speak about. More intimate, even, than sex. Or food. No, I take that back—food was my first taboo subject. Any goal I set always took a back seat to battling the relentless urge to eat. At thirteen, I weighed in at one hundred and eighty pounds, and my self-image was set in stone for years afterward. As the years went on, my teenage wish for a "spiritual vision" seemed to have been transformed into, "I want to have a spiritual vision . . . that will make me lose weight!" Throughout my twenties, I was a human yo-yo, alternating hours or days of stringent dieting with fasting and bingeing. Although I'd had two boyfriends and one girlfriend by the time I turned thirty, my primary relationship had always been with food and its attendant rituals.

Dear God: Are You There?

My eating disorder held the key to the next leg of my spiritual journey: sobriety from food. The woman I was with suggested that I join a Twelve-Step group that had helped her to lose thirty pounds. I did, and shortly thereafter, I left her, not for a man but for myself. I had never been alone before, and I saw how I had used projects and lovers as stopgap measures to halt my bingeing. During my first year of recovery, we were all encouraged to cultivate a Higher Power. I had left a personal God sense behind years before, along with the missionaries and the "savages." Can one really will oneself to believe in a so-called Higher Power? I didn't think so.

The old-timers at the meetings told us that the job of God was taken, and not by us, and that the power of the group could be our Higher Power ("G.O.D. stands for 'group of drunks'"). They said that the only thing you had to do in order to recover was to keep an open mind, or, in the words of one of the slogans, "Came, came to, came to believe."[1]

My longtime atheism was being challenged by one glaring fact: I wasn't abstaining from compulsive eating with will power. If will power had worked, I would have gritted my teeth, put my nose to the grindstone, and applied all the usual macho clichés—"just done it." Something else must have been responsible for my success, or perhaps, Someone Else. I was starting to believe in something (him? her? it?) simply because I felt a major shift in my daily consciousness, a personal, experiential miracle, perhaps what the literature calls "a spiritual awakening." No angelic voices sang, no clouds parted, but I hadn't "used" food as a drug for months.

The relief of having a smaller body and a clearer mind was just the beginning of a search for myself. My obsession had been my primary identity, and a secret one at that. Food had been a powerful sedative, as dangerous as narcotics or alcohol. And it was a stealth drug—cheap, legal, and easily obtained, a longtime favorite palliative for underdogs like women, queers, and the poor. And, I found underneath that fifty pounds a second mask, the "ism" of alcoholism: a tendency toward negativity,

[1] *Food for Thought* (Center City, Minn.: Hazelden, 1974), July 12 reading.

grandiosity, perfectionism, and isolation. Political self-righteousness was a great fellow traveler; it allowed me to reject the self-indulgent, bourgeois life of my more mainstream friends, but it was just another mask for social insecurity.

I struggled a bit with the Twelve-Step framing of spirit. When I asked a few others in my group about their views of this Higher Power stuff, I got various answers. There were Jesus people (originals and born-again) who were very loving and kind, but I had already OD'd on Jesus as a preacher's kid. Many of my friends were Jewish, valiantly sifting through the rampant capital-C-Christian references in the AA-based prayers and meetings. Many lesbians and other feminists prayed to a favorite goddess; no damning man for them, frowning and condemning. But no matter how we differed in our conception of a Higher Power, we believed that some force outside our own wills was keeping us sober. I liked the slogan, "If you're caught in a rowboat in a storm, pray as if it's in God's hands, and row as if it's in your own."

I agreed with the lesbian feminists that a humorless, angry male God image had to go, but I just couldn't picture a "She" in my favorite childhood comfort scripture, the Twenty-Third Psalm. On the other hand, "It" sounded much too sterile for the gentle shepherd who "leadeth me beside the still waters"; anything but the original "He" felt too arrogantly modern for those lovely, lyrical verses. But I was a feminist to the core, and it was crucial for me to make my Higher Power more of a comfort than a father-judge.

Dear God: Are You a Boy Or Are You a Girl?

Was God a "he" or a "she"? Did I have to pick?

Answering this question was the second leg of my journey, my bisexual spiritual quest. Once again, I turned to books. In the 1960s, Alan Watts wrote about the equation of spiritual ecstasy with sexual ecstasy. As he understood it, both experiences were a means of losing self in a sea of not-self. Watts was reacting to the male institutions of the West, which had declared Eve (stand-in for Nature herself) as Other and dangerous. With the exception of the odd comrade like Robert Graves, male forces had by and large stood at attention, steeled to face Woman in cosmic sexual warfare.[2] By the late 1970s, feminist spiritual thinkers had refined this pro-

[2] Robert Graves, *The White Goddess* (New York: Farrar, Straus & Giroux, 1948).

woman approach, addressing the changing reality of what it meant to be a woman, a man, and a spiritual seeker.[3] I was finally home.

I'd never been averse to a hint of sexual attraction to my Higher Power, since I'd always believed that mutual loving sex was god-given—quite the opposite of a sin. Why not have the perfect Lover/Friend/Coach/Mother/Father all rolled into one? Still, since I had been attracted to both men and women, how would I pick genders for God?

I decided that a picture that attracted me at the lust level might jump-start me to the spiritual level. Strong women and gentle men had always caught my eye, and postcards and photos of handsome androgynes like Georgia O'Keeffe, Rudolf Nureyev, and Frida Kahlo plastered my refrigerator (that most sacred of modern household altars). One day I saw a print of an Andrew Wyeth painting entitled *Nogeeshik, 1972.* A strong, gentle-looking Native American man with long brown hair and high cheekbones gazed out from wise, enduring eyes. I bought a copy, pinned it up over my breakfast table, and spoke to "Chief" whenever I needed to. He was almost an adult version of an imaginary playmate, a superhero who could swoop down and save me.

But, like all childhood magic, this power was not to last. Two or three years later, I started missing a female presence, a female picture, and I began looking for a similar image to talk and pray to. A few months later, a man walked by with a *Time* magazine, and there on the cover—it couldn't be—a picture of . . . him. The Indian, Nogeeshik. But wait . . . he was a blonde now, and he was a "she"! "Helga, Wyeth's Mystery Woman—Unearthed Treasures" read the headline in large red diagonal letters. I bought a copy, opened it up, and read that Wyeth had often used his neighbor woman and sometime lover, Helga, as a model for his pictures.

When I compared Helga to my old print of Nogeeshik, I saw the same thin lips, same Mona Lisa smile, same high cheekbones; with the right equipment, I could have superimposed them. How could *Time* magazine have known what it had done? It solved an impossible question, how to have a photo of a god/goddess that was both and neither. (I now know that

[3] See Charlene Spretnak's groundbreaking anthology *The Politics of Women's Spirituality: Essays on the Rise of Spiritual Power Within the Feminist Movement* (New York: Doubleday, Anchor, 1982); Naomi R. Goldenberg's *Changing of the Gods: Feminism and the End of Traditional Religions* (Boston: Beacon Press, 1979); Carol P. Christ's *Diving Deep and Surfacing: Women Writers on Spiritual Quest* (Boston: Beacon Press, 1980); Carol Ochs's *Women and Spirituality* (Totowa, N.J.: Rowman & Allanheld, 1983); and Starhawk's *The Spiral Dance: A Rebirth of the Ancient Religions of the Great Goddess* (San Francisco: Harper & Row, 1979) and *Dreaming the Dark: Magic, Sex and Politics* (Boston: Beacon Press, 1982).

I could have used a transgender person's picture, but I wasn't that informed back then.) Was Helga really the model for Nogeeshik? It didn't matter. Facts are not necessarily as important as Truth.

The Berdache in the Community

After about three years of recovery, I started noticing things—the fact that I worked thirty-two floors above the earth, for instance. I was typing away in my temp job at a downtown ruling-class gambling scam—I mean, investment company—and I happened to look out the window—really look. "My God!" I thought, "I'm thirty-two floors up here in space! What if there's a fire? This is downright unnatural!" I decided to change jobs, and God whispered one word, "Academia." I got the first one I applied for, staff assistant in one of Harvard's libraries. One of the job's fringe benefits was being surrounded by anthropology books. I read all about Native American spirituality, patching together bits and pieces in my imaginary spiritual playground, feeling like my recovery group was something like a tribal fellowship, with many of the same values of community and gratitude. One description of shamans echoed my experience of my Twelve-Step sponsor:

> It is precisely by demonstrating his own successful mastery of the grounds of affliction that the shaman establishes the validity of his power to heal. . . . Out of the agony of affliction and the dark night of the soul comes literally the ecstasy of spiritual victory.[4]

In many tribes, women, like the earth, were considered essential, not sinful or needful of control or invasion. In the tribes where the healers had suffered themselves, or where women were treated as equals, I rejoiced at having found early precedents for my ideas of personal worship. But nothing prepared me for one of the most profound instances I have ever had of recognizing myself in the cultural framework of a completely unknown subgroup of people; I learned about the shamans who were called *berdache*s (a word from the French *berdache* and the Spanish *bardaje,* now discredited due to its colonial meaning of "kept boy" or "prostitute"):

> The berdache among North American Indians may be roughly defined as a person, usually male, who was anatomically normal but assumed the dress,

[4] James Gabriel Campbell, quoting I. M. Lewis, "Approaches to the Study of Shamanism," *Wiener Völkerkundlich Mitteilungen* 22/23 (Austria, 1976): 74.

> occupations, and behavior of the other sex to effect a change in gender status . . . a totally self-sufficient "household" capable of both male and female activities . . . berdache category included some essentially asexual persons. . . . [Navajo] berdaches were essentially bisexual, engaging in sexual relations with males and females. . . . Mohave berdaches, especially females, were exceptionally powerful shamans . . . in Siberian shamanism, ritual homosexuality is believed to be at once a sign of spirituality, of commerce with gods and spirits, and a source of sacred power. . . . [They] drew respect because they were believed to possess qualities superior to those of a normal individual or at least particular qualities their societies needed for their own ends.[5]

I discovered that in these cultures, sexual differences were often accepted, not judged. In tribes in which Two-Spirit people existed, adults believed that children innately sensed their own path—that they "knew what they wanted to be when they grew up." They watched the children to see if they played with the other sex's toys, and, if so, they decided that the child was "choosing" to be Two Spirit:

> One of the important differences in Western and Native American cultures' view of roles and how individuals fill them has to do with paying attention to the spirit inside the person. It is the spirit rather than the anatomy that defines a berdache. Everybody mixes male and female, but some people do it in an extra-special, intense way. . . .[6]

Besides my anthropological reading, I stumbled on a recently written historical novel, *Hanto Yo,* which featured a shaman character called Winkte (also the Dakota Sioux name for *berdache*).[7]

Unlike *Hanto Yo,* many fictionalized accounts of past cultures were wishful thinking by privileged white authors. I knew that as a white borrower/trespasser, I could easily fall prey to an idealized conception of "Native" culture. To this day, sports fans see nothing wrong with the minstrel-show mentality of brandishing foam rubber "axes," shouting "war whoops," and sporting goofy-looking, big-nosed "Indians" on the backs of their jackets. Most white people need to educate ourselves about "Indians" in terms of real-world Native issues. By working with Native

[5] Charles Callender and Lee M. Kochems, "The North American Berdache," *Current Anthropology* 24, no. 4 (August–October 1983): 443–55.

[6] Jerry Snider, "The Zuni Man/Woman: Native America's Third Gender," an interview with Will Roscoe, in *Magical Blend: A Transformative Journey, Special Issue on Sexuality, Gender Politics, and Personal Identity* Issue 33 (January 1992): 46, in reference to Roscoe's book *The Zuni Man-Woman* (Albuquerque: University of New Mexico Press, 1991).

[7] Ruth Beebe Hill, *Hanto Yo: An American Saga* (New York: Warner Books, 1979).

American Indian activists I became aware of the results of our festive "Thanksgiving" myths and broken treaties: high early death rates, pervasive alcoholism, and the lack of education and jobs on the "rez."

Living in the Spirit

Living in the Spirit, the first gay/Native American Indian anthology, confirmed the fact that some contemporary Native Americans were also claiming their modern sexual identity in an archetypal context.[8] Although my inner life remained sacred, hence private, I too kept the Two-Spirit figure as my "biomythography," in the words of Audre Lorde. I shared this personal archetype's role in three major ways: as healer, artist, and twin-spirit lover. Recent books about these ancient shamans suggest that they would be helpful role models for today's queer activists:

> In the gay liberation movement, we try to emphasize that we are the same as everybody else except for what we do in bed. The American Indian cultures I studied do just the opposite; they emphasize the difference, but instead of seeing that difference as abnormal, deviant, or threatening, they see it as a "specialness," an extra gift.[9]

Most importantly, every single person—gay, lesbian, bisexual, transgendered, celibate, or straight—could benefit from learning about such healers. Kolhamana, a Zuni role model for the Two-Spirit shaman, raises powerful possibilities, especially for those of us who are bisexual and/or transgendered:

> Kolhamana, as an archetype, represents a form of sexuality and gender that is unrelated to reproduction. This meant that Kolhamana contributed a corrective influence upon the ruptures of social specialization and helped liberate individuals from the painful moral dilemma of opposites. . . . This "gatekeeper" aspect of the role became part of the berdache legacy. . . .[10]

Were there any Two-Spirit people still living? If not, where did they go? And who are the gender "gatekeepers" of today?

> The disappearance of the berdache is a result of Western civilization's determination to stigmatize gender mediation. . . . Given the increasingly omi-

[8] *Living in the Spirit,* ed. Will Roscoe (Boston: Beacon Press, 1988).

[9] Leigh W. Rutledge, *Unnatural Quotations* (Boston: Alyson Publications, 1988), 116, quoting Walter Williams, author of *The Spirit and the Flesh: Sexual Diversity in Ancient American Indian Culture* (Boston: Beacon Press, 1986).

[10] Snider, "Zuni Man/Woman," 45–46.

nous implications of what Jung terms the hyper-masculinity of the patriarchal hero, Kolhamana represents possibilities of gender reconciliation that Western societies can no longer afford to ignore.[11]

Until the arrival of "our wonderful missionaries," the Two-Spirit tribal member was not only not reviled; he/she was given a place of honor in the tribe for the gift of representing the sun and the moon, and of combining traditionally male and female roles. Bisexual and transgendered people, the latest groups to find a voice within the sexual politics liberation movement, are naturals for the role of modern gatekeeper. Within our ranks, any sexual choice regarding self or other is supported, not just tolerated. In defying culturally approved notions of being exclusively gay, exclusively straight, exclusively male, or exclusively female, we reflect and express the much-needed sacred middle ground:

> Berdaches had an identity that was separate, and it wasn't because they were persecuted into adopting it as a defense mechanism. It was a mode of expressing themselves. They took up the role like it was a paintbrush.[12]

At Seventeen . . .

One of Janis Ian's most poignant songs is called "At Seventeen." That was the age for impossible dreams and deep romanticism, especially for square pegs like me. I was seventeen when I confided to my diary that my number one wish was for "a spiritual vision." But back then, I wanted spiritual power over my enemies (parents, teachers, bullying kids), hoping that my superpowers would set me above and apart from everyone else. Becoming a feminist partially ruined that goal, for I learned that process in community was as important as product and competition, and therefore, that having power over people could never get me what I really wanted. At seventeen I had prayed to be invulnerable in a world where I'd been hurt by being called fat, loser, dyke, or weirdo. But today I can say that these names were a blessing. For as I grew older, being attacked with them drove me to explore what they meant for me. After I learned their flip side—the strengths they contained—I named myself. Imported shame turned into gold in a human alchemy of grace. Nzotake Shange said it best: "i found god in myself & i loved her/i loved her fiercely."

[11] Ibid., 46–48.
[12] Ibid., 96

In the end, I got my wish, but in a much more subversive way than I could have imagined. Instead of separating me from others, the discipline of food sobriety brought me closer than ever to other flawed human beings. Losing weight was a side effect, not a goal, for in order to "surrender my will" to binge, I had to rely on something larger than myself. I no longer worried about the opinions of some generic nemesis, "Them." When I stopped wearing a mask, sexual as well as emotional, there was work to be done. I wrote articles, I organized a new performing group, and I went back to school for a publishing degree. And I kept going to the same old meetings, year after year, just so I could hear once more that it was possible to "Be a Worker Among Workers," and to "Place Principles Over Personalities."

I don't worry so much these days about pictures of my Higher Power or imaginary spiritual worlds. I rely more on imperfect, living people than I do on perfect, imagined spirits. God may well be laughing at me, having watched me come full circle into my own version of my father's church. At fifty, in spite of my hermetic childhood, I am deeply enmeshed in my friends' lives, my queer community, my job, my Twelve-Step fellowship, and a small, socially active church. And, I have met the person whom I hope to make my lifetime companion, a transgender soul who, needless to say, understands and takes great joy in the twin-spirit life.

To paraphrase Oscar Wilde, "Watch out what you wish for; you will surely get it." I laugh at some aspects of my former twenty-something self, intrigued with the costumes and attitudes of outlaw sexuality, the more outrageous the better, for I'd lived in reaction to anything "traditional" or "normal." And as for sexual experience, that was easy to get in the seventies—all you had to do was be female and stoned. But experience and inner feeling are two different things.

At fifty I live with peace and restlessness. It's a good sort of restlessness, though, the kind that comes from living a life with no crises, no impossible demands (from inside or out), and no interest in charismatic but abusive personalities. It's an odd age—older than some friends who have died, a little more than half the age of other friends in their nineties.

My daily attitude of gratitude is based on a single insight: all of my life so far is gift. Why didn't I die at birth? Why didn't I kill myself as a depressed teenager with fifty extra pounds of needless shame and a head full of swirling, terrifying sexual identity choices? Why didn't I stay in that locked ward for more than three weeks battling suicidal depression, which was unmasked when I neared the age of forty? None of this life was promised.

"'Twas grace that brought us safe this far, and grace will lead us home." This day, this essay, this life is all gravy. I feel this message in my breath, every day, threaded through my being. My spirituality is no longer like a fake wood-grain top on a Formica desk; it is unconscious, accessible, and mischievous. As for my next forty years, anything goes. For to whom do I look for approval? Not to any one human being but to God. Just as I learned in Sunday school, God is love. And love is rare enough in any body, in any form.

Whereto My Beloved?

GANAPATI S. DURGADAS

I HAVE BEEN SO MANY SELVES—a pastiche of personas, some projected upon me, others chosen. Puerto Rican or Jew (through my parents), fat man and working-class slob, hippie and radical, street person and dope head, neo-pagan and Buddhist, activist and therapist, heterosexual and homosexual, even male and female. I smile and shake my head when I look at all the different people I have appeared to be, both to myself and others.

Sometimes I think I've been too many people in too short a time. At other times I realize that I've been portraying different roles in a play directed by an essence of me. In Hindu parlance, this essence would be called the unperceived perceiver, the unheard listener, or the unnoticed witness.

Yet, throughout my life, and within all of these characters, there flow twin streams: spirituality and sexuality.

Childhood in the Maelstrom

When I was growing up within my parent's interpretation of and indoctrination in the Judeo-Christian tradition, these streams stood in opposition to each other. Sexuality seemed to be spirtuality's subversive foe. Spirit loomed over sex like a secretly frightened bully, intimidating sexuality into a corner crowded with shame, whispers, and tugging hungers, dankly clutching at me with want and confusion.

During my childhood I had a long-held fondness for rocking myself in bed, singing songs aloud, songs in which I transported myself to faraway lands, became and interacted with a myriad of "make-believe" characters: some from television, others from comic books, still others from mythology. The worlds I explored were vivid and alive with an intensity not just inside my head but in the very air of my Brooklyn bedroom. My father thought I was crazy. He complained aloud and abusively about it. I was sent to a headshrinker through grade school. I eventually learned to drop my story singing, my inner world making, and became ashamed of my rhythmic body shaking amid the Gods. It was childish, nutsy, even worse, girlish. I realize now if I had been born in a different age or culture I might have been groomed to become a griot, shaman, or bard. I realize now that I had been shouted and shamed out of my spirituality as well as my sexuality. I was queer in each way. I had been duped into thinking they were separate from each other.

My father viewed me with distrust. During one of his periodic rages at my mother he told me point-blank that he seriously doubted I was his biological offspring. I suspect what rankled my father was my not being the man he was. Fact was, I only had a vague notion that I was a "boy," some pervasive social category into which I was supposed to assimilate myself, but was doing a halfhearted job at best. From the start I was possessed by a sense of maleness being something imposed from outside and not from within. I was aware of having a self, of being someone in a body, but not necessarily a boy child's body governed by a "male" character. I remember a definite interior feeling of girlishness. I knew I could not afford to let anyone discover it, though I feared it would be betrayed by the feminine fleshiness of my childhood fatness. Nonetheless, I tried hiding with indoctrinated shame.

I can't say I felt a complete "female" because I didn't know what that was any more than I knew what a complete "male" felt like. But I was terrified to realize that I was on the borderline, somewhere in the middle. I frightened myself into secrecy.

For my Puertorriqueno father, maleness was a God-given, predetermined repertoire which he expected would be automatically passed on with his genes. He was repeatedly enraged that I did not meet his expectations, acting as if I purposely refused to accede to them.

Coming of Age—Breaking Free

In spite of this, or perhaps because of it, I rebelled when able. I chased after sex to avenge myself upon spirit, which I had associated and confused with my parents' religiosity of learned guilt and twisted aggression. With innumerable male and female partners I felt like a shifting, shimmering presence within their embraces: a screen onto which they projected their own definitions of maleness and femaleness. What surprised me was their apparent certainty of being a man or a woman. I resented their sometimes implied, sometimes directly expressed demand that I reflect this same certainty. Almost every one of my lovers, with a few notable exceptions, had a surprisingly rigid inner gender schema, sprung upon me within the first moments of initiated intimacy.

Parallel to this sexual self search was a spiritual one. Coming to terms with my bisexuality and my conscious refusal to "be a man" helped me to realize fully both psychological and spiritual components of my being. A hopeless bibliophile, I sought solace in books during periods of isolation. Jungian psychology, gay liberation manifestos on genderfuck, bios of androgynous pop stars, and coffee-table photo books full of "shemales." I ransacked through stacks of mythology featuring twin-sexed gods like Dionysus and Yemaya-Olukun and discovered anthropological ancestors like the *hijra* and the *berdache.*

For me, the Divine was a "shemale." God appeared to be most at home in that borderland between male and female. I believed that most human beings had fallen into a spiritual exile, mistaken for reality, at either supposed gender extreme. For this reason occultism and mysticism developed a seductive hold on me. I began practicing meditation and mild yoga, and studied Eastern philosophy after a long fling with neo-paganism.

Once, just as I was entering sobriety following a heart attack, I found myself depressed and angry in a Tibetan Buddhist monastery, facing the abbot, Khenpo Kathar Rinpoche, sitting there wondering what I could possibly ask him. A male friend and occasional sex partner had brought me atop this mountain overlooking Woodstock. Maybe he thought just being there would help me. I doubted it then because the Rinpoche could barely speak English. Stupid me. I thought up some question, as that is what I understood was expected. Khenpo Kathar Rinpoche remarked that there is an unknown, invaluable treasure deep inside ourselves, and that I can find it only by making the effort. At that point, emerging from the drug and alcohol haze I had hoped would cloud and medicate my self-dislike, this was a key that gradually unlocked a me I could begin to love and respect. It led to twelve years of meditation and life as a Buddhist.

Facing the Death of the Soul

Despite the scope of this journey, the reconciliation I sought between spirit and sex could not fully manifest itself for me until the person created by those warring streams had died. A trip to San Francisco in the summer of 1990 catapulted me into the next phase of my rebirth.

I had been "in the life" for more than two decades by then, a countercultural veteran, overjoyed to have discovered a vibrant bisexual community, dedicated to restoring the radical sexual politics that had been one of the mainstays of a gay liberation movement not yet turned bourgeois.

Those ten days in San Francisco had a phantasmagoric quality. I shuttled from conference to street demo, from sex-club to bookstore, subconsciously searching for an explanation for the HIV-devastation around me. I kept remembering my friend Bill's commentary: "Don't you realize, most of the men our age in this city are dead or dying?" As a member of the AIDS direct action group ACT-UP, as a psychotherapist working with addictions, and as a queer, I had many HIV-infected persons in my life: clients, comrades, and sex partners. But on this trip something snapped. Maybe it was the protective wall of denial I had unconsciously erected. This time I truly felt the atmospheric presence of AIDS. Bill told me that more than fifty percent of the gay and bisexual men in the Bay Area were HIV-infected.

Sex and death were inextricably enmeshed here. I became a *Bhuta,* what in Hindu and Buddhist lore is called a wandering soul, lost among the *Pretas*, the hungry ghosts doubling as people caught up in the dance of desire and risk, outward defiance and inward quiet desperation. I had thought that I could synthesize calm Buddhist insight with angry queer street politics, and thus could handle anything, but it wasn't true. I was overwhelmed. I burned out.

When I returned from San Francisco I was disconsolate. Both Buddhism, which had opened me up to so much of life, and queer culture and politics, which had held so much promise, seemed to have failed me. Lost again, I wandered aimlessly.

The end of a disastrous affair, years after that fateful trip to San Francisco, completed my shift. My last fling in the face of encroaching middle age? Very likely, to some degree. Yet what had been loving three-way sex play soured into the poison of mutual manipulation and recrimination. He tried turning me against her; she turned against him and toward me, then returned to him. He ended up a year later psychiatrically hospitalized. She landed in a Twelve-Step program. I ended up emotionally spent, watching in the background. The affair seemed to have been a final catalyst. Somehow its death pairs with the pall of death in San Francisco.

I remember the day after the relationship finally collapsed. The week before had been full of burning, sleepless nights. I had felt as if my soul had poisoned itself. Sitting in the taxi riding to Albany's one Hindu temple, I felt the gentle warm breeze sweep in through the cab's open windows that early May morning. It had rained just before dawn, and the sun-kissed roads were still water-streaked, shimmering. The image of Mother Meera, an avatar, or recognized incarnation of the Divine Mother, appeared in my mind. Her image comforted me. I felt a sense of calm, an accepting and embracing love sweep over me. I felt strangely safe, almost ecstatic.

A Soul Reborn

On that day I recalled what my guru, Gurumayi Chidvilasananda, had once stated. To paraphrase her: Our most searing emotional agonies are often the effects of the burning away of a conflicted ego's most painful habitual patterns—patterns that the neurotic small self, the ego, tries to maintain in order to hold fast to the illusion of permanence. The alternative? Accept the impermanence of our patterns, and thus comprehend our true relationship with—call it what you will—Reality, Life Itself, or the Divine.

My first contact with Gurumayi Chidvilasananda had been in the late fall, after my return from the summer 1990 International Bisexual Conference and the Act Up demos in San Francisco. The *ménage à trois* affair had not yet begun, and I was a sexual freewheeler, with no attachments. Our initial conversation took the form of a confession. For no reason, except to be honest and to acknowledge my growing dissatisfaction with my sex radicalism, I revealed to Gurumayi my bisexuality and what effect that fateful summer in San Francisco had had upon me. Maybe I was expecting—at least, maybe my ego was expecting—a "logical" answer. I did not get it from her. What I did get puzzled me. My bisexuality was what I was anxious about. For me it was right in the middle of the mix of my spiritual and psychological crisis. Gurumayi simply called it my search for God, each and every bit of it. It sounds like a cliché, but the apparent simplicity of it caught me unawares, and even now it speaks an infinity of wisdom to me. Once again, a well-put, simple truth awakened me when I least anticipated it.

Now I had discovered my True Beloved.

I converted to Hinduism at that time, and in the process dropped out of queer activism. Though I had been living as a Hindu for five years before my taxicab experience, somehow that May morning marked a turning point in my practice. I realized then that God's love for us never decreases, unlike human love, and that the latter can only persevere if it is informed by the former. This is one of the main messages in the Hindu tantric understanding of sexuality, and may be the truest sex radicalism of all. I learned that declarations of and attempts at sexual revolution uninformed by God are just self-deceptions and quickly degenerate into replays of culturally conditioned fears, aggression, greed, and narcissism. If one's heart is not as open as God's, then the ego quickly belies all our high-flown rhetoric. The three of us may have started out as lovers, but we were really only in love with our small selves, our egos, our images of ourselves as sex radicals. Our inner dishonesty polluted our self-images, so that the basest ego-driven needs took control and corrupted the relationship. The affair's end taught me that only by opening myself fully to the Divine could I reflect liberation in the world—sexual liberation included.

I found, amazingly so, that much of what was taken away from me in childhood seems very present within Hinduism, its way of life so vast and polycentric, all the "experts" have trouble defining or categorizing it. A lot like I do, I guess. In it I see the Beloved I have always searched for, but only vaguely knew it until now. For you see, my Beloved is Lord Shiva, the God who is half woman. My Beloved is Mother Kali, who is sometimes female, sometimes male. Together they constitute the world's oldest deity.

I discovered Tantrism, the branch of Hindu and Buddhist spiritual practice characterized by shame/guilt-free sexual symbolism and an open acceptance of androgyny, which was shunned and suppressed in the West. Tantra is more than an assortment of schools of thought or an ancient collection of apparent sex manuals (as some Western populizers might have it). It is a mind-set, a way of life, in which one gradually withdraws from a learned dualistic and compartmentalized perception of ourselves and the universe. In withdrawing from false, imposed dualisms that attach constrictive and alienating identities upon us, Tantra offers a philosophy and a set of practices that enable us to merge with the underlying Divine Wholeness. Tantra returns one to the borderline between male and female, not as a "mistake of nature" but as an emanation of Sacred Reality. It was with tantric Hinduism that I finally felt as though I had come home.

Hinduism thrives heartily upon contradictions. The most ascetic sects live alongside the most sensual, with nothing more than a mild philosophical debate between them. More a way of life than a religion per se, conservatism coexists with the broadest sorts of acceptance. You can find the most sharply delineated sex roles assigned to biologically defined men and women. You can also find changes exerted by feminism and modernism. And, along with both of these realities, you will find a sanctified caste of transgendered people. All of these are accepted within the same spiritual social spectrum.

I can get away with wearing multiple earrings and nose rings, cosmetics and extensive jewelry (not to mention a chest and two arms full of god/dess image and yantra tattoos) along with my *dhoti* (a waist-gown, usually of cotton or silk) within a religious context. It doesn't hurt that Hinduism's main deities, such as Shiva, Durga, and Vishnu, are omni-erotic and pan-genderous. I achieve a fulfillment in Hindu community, in Hindu practice, in Hindu belief, that I never felt before. On the few occasions when I had come close, I had also felt hemmed in by a fear created by the clear and present fact (and danger) that such fulfillment was countenanced only among fellow outlaws. In my life as a Hindu I am given tacit spiritual approval. Sometimes I am even given explicit approval.

I feel I have somehow come home. For years I grieved the loss of my family to domestic violence, drugs, and racism. Now I find myself adopted into a family of immigrant South Indian Brahmins, my name changed legally, a member of the local Hindu community. I experience a sense of connectedness, a feeling of belonging I never felt before.

Therein lies my dilemma. I know I could easily disappear from visible queer life by entering fully into the Hindu community, cutting off all ties to the identifiable lesbian, gay, bisexual, and transgendered community. It is very, very tempting. My disillusionment with the latter community leaves me quite ready to abandon it. I find myself increasingly out of sync, if not alienated outright. I can cite continuing biphobia expressed by many lesbians and gays, through direct hostility, or through failing to acknowledge the existence or presence of bisexuals. I have my doubts about this ever changing, especially now that a mainstream element has virtually seized control of organizations and media, bent on assimilating into middle-class conformity. The result is a split in queer life where the liberationist and radically creative impulses are purposely marginalized, if not openly demonized. Bisexuals, like the transgendered, upset the drive for acceptance. Widely welcoming us would only derail the train toward assimilation.

Of course, there are conservative middle-class elements within the Hindu community, especially among South Asian immigrants influenced by the Anglo-Indian puritanism induced by colonialism. But Hinduism per se is not an erotophobic or homo/biphobic religion. Many of the divinities worshiped are so polymorphous and pansensual as to defy Western categories of gender or sexual orientation. And Hindu tolerance allows a large space for dissenting or nonorthodox religious sects and practices to coexist relatively peaceably. Faced with the mounting emptiness I feel within my former primary community, every day I take more and more solace and comfort from my growing identification as a Hindu.

Besides my discomfort with growing lesbian and gay conservatism, I am alienated by other aspects of the life I formerly so strongly identified with. After more than two decades "in the life," I've come to the angering conclusion that the assimilationist lesbian and gay community will never go beyond mere lip service and breast beating to actually address racism and religious bigotry. I suspect there is more segregation here than among heterosexuals, and that all the rainbow-waving talk about diversity is exactly just that—talk. Any feminist or queer liberationist stance against outmoded sex roles, erotic repression, ageism, or patriarchalism seems shunted aside as personal ads address people as commodities: gay men are as obsessed with youth as ever, lesbians power-broke, and every one tries deciding who's a top or a bottom. I seriously ask myself why I stay. Is the dance finally over?

Yet I remain. Somehow there persists that deep connection I sense and feel between my spirituality and my sexuality. Maybe it is my karma to be wedged between these two communities, undecided whether to leave one for the other. But that would mean the dance is far from over. When I ponder this, it seems to be what my Beloved wants. For Shiva, as Tandava, the Eternal Dancer, is the Source and Reconciler of apparent "opposites." As a follower of Lord Shiva I see the flow of life and everyone within it as really another aspect of him, the Actor and Dancer, who, along with his Consort, the Divine Mother, plays out as everything which is this universe. It seems they have placed me here, forever between worlds, for it is only when I am between that I feel most alive. Therefore I suspect the tension of my dilemma itself is part of the Dance.

I had been *brahmachari,* or celibate, for over a year before undertaking to write this. Originally I thought there was some weighty life decision I had to make. I had even been thinking about escaping the tensions of my dilemma via an arranged marriage. My alienation from queer life had been that strong. I planned to go to Kashi, or Benares, the sacred city of Shiva in India, for a *yatra,* or religious pilgrimage, or maybe an escape from my disillusionment. Again and again I have looked to my Beloved for an answer. And once more the answer was not in the obvious.

One evening, during an ecumenical spiritual ceremony at an area Metropolitan Community Church, I read to those assembled the story of Shiva's love affair with his fellow god Vishnu. Despite the latter's protestations that the love between two male deities could not be fruitful, Lord Shiva seduced him just the same. Then Vishnu trans-sexualized into the Mohini, a divine enchantress, and gave birth to the divinity Ayyapa. This god, the offspring of a homosexual union and transgendered birth, went on to triumph over the *asuras*, or demons, of ignorance and negative passions. The more I pondered this story the more it resonated within me.

The gods had wrought the possible out of the impossible. Maybe that is what my Beloved is telling me: conflict, inner conflict most of all, leads to its own sort of recreation of the new and vibrant and vital. The apparently same and the different are really not opposites. It is our hesitation about living life on life's often ambiguous terms that keeps us from taking true creative advantage of it. We want an easy road map for our spirituality and sexuality, a painless, tearless means for evolving new sorts of community. We create irreconcilable opposites often as an excuse. Yet the missteps, the stumbling, the fatigue, and the falls are part of Life's Dance too. If we just give up, if I just give up, opting for a kind of unilateral safety, hiding myself in the false security of resignation, I cut myself off from what life wants of me. The dance, life, my Beloved are inviting me to birth all the possibilities for living out of those very same projections of the impossible which I myself created from past failures, fears, hurts, and resentments.

No way am I stepping out of your Lila, your Dance, my Beloved. I am staying right here, forever in the creative middle with you.

From Darkness to Gateway: A Journey toward the Light

ANGEL THREATT

I AM AN AFRICAN-AMERICAN lesbian-identified bisexual. I am also one of a minority of people who feel a constant awareness of their presence on both the earthly and spiritual planes. I am at all times dual: both "here" and not here. I live with an intangible feeling of "difference" that cannot be attributed solely to my sexual orientation. I believe that my particular brand of spirituality is innate, a uniquely God-given gift, separate from "religion" and inseparable from my identity as a lesbian-identified bisexual. I experience this state as a finely tuned vibration. That vibration is defined by Malidoma Somé, Dagara shaman and author of *Of Water and the Spirit,* as something that is unique to gay, lesbian, bisexual, and transgender (GLBT) people.[1] Mr. Somé states that within the culture of the Dagara of West Africa, it is known that "gay" people are the "gatekeepers" of the society, the ones who hold open the gates between the earth and the spirit world.

I have always been aware of my difference, as have my family, my teachers, and many of my schoolmates. I was a serious child, and family members accepted my need for silence, my quiet "brooding," the long spells when I would wander off by myself into the woods behind my grandmother's house, my "booking"—rocking against the back of a chair or couch (when my mind would wander wherever it chose), my voracious reading appetite. When engaged in these activities I often did not hear my

[1] Malidoma Patrice Somé, *Of Water and the Spirit: Ritual, Magic, and Initiation in the Life of an African Shaman* (New York: Putnam, 1994).

name being called or a person speaking to me. I was never more than mildly chastised and was either coaxed back into the present or left alone. My fourth-grade teacher allowed me to read or write while she was giving her lectures to the class. A classmate once asked her why it was all right for me to do that without being chastised, while other students were reprimanded for "not paying attention." I looked up from my book and waited curiously, along with the rest of the class, for her response. She replied that she knew that I was paying attention, and that she was aware that I could do two things at once.

Today, when I meditate and talk to the ancestors and come closer into my spiritual center, it becomes even more apparent to me that I live between two worlds, and that this is where I am supposed to be. It was not always this way. I was not always aware and proud of myself as a lesbian/bisexual woman. Nor was I always aware of myself as a spiritual being. In fact, for many years I believed I was not spiritual when in fact I was simply not religious. Now I understand that during my childhood walks in the woods, I was connecting with God and with the spirit within myself and in nature.

I have learned to cultivate and value my need to be of "two minds," my propensity to daydream. I have learned to pay attention to the quiet, still voice within. I do this by meditating, by writing, by listening to and trusting my intuition, by finding wisdom and truth in astrology and spiritual teachings including Yoruba, Christianity, Buddhism, and paganism, by communing with the trees, the rivers, and the streams, by valuing the wisdom and insight gleaned from the depths of depression, and, finally, by understanding depression to be ordained by Spirit as an alert to her/his presence and a reminder of my divinity.

As a spirit, the earth feels foreign to me. My body feels foreign to me. Even the idea of genders is foreign to me. I believe that my soul has spent quite a bit of time on astral levels or perhaps on other planets, where gender and other aspects of current "reality" do not exist. I also feel very strongly that my soul was born into this body, on this planet, at this time, for a reason. The life that I was born into, my sexual identity, my experiences and feelings, my talents and shortcomings, all exist for a spiritual purpose. I believe that we are souls in bodies and that we make a choice as spirits when and where to incarnate. The Dagara concept of gatekeepers, along with the Native American concept of Two-Spirit people perfectly describes the way I experience the confluence of my sexuality and my spirituality. As Malidoma Somé says:

> The Earth is looked at, from my tribal perspective, as a very delicate machine or consciousness, with high vibrational points, which certain people must be guardians of in order for the tribe to keep its continuity with the gods and with the spirits that dwell there. Spirits of this world and spirits of the other worlds. Any person who is at this link between this world and the other world experiences a vibrational consciousness which is far higher, and far different, from the one that a normal person would experience. This is what makes a gay person gay. This kind of function is not one that society votes for certain people to fulfill. It is one that people are said to decide upon prior to being born. You decide that you will be a gatekeeper before you are born.[2]

A World beyond Labels

It makes sense to me now that I opened fully and consciously to Spirit during my coming out process. Understanding what the role of the gatekeeper entails—holding open pathways between worlds—and understanding how this role may be linked to sexual orientation, I now see how coming out initiated the integration of my many-aspected self. Coming out was and is a process of transcending perceived limitations, a process that enabled and continues to enable me to see that I am more than a word that can be held in the mouth. I do not believe that any of our souls can be defined by the temporary vessels we inhabit, or by the temporary reality that the All has created for us to exist within. I am an expression of the everything, the all; thus, I am, theoretically at least, bi-gendered, bi-sexual, multi-gendered, multi-sexual, yet I am at times non-sexual and no-thing.

I have identified myself at different times as lesbian, as bisexual, as pansexual, as asexual, and all of these things have been true. But I believe that we must be careful not to allow the labels we adopt to separate us one from another even within the GLBT community. While labeling our realities may be necessary and empowering at this stage of human development, such separation of human beings one from another is artificial. Indeed, the separation of one aspect of the self from another is unnatural.

Perhaps I call myself bisexual because I know that the complexity of

[2] Bert H. Hoff, "Gays: Guardians of the Gates, An Interview with Malkidoma Somé," *M.E.N. Magazine* (September 1993). Online. Internet. 29 July 1999. Available http://www.vix.com/pub/menmag/somegay.htm

myself cannot be defined by my genitalia or by my sexual expression. I want to challenge the GLBT community to look at its own exclusivity and prejudices. I am willing to risk my level of inclusion in and acceptance by the very community I struggled and dreamed my entire life to find, in order to move us all forward into a world without labels, without barriers. And, though I continue to identify myself primarily as lesbian, I recognize that even this label has a cultural origin that does not address all of who I am as a woman of African descent, as a spiritual being, as a woman who has loved men, both sexually and non-sexually, as a woman who would like to spend the rest of her life with another woman, as a woman who wants to bear a child who has a loving relationship with his father. Because of this, I look toward a future where we are to evolve fully into who we are, "coming out of the closet" as a spiritual people and adopting another language which focuses on connection and wholeness.

In one of its most damaging manifestations, we can see that the separation of the sexual from the spiritual holds us hostage to a stale worldview. Spiritual/sexual energy is energy for creation, for survival, for living, regardless of what form that creation takes. And, just as there is little societal support for a fluid sexual identity, there is little social support for a fluid and oceanic spirituality. When we have learned to embrace a spirituality that need not be hindered by religious persecution, when we have learned to embrace human difference and not to demand or expect that black gays "choose" which identity is more important to them; that bisexual people "choose" between a heterosexual and homosexual identity; that interracial people "choose" which race they will identify with, perhaps we will have come closer to a world in which we accept our wholeness. Through integrating the various parts of ourselves, we become whole. In our fragmented, postmodern world, perhaps we should look back to indigenous societies, not for an imagined utopia but for visions of wholeness that we can translate into a modern-day new world. This wholeness of individuals and of community is expressed this way by Somé:

> Again, in the culture that I come from . . . [gay] people are looked on, essentially, as people. The whole notion of "gay" does not exist in the indigenous world. That does not mean that there are not people there who feel the way that certain people feel in this culture, that has led to them being referred to as "gay." The reason why I'm saying there are no such people is because the gay person is very well integrated into the community, with the func-

> tions that delete this whole sexual differentiation of him or her. The gay person is looked at primarily as a "gatekeeper."[3]

As I hold this vision of a world focused on connection instead of separation, I realize that this work holds the gates between this world and the next. I realize that I am the heir to my African-American, my Native American, and my GLBT ancestors who have done this work. I am reminded of my grandmother, who prayed for me through my years of depression, when I didn't believe in a "God," who called me constantly to wake me from depression's fog. As my grandmother prayed for me, it is now my destiny to pray for my family, my friends, myself, and the world. Though I often feel trapped between two worlds spiritually and physically, or between two or more realities socially, I recognize and accept this as my path and life work. Though ultimately my "difference" escapes definition, I am beginning to see that it is my difference and the difference of others that keeps us in the margins, which is really in between worlds. Perhaps we will one day be gatekeepers all, and on that day our souls will return home.

[3] Ibid.

I Can Love All the Faces of G-d

Gilly Rosenthol

As an observant Jew, I often feel as though people expect me to feel a conflict between my Judaism and my bisexuality. Ironically, the only area in which I feel any such conflict is in the assumptions and expectations of other people. I personally see more parallels than contrasts between the two.

One parallel is that I didn't choose to be Jewish, and I don't honestly think I would have chosen it had I been born otherwise. But being Jewish is an integral part of who I am, a part that I value. The same is true of bisexuality. I don't feel that I chose it, but it's who I am, and I'm glad for that.

Why wouldn't I choose my identities? Quite simply, it's not easy to be either Jewish or bi in such a Christian, heterosexual society. Even if there were no negative value judgments made about either, the United States is set up to assume both heterosexuality and Christianity as the norm. For example, In Boston, where I live, you cannot buy alcohol in a store on Sunday. Why? Because Sunday is the Christian Sabbath, and Boston was a Puritan city. Also in Boston, two female friends of mine just had a child together, and they had to jump through all sorts of hoops to make sure they shared legal parenthood of this child whom they had brought into the world together. Why? Because the United States is a nation that does not honor the validity of same gender unions—a reflection of institutionalized heterosexism.

This essay began as an interview/discussion with Amanda Udis-Kessler; my thanks to her for suggesting topics and issues.

One way that my bisexuality has supported my increased awareness and wholeness as a Jew is that before I came out to myself as bisexual, I was never aware of such inequalities. I hadn't noticed many of the difficulties that still face African-Americans, or the physically disabled, or people who happen to be larger than average, or any number of groups that fall outside the range of the "average American." In fact, now that I have come out, I believe that I even notice "Christian-centrism" more than I used to.

I think I used to take it for granted that the rules were made to favor the majority group. Now that I have learned to work for equal rights as a bisexual, it occurs to me that I deserve them as a Jew as well. Moreover, it also occurs to me that social justice is at the heart of Judaism—loving the stranger as yourself, *tikkun olam* (fixing the world), leaving the edges of your field for the poor to glean. These are the mandates of a system founded on egalitarian principles—radical in their day, and many of them radical to this day.

Since coming out, I feel as though I've had blinders removed. That has given me not only the ability to empathize with others who face prejudice but also the freedom to really look at how our society works, to question it, and to work for change. I think I'm a more sensitive and open-minded person for having gone through the coming-out process. In the process I have found it interesting that members of minority groups are no less prone to making assumptions than anyone else. Many of the Jews I know presume that everyone is heterosexual until proven otherwise. I've certainly assumed that even fairly close friends were Christian until they mention being Jewish. I still have plenty to educate myself on, but at least I'm learning to question my assumptions.

Another parallel between my two identities is that as often as I come out as bisexual, I find myself coming out as Jewish, and it truly is a coming out. I'm always nervous about how people will respond, and I get tired of explaining myself. There are times when I go out to eat and I'm tempted to just say, "I'm a vegetarian" instead of "I keep kosher." When I say the latter, I have to be prepared to launch into an explanation of what that means and why I do it, because people usually ask.

But I come out as bisexual in part to educate people, to show them that bisexuals do exist and that we're not as different as they might think. It's the same for Judaism. I've found that people have certain assumptions about observant Jews that don't always fit me. When I am open about who I am, I can help them to open up to the wonderful range of people who are out there, outside of their experience. I particularly like to be out as a

Jew in queer settings because I like to show people that a person can be religious and still be accepting of others with different beliefs.

Learning not only to accept but also to value being a member of an "oppressed" group, the queer community, has also helped me to value my Jewish community. I am sometimes concerned about how my non-Jewish or nonreligious friends view my traditions and rituals. I know that sometimes they see them as bizarre and antiquated. They try to be supportive, and I know that the way I stick to my beliefs is something that they respect about me, but I'm always very conscious of being different. Finding a Jewish community and being able to celebrate those rituals with a group have reminded me that I'm not alone, that others do share the same values and beliefs. It's wonderful to feel that even though we may have very different Jewish backgrounds, we're all coming from the same place, with the same values, and that we can share these things together as a community.

That sense of community is something that is important to me in both bisexuality and Judaism, and it constitutes my final comparison. I like being part of the Jewish family, of knowing when I light candles on Friday night that women all over the world are doing the same thing; that for hundreds, even thousands of years, women have shared that same moment of peace as they say the blessings over the candles and bring in the *Shabbat.* I also like being in a queer community. One of my favorite events of the year is the Gay Pride parade. I love watching the thousands of people filling the streets and feeling an instant connection with every one of them, knowing that we are, in a sense, family.

As in many families, sometimes I feel that my "in-laws" can't get along, and that's a shame, but they're still both family. I think they don't have any problems with each other as people, but when they see each other as groups, there's this clan feud going on. Many people in the queer community, perhaps through bad experiences in their own past, think that all religious people and communities will reject them. Many Orthodox Jews have difficulty accepting homosexuals because male homosexual acts are condemned in the Bible and Orthodox Jews have little or no experience with gay people who are also religious.

It hurts to be caught in the middle when both sides are me. I *can't* give up one or the other, and it infuriates me, because nowhere in the Torah is there any prohibition against female homosexuality. Only male homosexuality is mentioned, and even for that I've heard a number of alternate ways of interpreting those few passages. I personally can't believe that HaShem would create people to love a certain way and then condemn them to death for it. I don't believe the actions that are condemned in the

Torah equate to our understanding of homosexuality today. Despite the silence regarding women, and despite these alternative explanations, so many Orthodox people say that who I am and what I do is wrong. It seems to me that they are not even willing to look at their own sources—*our* own sources—to understand this question. I have to wonder when the prejudice of humanity became more important than the word of G-d?

Despite some of the difficulties I have had with balancing my Judaism and my bisexuality, I know that coming out as bisexual has forced me to look deeper into myself than I might have otherwise, and to have faith in myself. It was scary for me to question who I was, to say, "This is who I've always assumed I am, but maybe not." When I started recognizing my feelings for women, I was terrified. I knew nothing about homosexuality and had never even heard the word bisexual. I knew what it meant to be straight, but I could not even begin to picture what my life would be like as a lesbian. It took me years to go from accepting that I had feelings for a particular woman to being comfortable with taking on the label "bisexual."

Going through that process, and learning to allow myself the freedom to change, helped me to face the fact that traditional Orthodox Judaism was not for me. More than just being Jewish, being Orthodox has always been a huge part of my identity. I was afraid that if I started to question that, I might discover that the Jewish traditions that shape my life really had no meaning for me, that I was practicing out of habit and pressure. I honestly can't picture my life without keeping kosher, keeping *Shabbat*—I think I really would be a different person. Yet, when I found the strength to look deep inside and examine what the traditions mean to me and how they fit into my life, I found understandings that I had never even imagined.

I now embrace a Judaism that is much more personal. Now when I smell some bacon and find my mouth watering, instead of feeling deprived that I can't eat it, I know that it is my choice to keep kosher, every time, and that means a lot more than doing it because someone else says I have to. I've discovered that the parts of Judaism that I have trouble with are the ones that I can't reconcile with my feminism. Since I was a child, I've had trouble accepting the role of women in Orthodox Judaism. It hurts me to go to synagogue and not be counted as part of a *minyan* (quorum required for prayer) just because I'm a woman. I feel invisible—much as I do when people assume that I'm straight, or Christian.

Having some Jews, even some rabbis, who have accepted me as I am—as an observant egalitarian bisexual female Jew—has helped a lot. I worked for three years as an office manager in a synagogue and formed a close relationship with the rabbi there. I got the impression that bisexuality is not what she would have wished for me, but she didn't seem to think of it as bad or wrong, just difficult. If I were to become committed to a woman, I know that she would help me mark the occasion in a Jewish way, just as if I married a man she would help me to create a Jewish ceremony that was both legal and reflected my beliefs about marriage and relationships. She would dance at my *simcha* in either case. (*Simcha* is the Hebrew word for "joy," used for events such as weddings. It is a *mitzvah,* a commandment, to dance at one.)

Family is extremely important to me. I look forward to finding a life partner and having children, and I want to raise them in a Jewish home, whether I build that home with a man or a woman. I want to have a Jewish family. It makes me smile to picture lighting *Shabbat* candles together with my wife, or wearing a *tallit,* together with my husband in the synagogue.

As valuable as this growth has been, and as much peace as I have managed to achieve within myself, that yearning for family and community was an ongoing struggle for a long time after I came out. Four years ago, I figured out how to integrate what was happening for me on the inside with what my world looked like on the outside. On that day, for a few awesome moments, my identity as a Jew, my identity as a bisexual, and my identity as a woman came into an alignment so profound that I feel it today as if it happened just moments ago.

I finally came out to my mother in 1994. It was one of the most difficult and frightening things I've ever done, and it was painful for both of us. Even so, it left me feeling freer and stronger and very proud of myself, and I felt a powerful need to mark the occasion with a ceremony. So the next Saturday, I went to synagogue, and when I got there, I knew the perfect way for me to celebrate.

I was brought up Orthodox, and in that tradition men and women have very different roles in ritual. Only men are allowed to go up to the Torah during the service and say the blessings over the reading—this is called an *aliyah,* and it's considered an honor. The synagogue I attend now is egalitarian, so women and men have equal roles, and it's quite common for a woman to have an *aliyah,* but I had never had one before. But when I got to *shul* (synagogue), it suddenly hit me that taking an *aliyah* was just what I was looking for. I was there early, and I approached a woman in the hall and asked her how one went about getting an *aliyah.* She said, "I don't know, I think they may have already assigned them." When she saw my disappointment, she asked, "Was there a particular reason you were interested?" I took a deep breath, nervous of her reaction, and said quietly "I just came out to my mother as bisexual." And instead of the dismissal that I had half expected, she gave me a great big smile and said, "Mazel tov! That's wonderful!" And another woman who had been standing nearby overheard us, and came over to say, "How did it go? Do you know about the Bisexual Resource Center? They might have some helpful information for your parents." And someone else turned to us and said, "What about P-FLAG? They're pretty good."

Instead of being cut off from my community, I was surrounded and supported and loved and respected. It felt so wonderful. Everyone made sure I got my *aliyah.*

My Hebrew name was read to call me up—Gilana Mia bas Abba v'Sara Leah, Gilana Mia daughter of Arthur and Sandie—I felt as though G-d himself were calling me. I stood before the Torah in front of the entire congregation, wrapped in a borrowed *tallit,* just as my father had wrapped me in his when I was a child. My voice was trembling with emotion as I sang the prayer, but it felt to me as though it filled the room and beyond to Jerusalem. Tears filled my eyes so that the Torah in front of me shimmered and the words danced—tears of sorrow for those parts of me I had denied for so long, and tears of joy for that perfect moment that allowed me to finally be all that I am.

As one who can love men and love women and love the Torah too, I did not choose to be a bisexual Jew, but it has brought me a special wisdom and strength. I guess you could call it a blessing.

Even though I know that G-d is not a gendered person, it's easier for me, as a bisexual Jew, to envision Him/Her/It as having masculine and feminine sides. Just as I love and appreciate men and women for their differences and similarities, I love all the faces of G-d that I can see.

Look to This Day

LYNN DOBBS

Look to this day!
For it is life, the very life of life.
In its brief course lie all the verities
And realities of your existence:
The bliss of growth,
The glory of action,
The splendor of beauty;
For yesterday is but a dream,
And tomorrow is only a vision;
But today, well lived, makes every yesterday
A dream of happiness
And every tomorrow a vision of hope.
Look well, therefore, to this day.
—Attributed to Kalisdasa[1]

In the Beginning

THE FIRST FORTY YEARS of my life's accumulated yesterdays live in my mind as a poorly plotted, badly written melodrama of epic proportions.

My story is hardly unique. In childhood, my life was awash in guilt-inducing, trial-and-error lessons about an incomprehensibly inconsistent

[1] As written in *Singing the Living Tradition* (Boston: Unitarian Universalist Association, 1993).

social morality. Adults used whatever physical or psychological tools were at hand to instill "the fear of God" in me. The lessons were based on conflicting interpretations of God's laws for correct Christian thought and behavior. Sunday school lessons about turning the other cheek, the golden rule, the virtue of meekness and the quest for unconditional divine love were set against the backdrop of physical and emotional violence perpetrated against me by my parents and my Lutheran school teacher. These moral contradictions invariably led me to ask why things happened as they did. I desperately wanted my world to be consistent and understandable.

Sexual desire, being such a strong force in a young life, provided the perfect example of this. Without understanding the concepts, I knew that genital touching, hugging, kissing, and other behaviors felt good. When I was eleven, my sex drive was strong and not gender-restricted. I was a young hedonist. In fact, I was caught with my best friend's cock firmly in my hand. The stiffness of my punishment made it crystal clear that touching cocks was a serious sin. In my child's mind, the solution seemed clear —keep secrets and pretend.

As a teenager, I continued to base my daily choices on the principle "What they don't know can't hurt me." Necessarily, I chose a path that kept me emotionally distant from others. This provided the illusion of short-term safety and the reality of long-term tragedy. Well hidden within my emotional fortress, I vainly attempted to unravel an obfuscated tapestry of religious truth and moral order. I continued to question God's reasons for creating misery, pain, and death. Questions led to more questions. I was mired in a swamp of confusion.

Though I might not have had any answers to those questions, by the mid-1960s I knew what publicly acceptable behaviors were associated with romantic relationships. My concepts of love, relationships, and the ideal family were fashioned by 1950s and early 1960s television. Not only did I believe that *Ozzie and Harriet, Gunsmoke, Father Knows Best,* and *Leave It to Beaver* were entertaining; they served as my models for interpersonal relationships. I knew my family didn't fit the pattern, but that was only one data point in the face of all those television families. I felt like a sitcom character searching for a more appealing story.

I also knew that romantic relationships were always between one boy and one girl and that both needed to be pretty. Since the feelings I was having for both boys and girls didn't fit that picture at all, I assumed my feelings weren't romantic love. By age sixteen, I knew that sexual desire existed outside the framework of sitcom love, but my view of moral and social correctness never allowed lust and only permitted sexual behaviors under tightly controlled conditions.

I was embarrassed by sexual desire in general and ashamed of my own. The societal taboo against discussing sexuality left me with the certainty that I alone faced these torments as a vengeful God's punishment for some unknown, egregious sin. Increasing feelings of shame forced me deeper into my emotional fortress. I angrily questioned God and God's love in the face of such emotional torment. I began to hate God for what he had done to me. Late in my sixteenth year, I declared myself an atheist as an act of rebellion.

Searching for Universal Morality

But I longed for simple rules with well-defined rewards and punishments, which seemed to be the promise of religion. I assumed that my inability to conform to what I imagined were society's expectations was based primarily in my failure to understand the complex moral code. At eighteen, I joined a Lutheran church with a new determination to learn and understand the meaning of and purpose for my life and life in general.

I asked theological and moral questions of the minister and congregational members. The answers to my whys seemed evasive. The minister often said, "There are many things we aren't meant to know." This was an entirely unsatisfactory answer. The clear inference was that there is something to know but that we mere mortals—or, possibly, just me—are incapable of understanding the complexity of God's plan. For the first time I began to realize that there might not be a plan or a God. Once again I declared myself an atheist, but this time I believed it. For years, my atheism included an overt antireligion vehemence.

At nineteen, still looking for the simple set of moral rules I craved, I joined the navy. Life was unpleasant most of the time, but it was consistent. Predictability seemed a safe haven. It was easy to remain emotionally distant under the hyper-masculine rules of self-reliance and stoicism. For the first eighteen months of training, the navy controlled much of what I saw and heard. I slipped into a routine that required little thought, less consciousness, and no emotional display.

As the months passed, my feelings of loneliness and aloneness deepened to the point where they could no longer be ignored. I fell into a chronic, but not entirely hopeless, depression. I was no longer an active participant in my life. For the next twenty years, I watched life as if it were someone else's home movie. I married, raised a child, completed a navy career, and divorced with little interest, less love, and no compassion. The predominant emotion in my life was anger. I was hostile to a world that had seemed intentionally thickheaded and violent in all its interactions with me. "Vengeance is mine," sayeth the Lynn.

Even though I was sleepwalking through my life, there were times of joy, love, and intimacy. As I look back, I can see they were attenuated emotional moments of openness. At the time, I accepted the feelings without reflection. I chose to live rather superficially. Yet, with the exception of my early relationship with my ex-wife, I didn't recognize that my emotional states contained sexual desire. I found nothing sexual about my relationship with my shipboard friends because I was hungrier for feelings of belonging than for sex. And I still held sexuality in an extremely negative context.

I looked back after my divorce at my few attempts at affinity and intimacy and was shocked to discover that these feelings had been strongest for members of my own gender. My deep friendship with a fellow sailor during one deployment was electric with sexual energy, but I was completely unaware of my attraction to this man. Sexuality had long since lain dormant in my body and been held in contempt in my mind. I felt totally unprepared to explore this revelation. My rising shame temporarily pushed thoughts of sexual desire out of my mind.

Discovering Complexity in Human Beings

In my youth, I created myself as a hammer in search of nails. I treated every "problem" as something to solve unemotionally with brute, and often brutal, force. I raged against the world in incoherent tirades. By the time I was thirty-five, I knew that my anger was my method of distancing myself from other people. I had created a coherent philosophy similar to social Darwinism or Objectivism that rested on a soulless foundation and that considered mystical aspects of being to be abdications of personal responsibility.

It wasn't a satisfying philosophy, though. I knew that I wasn't cut from cloth that would ensure my survival if I relied on personal ruthlessness and strength. For five years I struggled to find the truth in my philosophy, but felt more and more insecure with the basic concepts. I discussed these issues with the people around me but only found agreement in the military.

After my divorce in 1991, I learned about bisexuality through connections I made on the Internet. Several outspoken bisexual contributors in a newsgroup I subscribed to introduced me to terms like "sex positive," "bisexual" and "polyamory." Despite my suppressed sexuality, I felt compelled to join the conversations about morality, sexuality, tolerance, and the meaning of intimate relationships.

Up to this point in my life I hadn't argued my position with philosophers, historians, social scientists, or theologians. My new friends asked questions that ripped my arguments and my philosophy to shreds. Every exchange generated more questions than answers about individual responsibility to the whole of our communities. When I finally surrendered to uncertainty, the opening was created for me to consider the nature of soul.

The question that eventually undid my philosophical house of cards concerned the nature of ritual and the purpose of shared rituals. I had previously dismissed rituals by defining them only in terms of "primitive and superstitious religions." In discussions about ritual, I found a rich mix of religious traditions that spoke to the same sense of interconnectedness in life. A deep longing to be connected found a voice in these concepts. I also found the roots of my own sexism, genderism, racism, and heterosexism.

Discovering that my definitions of sex and gender were artificial and capricious was a transformational moment. The television model of a proper man and a proper woman on which I had been weaned now horrified me. I instantly saw the insidious nature of sexism and racism. My objectivist notion of individual responsibility was seriously flawed and simplistic. It was as if an all-consuming fog had lifted. A feeling of happiness unlike anything I had ever felt washed through me.

I began arguing for collective responsibility to end institutional biases against women and people of color. For the first time, I felt a connection with large segments of humanity. Previously suppressed emotions, including love, rushed to the surface and flooded over me. I claimed a corner of the progressive social movement and staked out a political stance for equality before the law for everyone. I couldn't explain the nature of the connection I felt (and still feel). It was a mystery I didn't explore. I was too intoxicated with the feeling.

Suddenly feeling as if I was part of the species raised my long dormant sexual appetite. I noticed that my attraction criteria were based on politics and social conscience rather than appearance and gender. I loved lots of people and wanted deep emotional and physical relationships with them all. I adopted the descriptive label: politically progressive, polyamorous bisexual.

But I still felt alone and insecure. My new sexual awareness brought fear and shame with it. Now I was forty and had the interpersonal skills of a ten-year-old. My Internet friendships lacked sufficient corporal contact, so I searched out local connections. I discovered the BiForum, a local bisexual discussion and support group and my introduction to the queer and pagan communities. I talked to activists in the transgender, lesbian, gay, and pagan communities. I met people who were exceedingly sex positive. In a short time, my attitudes about sex and sexuality were challenged and reversed. But my fears about being sexual lingered.

In the pagan community, I found the concept that sexual behaviors can be honoring of one's self and one's sexual partner rather than a debasement of either. I also discovered a different set of definitions for "divine" and "divine love." The mystery of why and how that had tormented my youthful attempts to find spirituality were replaced by a more Eastern attitude that the divine is within all living things. A new meaning for "spiritual" entered my consciousness.

I was experiencing an integration of body, mind, and spirit even though body and spirit were still somewhat vague. Once I embarked on this exploration, though, vagueness vanished quickly. The feeling of belonging enraptured me, so I created a label to show my clan: a sex positive, gender-anarchist, pagan, peace and pleasure activist.

Throughout this exploration, I steadily increased my activist participation in progressive causes. I began to recognize the privileges I had merely because of the color of my skin, my perceived gender, my perceived orientation, and my physical size. I became convinced that people are entitled to self-determination and that society has at best only limited authority to set a moral standard for private behavior.

Activist organizations filled my desire for community. Working internationally for peace and social justice, nationally for human rights and nonviolence, and locally for bisexual visibility brought me in contact with people who could and did speak eloquently and persuasively about the philosophy of love, compassion, and diversity.

Locally, I was privileged to work with two social justice activists for whom I have the greatest respect, Wendy Bartel and Michael Triompo. I was enthralled by their way of being, even in the face of tremendous obstacles and hostility. They exhibited a gentle insistence that all people deserved love and respect. I watched them act as peacemakers in highly inflamed debates. They seemed as unflappable as I imagined Jesus or Buddha might have been. Just being in their presence made me feel comfortable and peaceful. It was a trait I wanted to cultivate for myself.

As I grew to know them better and to count them as friends, I discovered that they had the First Unitarian Universalist Church of San Diego in common. They talked about the social justice work of the church and the loving nature of the congregation. Plus, the church welcomed people of all sexual orientations. I found it hard to believe the description could be real, so this one-time vicious atheist found his way to church for the first time in twenty-five years. I decided to give this place a chance, so I planned to attend for a few months.

Surrendering to Chaos

When I first attended this Unitarian church, I found that the church-sponsored Gay and Lesbian Outreach (GLO) group had been fostering a climate of queer acceptance for twenty years. I also found that while the church was strongly welcoming, it wasn't perfect. As Tom Owen-Towle, one of the parish ministers, once told me, "We have our warts." I quickly noticed that bisexual inclusion, or even understanding, was not to be found. It was another opportunity to educate, and my partner and I dreaded the expected long battle to create bi awareness.

We were taken completely by surprise to find people with open minds who would listen, evaluate, and change their minds and hearts. People from both ends of Kinsey's scale were interested in learning about bisexuality and growing in their understanding and acceptance of all people. I was asked to speak on bisexuality in the church's annual Pride Celebration worship service, and, shortly after, the Gay and Lesbian Outreach committee unanimously agreed to change its name to Rainbow Outreach. After five months, I felt it was time to join the church.

When someone in the congregation at this church dies, the following Sunday's service includes a ritual in which one minister says, "In mystery we are born; in mystery we live; and in mystery we die." This statement carries no hint of questioning; it is simply a statement of fact. I immediately understood that the mysteries are unsolvable and require only the acceptance of reality rather than faith in any God's plan.

In my youth, I wanted answers to the mysteries. I wanted to know why I was born and how the universe was created. I wanted to "know God." I was completely unsatisfied with the early answers of "We aren't supposed to understand God's plan." Unitarian Universalism doesn't insist that there is a plan, just a mystery. It is that mystery that occurs to me as spirit.

The cycle of birth, life, death, and rebirth that connects all living things is the shared consciousness that defines the spirit aspect of "body, mind, and spirit." It is the acceptance of our common mystery that creates the unspoken need for connectedness that serves as the foundation for many of the world's religious teachings.

Likewise, accepting my bisexuality as my natural state which "just is," allowed me to move beyond the feelings of shame and separateness that had hounded me for years. Why stopped being an important question in my life. A new picture of a universe without the concepts of good/bad, right/wrong, moral/immoral formed in my consciousness. I had to reshape my worldview.

Unitarian Universalism encourages followers to explore and find their personal truths, rather than *a* universal truth. We are charged, as individuals, to create the context for our lives within the basic framework of seven principles. Two of the seven have been particularly important in creating my current values and activism. I affirm and promote the "inherent worth and dignity of every person" and "respect for the interdependent web of all existence."

Before I could gain a deep understanding of these two principles, it was necessary for me to abandon the search for an intrinsic purpose to life. My early quests for understanding had ultimately rested on the belief that the universe, and therefore I, had been created for a purpose. I believed that there was a plan and that life existed as a vehicle to travel from some point in the past to some more important and powerful point in the future. I had been taught that I would be tempted to stray from the path and that life would be a constant struggle between good and evil.

The very question of intrinsic meaning has become immaterial in my life. I no longer need to ignore it or confront it, for it carries no weight in my heart. The phrase "in mystery we live" has allowed me to examine life as if purpose and meaning are human fictions. It is a powerful and liberating perspective.

As a young Lutheran I learned that God's love for humanity had provided, through Jesus, for my salvation and eternal life. But if Jesus isn't the source of my salvation, who is? Rather than scaring me, this question now seems like dawn after a long, cold night. In the growing light, I found my first truth.

If I can't count on an external factor to save me and give me direction, then I must be responsible for my own life—not only in day-to-day survival but in the deeper sense of creating meaning from a meaningless and amoral universe. But what is the nature of "meaning" if it isn't based in a universal truth? And how does one create it?

I started by discarding the notion that I needed to fix the broken bits of my life. I had no intention of creating a repair and maintenance plan for the corrupt philosophy that had utterly failed to bring joy and satisfaction to my life. To create a new philosophy, however, I needed to begin in a clearing, an empty space. It became necessary for me to build a container for my life, that is, a context from which I could examine each aspect of a budding philosophy.

Creating an Orderly Response to Chaos

My philosophy, by intention, had to be internally consistent and externally transparent. I wanted the people who knew me to be able to predict my actions and reactions in any given circumstance. Further, I wanted a life in which I did not need to hide my emotional, spiritual or physical self. These were the initial boundaries of my philosophical container.

The concept of transparency was born from my need to normalize the range of human sexuality. It was important that I never close a closet door on my sexual orientation. "Queer" exists only as a measure of difference from some imagined norm. I wasn't the only person watching TV in the 1950s and 1960s or hearing anti-sex messages from many churches, so I wanted to shine like a beacon of freedom for other hidden bisexuals.

> *The first rule, borrowed from my childhood, for examining each aspect of my being was to ask, "If someone did this to me, would I like it?" Consequently, the first plank in my philosophical platform became nonviolence.*

Defining violence, however, was a struggle. The first of the Unitarian Universalist principles—to promote and affirm the inherent worth and dignity of every person—became the standard by which I could measure violence in my actions. And, because my bisexuality presents me with attractions based on criteria other than genitalia, I saw it as essential to extend the same worth and dignity to all, regardless of gender. In fact, gender isn't an obvious dividing line between people for me. My bisexuality makes me very much aware that the gender line has been drawn by societies. I believe that artificial and capricious categories such as gender separate people from one another and diminish us all. Moreover, what most people clearly see as fixed, I see as muddy and fluid.

Another element of my nonviolence platform flows from my bisexual visibility and human rights activism. To be effective, my activism must be respectful of people who would ignore me, work against me, or threaten me. To be respectful, I must assume that violence, even if intentional, cannot arise from an intrinsic evil. In this light, I can no longer demonize those who commit violence against me. "Respect for the interconnected web of all existence" demands of me that I strive continuously for reconciliation. Building bridges of understanding, creating a climate of tolerance, and celebrating diversity aren't tools I use to shape the perfect future; they are the way I live the perfect present.

"Respect for the interdependent web of all existence" also demands that I articulate a very specific lesson I have learned as a bisexual. I have come to understand that because we are all parts of a greater whole, most people can form emotional and/or sexual attachments regardless of gender identity or expression. This understanding lives in direct contrast to those who would assert that queerness is "other" and is therefore wrong. Ironically, as one part of the interconnected web, my love for other parts more closely resembles self-love and high self-esteem.

The second element of my philosophy is this: I do not know what tomorrow will bring. In mystery we are born; in mystery we live; in mystery we die.

In my understanding of the universe, all I have is each moment. I must find my happiness, my joy, and my connection with all existence in the circumstance of this moment and the next moment and the next. For example, I am not vested in the outcome of my activism, but I am committed to being active and to living fully and authentically in each moment.

In the context of these principles—nonviolence and mystery—I examined my beliefs around gender and sexuality. It was inevitable that I would also consider the nature of love. I wanted to understand why there were a handful of people I loved, several I liked, several I didn't like and many more toward whom I was completely indifferent. In what way was I holding the concept of love that limited my ability to give and receive love generously? There is one norm that suggests compulsory monosexuality. As a bisexual with a fuzzy gender identity, the concept of love became more crucial with time.

What if love exists in one pure state and gets saddled with a lot of baggage by our negative experiences and by our childhood lessons? If we misunderstood our experiences and the lessons were wrong, then love needn't be rationed. Maybe it isn't limited at all. Further, maybe sexual behaviors are merely extensions of affectionate displays. There are plenty of social rules about the appropriate displays of affection. For example, football players can pat each other on the behind during a game but not at the local sports bar. Clearly we learn these behaviors and we learn to limit our displays of affection.

I think most people live their lives as if love were scarce. Some people live as if they mustn't give any love away before they find out if it will be returned. Others are afraid that their love will be stolen, leaving them alone and lonely. For romantic love, our language and culture are filled with sayings and images that presuppose there is one and only one true love for each of us. Our society considers each relationship that ends before death a failure. Monosexual identities might be used as a protecting filter to limit giving love rather than a statement of true attractions. Bisexuals who prefer dating other bisexuals might be filtering for the same protections.

My old rules for giving love, which I did rarely, included gauging the level at which the person might hurt me and what social risk I was taking to express my love or affection. When I examined that notion, I found that I was building expectations around the person's responsibility to me if I loved that person. Would that person love me as much, and would that person protect me from the evil in the world? In other words, would that person make me safe? I made all my love conditional. If you don't "take care of my love," I will take it back. I treated love like a solid yet fragile entity. In my new philosophy, transparency and respect for others made this totally unacceptable.

So I tried a few experiments about loving people. I started giving love away. I started listening and sharing my life's story with people. I began to be real with people. In that authenticity, I discovered that all the feelings of love I shared with one or two people were available for and from nearly everybody I knew and have since met. As I experimented with this, I discovered what might be a more accurate orientation label for me: anthroposexual, or attracted to humans.

Because I have dared to risk love, I have come to believe that mutually supportive love is the underlying natural state of interactions in human communities, yet our lives are crowded with a wide variety of fears, worries, and concerns that prevent us from really noticing one another. Our expectations—the demands we place on love—prevent us from sharing easily with the people in our lives.

Expressing love for people can be as simple and as difficult as being authentic with them, listening and responding with respect for their worth as a fellow traveler. For me, it has gone far beyond a willingness to interact with honesty.

My church has an aspiration that we recite at each service: "May love be the spirit of this church, may the quest for truth be its sacrament, and service be its prayer. To dwell together in peace, to seek knowledge in freedom, and to help one another in fellowship, this is our aspiration."

Lately I have been exploring the "service be its prayer" aspect of this shared yet personal aspiration. We have many examples from history and other mythologies of great spiritual and social leaders who found lives of service. Albert Schweitzer said in an address to students, "I don't know what your destiny will be, but one thing I know: the only ones among you who will be really happy are those who have sought and found how to serve."

I am unable to determine the extent of this particular truth, but I know that the hours I spend in service—an expectation-free giving of myself—creates an expansive feeling in my soul and increases my capacity to love. And increasing my capacity for love has directly increased my joy with life. So I would count the following as the third plank of my philosophy:

Service be its prayer.

Even though in my activism I live in the midst of environmental degradation, nationalistic saber rattling, ethnic genocide, corporate greed, and other violations of the human heart, I live in peace and joy. Using a perverse interpretation—living well is the best revenge. I am convinced that when we increase our own capacity to give and receive love, we transform the world. As Hazrat Inayat Khan realized, "With love, even the rocks will open."[2]

[2] Hazrat Inayat Khan, *Spiritual Liberty,* The Sufi Message of Hazrat Inayat Khan Series (New Lebanon: Omega Publications, 1979).

Is It Too Much to Ask?

ROSEFIRE

He who knows his self knows his Lord.
—Muhammad

I DON'T KNOW HOW MANY TIMES I said it. It was my one-liner introduction to the issue. "If someone had a choice, why on earth would any rational person choose to be gay?" The subtext, which I never said aloud, was, "So, if you're bisexual, then you have a choice, right? And if you have a choice, there is only one choice—again, right?"

> Because of these and similar practical handicaps, it is a kindness to advise people whose drive could be channeled in a heterosexual direction to go in that direction if at all possible.[1]

I kept coming back to the idea that if you were really gay, the ethical ideal was a long-term relationship. If you weren't gay, you got married. In either case, fidelity was part of the package. The Christian Association for Psychological Studies supported this view in their 1975 meeting. Specifically, they proposed that promiscuity, fornication, and adultery should be regarded as sinful for both homosexual and heterosexual people, but that a loving, committed, permanent relationship between two persons of the same sex was in a different category, and was not condemned in scripture.[2]

I struggled also with the common misconception that bisexuals are promiscuous. Since I was far from promiscuous and had tons of self-

[1] Letha Dawson Scanzoni and Virginia Ramey Mollenkott, *Is the Homosexual My Neighbor? A Positive Christian Response,* revised and updated ed. (San Francisco: HarperSanFrancisco, 1994), 144. This quotation is from a comparison of approaches to homosexual morality taken by the theologians Charles Curran, William Norman Pittenger, and John J. McNeill.

[2] Ibid., 140.

discipline, it was obvious to me that I couldn't be bisexual. This made the rest easy. I was either gay or straight, and, given those options, well, I was straight. Sexual behavior was morally independent of sexual orientation. No problem.

In my early twenties, when I was most concerned with this issue, I was mostly celibate, with brief, restrained, half-terrified attempts at relationships. Overwhelming surges of lust usually inspired these, rather than a sense of intimacy or emotional connection. Having struggled with attempted celibacy and failure, I modified my goals from celibacy to chastity. With a little tweaking to come up with a version of chastity not quite so incompatible with a single lifestyle in the 1970s, chastity became not rushing into things, thinking with my head. It was a sincere attempt to evaluate the psychological health and probable durability of a relationship before making any emotional commitments or getting involved sexually. The goal was still a long-term faithful relationship.

Chastity was a big word for me, even if I didn't really understand what it meant. From age twenty-two to twenty-four I was a novice in the Secular Franciscans. The heart and soul of being a Franciscan were the three vows—poverty, chastity, and obedience. I had become a Secular Franciscan because I believed equally strongly that I had a calling to a sincere spiritual vocation and to be a mother. If anything, the second belief was the stronger. As a rural Catholic girl in the 1960s, I did not know of a way to reconcile the two. A priest friend mentioned the secular orders, and there I went, off and running. A seeker, a novice.

While I did not grasp the meaning or significance of the three vows, what attracted me was the idea of spiritual osmosis as opposed to evangelism—to live one's life as morally as one can, to attempt to set a good example, and to communicate the faith only when asked. Although I didn't remain a Franciscan, I kept in mind spiritual osmosis and the three vows. I struggled with these, and from time to time would go back to talk with the man who had been my novice master. We talked about issues of spirituality and sexuality, but we managed to avoid bisexuality or homosexuality. Despite that, he gave me a great spiritual gift, one that enabled me to live with myself until I was ready to take a closer look. His gift was a way to make compromises.

> At its Latin root, the word religion is linked to the words ligature and ligament, words having both negative and positive connotations, offering both bondage and freedom of movement.[3]

[3] Kathleen Norris, *Dakota: A Spiritual Geography* (Boston: Houghton Mifflin, 1993), 133.

In the parochial schools I attended during grade school, the idea of sin was presented as black and white. Something was a sin or it was not. If it was a sin, that was it. You didn't do it, or you promised not to do it again. The idea that some sins might be worse than others wasn't addressed. The subtlety the teachers missed was the distinction between venial and mortal sins. It was this that my novice master clarified. Mortal sins were bad things that weren't possible for someone whose spirit was healthy and whole. They required severe damage to the soul before you could make yourself do them, or they created severe damage to the soul. Venial sins were bad things one did that nibbled at the edges and weakened one's overall moral strength, but didn't cripple, didn't break the spirit or soul.

So how did venial sin save my sanity? It's been a while, so let me try to do justice to my novice master's message. Birth control is one of the Catholic Church's big no-no's. My novice master explained that using birth control is a sin. Something about a focus on lust rather than cherishing and respecting your partner, and decisions of birth and death belonging to God. Despite this, as long as it is a shared and mutual decision, the use of birth control is a venial sin. Why? Because having more children than you can care for responsibly is a mortal sin, and a selfish act.

I finally understood that there is a hierarchy of sin—some sins are more harmful than others, and the main distinction is who gets hurt. Now the challenge was to apply this hierarchy in my own life. I reasoned that getting physically involved with someone because of lust (however camouflaged) would eventually hurt the other person, and likely yourself as well. Getting involved with someone who was committed to another person was the same, only more so and hurting more people. Getting involved outside of your own committed relationship would be unfair to the other individual and your partner. Getting involved or committed quickly meant you couldn't know the other person well enough not to be fooling yourself about whether or not it was lust.

This discussion arose in my memory a few years later as I struggled with my first deep attraction to a woman, a married woman. How could I reduce desire enough to avoid making an impulsive and hurtful decision? How could I ever make sense of my sexual choices? My solution, choosing the venial sin over the mortal, was to masturbate as I bawled my eyes out in a hot shower trying not to think of another woman's eyes and mouth. I relied on this solution over the next dozen or so years as a last-ditch act of desperation whenever I was tempted toward an uncertain and unwise course of action. Sensible sexual behavior remained a struggle for me, a struggle I was determined to win.

> Is it too much to ask, that you should be my servant. . . . (Isaiah 49:6)

I believe in the sacramental nature of marriage, and I believe in marriage as a form of spiritual vocation. Maybe it is because I was raised in a fairly conventional manner, or maybe because I'm a woman, but I really do believe that an important part of marriage or any committed relationship is fidelity. I believe you can learn a lot from fidelity. As in writing a sonnet or a fugue, the form forces you to discover new depths to your creative ability—not to mention that fidelity is one of the Ten Commandments and that the Ten Commandments have a lot of common sense.

As for my predicament with the married woman, life made it easy. Well, life made it easy to avoid the issue. We headed off to different graduate schools. After a few months of crying myself to sleep, wishing that I had kissed her just once, I intentionally stopped thinking about her. New plan—I was going to have a career, marry a career man, and have kids with the man I married. Any relationship not going that direction just wasn't going to happen. But before I put the alternatives out of my mind, I made one small promise. If I was single when I turned sixty, I was going to come out, and shack up with another little old lady. Somehow, I would hold out until sixty.

> And learn whence is sorrow and joy, and love and hate, and waking though one would not, and sleeping though one would not, and hating though one would not, and falling in love though one would not. And when you have closely examined all these things, thou wilt find Him in thyself, one and many, just as the atom, thus finding from thyself a way out of thyself.[4]

Four years later, I became engaged, and I married in another two years. Before the wedding I warned my husband-to-be that fidelity was an issue for me, in both possible interpretations: that I would not tolerate infidelity from my partner, and conversely that I expected to find myself tempted. I also told him that I refuse to act on these impulses. He already knew of my self-discipline. Not long after the wedding, a couple of friends

[4] Monoïmus. (The version quoted here is one I memorized as a teen. I no longer have access to the original. The citation here is for the same text in a different translation.) See Hippolytus, *Refutation of All Heresies,* book 8, in *The Gnostic Society Library* (http://www.gnosis.org/library/hyp_refut8.htm).

met my husband. They moaned, "How could you do it? How could you marry a man?" By that point I had forgotten a great deal and had invested a great deal in the forgetting. I replied, "I have this little problem, ladies—I'm straight. Remember?" A comment that they wisely overlooked, and of which they have graciously neglected to remind me.

Over the years, our marriage suffered. During grim years, I clung to the memory of a particular moment after the wedding and before the reception, when, I believe, I felt the sacramental grace of the wedding take hold, the moment in which the marriage was truly sanctified. I sincerely believe that no matter how ludicrous or inappropriate our marriage sometimes appears God wishes us to be a couple, and that there are lessons he intends each of us to learn through being with the other. I refuse to divorce my husband, no matter how awful things are, so long as there is still something for me to learn, and so long as the children aren't the ones being hurt.

Eventually, it became clear to us that change was necessary, and change we did. As we did, everything around us also changed. Life was good at last. We both had good jobs, a lovely home, enough food, and money for clothes and necessities. We could even justify a few small luxuries. As the pressure lifted, my husband and I found time for each other in a way that had never happened before. Sitting under the trees in our back yard holding hands, we discovered the comfort of being a partner, of having a partner, of having known someone through bad times and good. We discovered that comfort is its own blessing. I had prayed often and prayed hard, and now my prayers were of thanksgiving.

> Our love has been anything but perfect and anything but static. . . . There have been times when we have misunderstood each other, demanded too much of each other, been insensitive to the other's needs. I do not believe there is any marriage where this does not happen. The growth of love is not a straight line, but a series of hills and valleys. I suspect that in every good marriage there are times when love seems to be over.[5]

My new job included a comfortable level of business travel. At one of the professional meetings, I noticed a woman on one of the panels. She was tall, strong, and wore a lavender jacket, which I kept noticing during the rest of the conference. It wasn't until the drive home that I figured out I

[5] Madeleine L'Engle, *Two-Part Invention: The Story of a Marriage,* Crosswicks Journal 1 (San Francisco: HarperSanFrancisco, 1989), 100.

had been keeping a very close eye on her. I found I had a powerful attraction for the woman in the lavender jacket. What horrendous timing—just as I thought I finally had my life worked out and was looking forward to a breather. I could no longer deny that I was . . . something. What is the old saying? If I say something three times, it must be true. How many times did my body and heart have to speak of same-sex attraction, before I could hear what they were telling me?

> Que est ista que ascendit sicut aurora consurgens,
> pulchra ut luna, electa ut sol,
> terribilis ut castrorum acies ordinata?
>
> Who is she that ascends like the rising dawn,
> beautiful as the moon, bright-shining as the sun,
> awesome as an army in battle array?[6]

After years of struggling to strengthen my faith and downplay my physical side, these two aspects were about to come together, obviously and with emphasis! They would explode in a far richer connection than in the "chastity/celibacy" debate of my early twenties. On National Coming Out Day, twenty-five years after my first attraction to a woman, my husband and I went for a walk, our path cutting through the edges of a Pride Rally. As we passed the rally, I convinced my husband I was bisexual.

This has been traumatic for both of us. Clouds of turmoil, anger, and fear surrounded us. We were again unsure our marriage would survive. He worried about my influence on the children. I worried that if he could not find a way to accept me the children would lose either a father or mother or both. Concerned friends mentioned that some men killed their wife rather than cope with such a threat to their masculinity. I found myself watching my husband with fearful eyes, just in case. My husband remains terrified that someone will find out about me.

For the first time, I felt that God had abandoned me. Nothing made sense. Why her? Why now? Why at all? I could not find a reason for what was happening. While part of me found that life finally made sense, another part felt bitter and lost, wishing none of this had happened. I could cope with death and disaster, but this was different. I felt ashamed, that everything I had ever said or done was a lie, even if mostly to myself.

[6] Assumption antiphon "Que est ista." Translated by Susan Hellauer, from *Anonymous 4. Lammas Ladymass: 13th and 14th Century English Chant and Polyphony* (Arles, France: Harmonia Mundi, 1998).

I wanted the lie back. I began to believe that every problem we had ever encountered in our marriage must be traced back to my own insecurities, my own subconscious. I detested myself and felt even more unloved and unlovable than at the worst times of our marriage. I felt ugly. I could not think of an uglier word than "bisexual."

> Theologians, philosophers, and clinicians alike have alluded to the idea that persons who are hopeless misperceive to the spiritual or transcendent. . . . What is perhaps most characteristic of persons who present with feelings of hopelessness is a particular muteness, an inability to cry out to a Higher Power or to others around them.[7]

This phase lasted three months. Only three months, but still, three months of fear, paranoia, ugliness, and loneliness—violent mood swings and irrational urges, drawn toward fragmentation and dissolution, attempting to show no significant change in the face I showed the world. Lucky for me, I had a family to live for. Lucky for me, I'm not the first person to go through this, and there are writings and artwork in which others have struggled with similar issues, others who reasoned with the mind, heart, and soul toward solutions that enabled them to survive and love themselves. As I began to discover and explore others' solutions, I shared bits and pieces with my husband, opening a new dialogue with my spouse.

This helped, helped a lot actually. But it wasn't everything I needed. For one thing, most books I found were written by and for gays. I found some bisexual titles in Amazon.com, but didn't feel brave enough to order them. The few bisexual books at the public library seemed to always be checked out, and again I didn't feel secure enough to place a special request and risk attracting attention to myself. So it was a start, but not quite what I hoped for. When I finally worked up enough guts to ransack the shelves at a local bookstore, what I found confused me more.

I wondered, Was I bisexual or was I a lesbian? I kept digging at the idea, circling around and around, and coming back to the same place. Part of me acknowledged and embraced the beauty of lesbian life. Part of me. The attraction I felt for my husband and for other men was as true as what I felt for women who also attracted me. Truth: attraction was different from love. Venn diagrams. Love and attraction sometimes overlapped, but there

[7] Carol J. Farran, Kaye A. Herth, and Judith M. Popovich, *Hope and Hopelessness: Critical Clinical Constructs* (Thousand Oaks, Calif.: Sage, 1995), 29–30.

was nothing that said they had to. Attraction was only part of what I needed to understand. I still had a lot to learn.

> Beware of prejudice; light is good in whatsoever lamp it is burning. A rose is beautiful in whatsoever garden it may bloom. A star has the same radiance whether it shines from the East or from the West.[8]

Having reached an understanding of how homosexuality could be a beautiful, spiritual lifestyle, I now sought a similar understanding for bisexuality. This was more difficult. Many people I knew believed that bisexuality is a cop-out. For me, to be bisexual and maintain truth, integrity, and honor were far more difficult than to be either straight or gay. Bisexuality adds a layer of complexity not present in being either straight or homosexual. It adds an easy out, an option of being true to oneself, but not wholly; a way to conform and also hide from one's self. Bisexuality offers the opportunity to make a choice, like the apple in the Garden of Eden, but a choice with a rotten core. To take the easy out requires that one flatten one's interior landscape, disown whole truths, whole nations, as if they never existed. Or, bisexuality offers the option to make a choice, and to keep making choices.

> My own heart let me more have pity on; let
> Me live to my sad self hereafter kind,
> Charitable; not live this tormented mind
> With this tormented mind tormenting yet.[9]

Once, as an undergraduate, an upper-level psychology course had us take a test indicating our adherence to socially defined sex roles, the normal male role (masculinity) and the normal female role (femininity). Of the entire class, I scored higher than anyone else on both measures. Later, the teacher asked everyone who thought in words to raise their hands; then asked for everyone to raise their hands who thought in images or sensation. I was in the front row and couldn't see the rest of the class, so I was surprised to find I was the only person who raised my hand both times. At the time I saw this juxtaposition of traits in my poetry. As I compose, I feel as if I am translating, attempting to sculpt an emotional response in the

[8] Abdu'l-Bahá, as quoted in Gloria Faizi, *The Bahá'i Faith: An Introduction* (New Delhi: Bahá'i Publishing Trust, 1971), 39.

[9] Gerard Manley Hopkins, *"God's Grandeur" and Other Poems* (New York: Dover, 1995), 48.

reader through my words, attempting in fact to recreate the sensation of my own emotional response which led to the creation of the poem in the first place.

I wonder if this isn't the core of my sexual orientation experience. Perhaps being bisexual is being a translator or bridge between different ways of being, loving, thinking. Perhaps being bisexual is to embrace and embody as many differences as possible; to show through the example of our own difficult challenging lives ways in which everyone could embrace contradiction and still be whole healthy creative individuals. And then to communicate this experience to the whole community, by osmosis—the witness of those lives which touch our own. Perhaps it is part of my duty in this life to set the example of balance between opposites, to straddle the teeter-totter of my life and make as great a harmony as I can out of opposites. Perhaps I am bisexual to deny me easy choices and easy solutions, forcing me to closely examine each step along the way. Perhaps being bisexual is to look at the yin/yang symbol and identify with the seed germ dots within each teardrop.

> The words gay and lesbian do not exist in the village, but there is the word gatekeeper. Gatekeepers are the people who live a life at the edge between two worlds—the world of the village and the world of spirit. . . . The gatekeepers stand on the threshold of the gender line. They are the mediators between the two genders.[10]

When confronted about my religious identity, I tell people I am a Zen Catholic pagan. Some folks have no problem with this, but they are few. To most, the phrase itself is an incongruity, as much of a contradiction as the concept of being bisexual and married. To me, this incongruity, this contradiction is a natural blend of three spirit paths, unified by an emphasis on intimate contact with Deity in all aspects of life, and through the practice of hearing the Deity's voice in still spaces. Also, these three have in common a wry understanding of spiritual benefits from incongruity itself!

I find myself very glad that I was raised as a Roman Catholic, one of the few religions with both masculine and feminine forms of Deity, in the forms of Jesus and the Virgin Mary. I am glad to have been a Franciscan and learned early on the value of osmosis in a social and ethical context,

[10] Sobonfu Somé, *The Spirit of Intimacy: Ancient Teachings in the Ways of Relationships* (New York: William Morrow, 1999), 132–33.

quietly living one's life as best as one is able and letting that speak for itself.

From the earth religions more commonly known as pagan, I cherish the personal unique and sacred identity in every natural place and thing. I relish the fact that remnants of earth religions remain a part of Roman Catholicism, through rituals, music, and the saints. I marvel at the intellectual intricacy and emotional balance of the visual and poetic symbolic languages used in both Catholicism and astrology, much of which originated with historically earlier faiths and belief systems. Marveling includes a sense of awe at the miracle of truth that is the macrocosm and microcosm, that dynamic and active link between the great and the small, the sense that choices we make in our lives can change the pattern of the stars and vice versa.

In astrology an opposition is two planets that stimulate contradictory and complementary areas of the person's nature. Awareness of an opposition begins as an almost unbearable, painful tension, feeling somewhat as if a horse is tied to each arm, running in opposite directions. Being out of control, with wild oscillations between two extremes, is more likely if one side or the other is being denied or repressed. If the lesson represented by the opposition is learned, eventually the person learns a balance between the two contradictory areas. Instead of being pulled in two directions, one centers over the fulcrum of a teeter-totter, shifting slightly one direction or the other.

Zen and Pagan traditions offer the coalescence of a sense of duty, choice, and connection extending from one lifetime into another in the principles of karma and reincarnation. These truths help me to make sense out of apparent imbalances in my life. Zen centering and stillness-that-is-not-silence fill me as they extend a vibrant awareness as far as the senses reach. I find the Zen wordplay incongruities known as koans uproariously funny. I learned that, presumably intentionally, there is a great deal of similar incongruity in Christ's teachings, especially in his parables. I love the idea from both Zen and Aikido that the best way to learn spiritual lessons is to teach them to the body, and eventually the body teaches the spirit and mind. This allows me to trust the voice of my body as it tries to tell me this particular something that I have refused, until now, to hear. My body teaches my mind that I am bisexual.

It is at the points where these spirit paths link that they become most strong and that my sense of spirituality becomes most sure. It is the flexibility and openness of moving along those intersections that allow me to maintain a sense of being anchored even as my entire life and sense of personal identity shift wildly. It is this, perhaps, that has been the most important lesson and gift from each of these paths—that the path changes, that it can contradict what seemed sure only moments before, and that to understand the path completely is not a requirement for following the pattern in faith.

> God exists in the mind. In your mind. "The Kingdom of God," wrote Luke, "exists in your mind." Zen and Christianity, the East and the West, are like two separate highways. But sometimes I come across points of interchange, intersections, crossroads between the two. Deep ones. If you do zazen you will find the complete, the total Satori. The same Satori as Christ's. The same as Buddha's. . . . The object of concentration is very important. Not the Santa Lucia—not during the sesshin. Here-and-now zazen posture. Here is the true Kingdom of God. The true Santa Lucia. You don't know the meaning of Santa Lucia?[11]

Choosing marriage the way I did represented both a conscious commitment and an unconscious denial. While our marriage would have been difficult in any case, this certainly did not help. By denying a significant aspect of my sexual and affectionate nature, little by little I closed off more and more of any affection or sexual expression. Perhaps it shouldn't have been a surprise, but surprise me it did, when, in accepting my desire for women, I rediscovered desire for my husband. For several years prior to this, my husband and I lived in grudging celibacy, each feeling rejected by the other. I value the celibate lifestyle, but do believe it should be chosen rather than imposed.

Now I face a different kind of celibacy. To remain faithful to my marriage vows requires that I not explore the physical side of my bisexual identity. I know those who consider that idea a betrayal of the essence of bisexuality. Nonetheless, I believe that the full meaning of a vow is never clearly understood at the time the vow is taken, but rather unfolds over time through exactly this sort of testing and trial. I confess I don't know if I can manage it. I agonized over this, talked it through with friends. I have heard a number of times, "How will you ever know, unless you, well, you know." Well, trust me—I know. I have absolutely no doubt of being bisexual.

How do I know what's right? That's hard. We are never ourselves the

[11] Taisen Deshimaru Roshi, *The Voice of the Valley,* ed. Philippe Coupey (Indianapolis: Bobbs-Merrill, 1979), 177.

ones who know what's right. Whenever I decide what's right and set my feet stubbornly on a path, God lets me know how close I got this time. This doesn't work the same for everyone, but in my life, if I've got the wrong idea, everything gets harder, impossibly hard. I can pray as much as I want, cry as much as I want, no difference. My own solutions run me up against brick walls. It feels as if my prayers aren't being answered, or the answers paint me into a corner and I don't see windows.

Over the last twenty years, I have struggled to learn to listen to God, to see his hand shaping my life. I find when I pray for the right thing, it can be downright eerie how quickly and clearly some of those prayers are answered. So far, each time I was tempted toward infidelity within my marriage and prayed for strength, I have received help. Believe it or not, "temptation's car" has been known to break down at the darnedest times! Because that happens, and keeps happening, I believe that God wants me to continue to explore the challenge of fidelity. He doesn't seem to have any problem with setting temptation in my path, but has so far always given me a way out.

> The first step to spirituality, it seems to me, comes in contemplating the mystery, not in resolving it.[12]

Every spirit path I know takes quite seriously the issue of making a vow, recognizing there may be conflicts between a vow taken and future life paths. This doesn't invalidate the vow as a source of spiritual growth. For inspiration, I look to all celibates challenged in maintaining their vows, but especially Gerard Manley Hopkins. He also encountered a trial of identity in living his priestly vow of celibacy within a mostly hidden homosexuality. In Zen tradition, while celibacy isn't usually asked for throughout one's entire life, there is an understanding of the value of self-discipline and denial in various forms. While I don't know of a parallel in the pagan traditions, I have encountered a belief that betrayal of a vow and the resulting injury of another build an obligation that crosses from one life into the next.

In developing a personal identity in faith, I learned to trust a strong internal sense that seemed to ring like a bell upon hearing a truth that spans cultural boundaries. Naturally, internal chaos deafens the spirit even more than external chaos. I find myself, as I seek to learn more about being bisexual, also seeking to learn more about my unique blend of faith

[12] Frank Browning, "The Way of Some Flesh," in *Wrestling With the Angel: Faith and Religion in the Loves of Gay Men,* ed. Brian Bouldrey (New York: Riverhead Books, 1995), 102.

and spiritual practice. Having neglected zazen for some years, I now hunger after it, yearning for balance and stillness. Having been timid in exploring my connection to paganism, I now seek out persons with a strong pagan faith and practice. I also seek out persons who helped me define my faith earlier in my life, and as I redefine my own personal identity, I renegotiate my faith identity.

I continue to be hesitant about exploring this issue within the Catholic Church. I did make an attempt to bring it up to our pastor, but he reacted badly, as if frightened. Even observing activities within our parish, however, I begin to see possible connections to my life, examples that show I may not be unwelcome when I find the courage to come out: the gay tenor who pretends to straighten his bra straps during practice, solemnly playing the organ on Sunday; the young priest preaching his own analogy for confronting difficulty—coming out of the closet; the married-with-children choir director who refers to God as "She."

I find a different kind of balance in bisexuality—not so much dyadic as triadic. Hold the hand of a woman. Hold the hand of a man. Connect the two, through myself. In faith, also, seeking the deep intersections between spirit paths that seem superficially unrelated. Like loving both men and women, they are connected, in my very being. In my being, I struggle to make a single faith out of what appear to be contradictions. I attempt to live a life that, while superficially a paradox, when lived deeply discovers unity.

On a path I avoided, I learn a great deal! My husband, likewise, learns. I don't know how our relationship will develop from this point. I don't know if we will continue to learn together, or if one or the other of us will reach a point when we say, "No more." I do know, as part of being able to live with myself as an ethical human being, I must make a concerted and sincere attempt. I have faith that there is a way to do this, that because God made me the way I am, there is beauty and harmony to be found, so long as I keep seeking, so long as we both keep seeking. What is it I seek? The strength, courage, and wisdom to do these three things as wholly as possible: celebrate diversity, embrace contradiction, embody paradox—within love.

> Bless, O God, the thing on which mine eye doth rest,
> Bless, O God, the thing to which my hope doth quest,
> Bless, O God, my reason and what I desire,
> Bless, thou God of life, O bless myself entire. . . .[13]

[13] "Rest Benediction," from G. R. D. McLean, *Praying with the Celts* (Grand Rapids: Eerdmans, 1988), 69.

Jesus, Bread, Wine and Roses: A Bisexual Feminist at the Catholic Worker

LAUREL DYKSTRA

I AM A THIRTY-YEAR-OLD CANADIAN of European grandparents. I am a woman who is sexual with both women and men. I call myself dyke, bi, bisexual-lesbian, or queer depending on the circumstance. I was raised in the Anglican Church of Canada, nurtured and damaged by my upbringing there, and I identify as Christian. But when asked what denomination I am, I usually say Catholic Worker.

The Catholic Worker is a radical Christian anarchist movement begun in the 1930s. Most communities focus on the Works of Mercy and the Works of Justice, practicing hospitality, voluntary poverty, and activism of some sort. Praxis (how we live, the actions we take) is key.[1] We publish newspapers, farm, run soup kitchens, organize for social change, and open our houses to homeless people. Because the Catholic Worker is an anarchist movement, it is possible for me to speak only from my own experience, living in and around the communities in Toronto, Ontario, and Tacoma, Washington, for the past five years. I am confident that some houses and communities do not share my views on plenty of issues, including sexuality.

My spirituality and my sexuality have a profound impact on my work as an activist, an artist, and a scholar. But because of my long awareness of what it means never to be one or the other—a Canadian living in the United States, a bisexual person, a theologically educated lay person,

[1] The Works of Mercy and the Works of Justice are practices of hospitality and action derived from Matt. 25:31–41.

always living in the in-between spaces—I am acutely conscious of how every assertion I make veils, negates, or absolutizes some truth. Simple questions unravel me: Where are you from? What do you do? Are you a boy or a girl? How can I answer and not deny some fragile self? But, responding with silence or with a formula is another kind of lie. So I tell my story, knowing that I will tell it again and tell it differently, but that I will always tell it true.

By Our Lives Be We Spirit[2]

Several years ago I was listening to Tracy Chapman's song "All That You Have Is Your Soul," when the meaning of the words unraveled and I heard not "the only thing which is truly yours is your soul" but rather, "your soul is comprised of all your possessions."[3] I took this temporary rearrangement of meaning as a message of sorts—a cue from the universe that has helped me frame my understanding of spirituality.

I find that I often don't know what people mean when they use the word *spirituality.* The term *spirituality* frequently refers to praying, meditation, church, or women's circle—a separate and special aspect of our lives, distinct from the time spent eating, playing, or working. I see this thinking as capitulation to a dualistic mind-set that divides the world into spiritual and profane.[4] I believe something quite different—that we are a packaged deal, all of a whole. I define my spirituality as whatever I invest myself in: possessions, family, community, business.

Again, the Tracy Chapman verse reverberates: *"All that you have is your soul. . . ."* If this is true, then I am obligated to take great care in choosing what it is that I have, what I own. I have no choice but to struggle with issues of simple living, wealth, and voluntary poverty, and that is a spiritual struggle. Spirituality pervades all that I, all that we, do. Much like Audre Lorde's now classic description of the erotic pervading all of her life, my understanding of the spiritual is that there is no aspect of our lives that is not spiritual.[5]

[2] Lyric from a Ferron song, "Testimony," from the album of the same name, *Testimony,* Lucy Records, Nemesis Publishing, Vancouver, B.C., 1980.

[3] Tracy Chapman, *Crossroads,* Elektra, New York, 1989.

[4] Kathleen Bennet, "Feminist Bisexuality: A Both/And Option For an Either/Or World," in *Closer to Home: Bisexuality and Feminism,* ed. Elizabeth Reba Weise (Seattle: Seal Press, 1992), 219.

[5] Audre Lorde, "Uses of the Erotic: The Erotic as Power," in *Sister Outsider* (Freedom, Calif.: Crossing Press, 1984), 53–59.

Similarly, Audre Lorde's description of the erotic is true for me. I understand my sexuality to be something that pervades all aspects of my life, not merely the time I spend in genital contact (or even nongenital fleshy embrace) with lovers. In fact, when I was a bright and shy child, some of the first rushes of that joy and fear I came to know as eros broke into my life in classrooms and in churches. Sermons and lectures gave me a fierce joy and a physical sense that I was connected outside the boundaries of my skin. I developed "intellectual" crushes on teachers and priests whose ideas I loved, who introduced me to poetry, who were passionate about G*d.

Passion is a part of my daily life, alive in my interactions with neighbors, partners, pets, friends, trees, tasks, worship. Because spirituality and sexuality are such pervasive parts of my life, they are almost necessarily related. In fact, it is difficult for me to separate what is spiritual and what is sexual in any situation. Both concepts have to do with passion, connection, and boundaries. I imagine that my spirituality and my sexuality are flower and fruit of a single tree.

The World Will Be Saved by Beauty

Friday morning, Sarah and I painted a huge sunflower on the driver's side of the Zacchaeus House van with this Dostoevsky quotation in the stem: "The world will be saved by beauty."[6] The van is used to deliver bread from the community bakery, to transport previously homeless guests and former guests of Zacchaeus House, and to carry community members to demonstrations, court appearances, retreats, actions, and meetings. Paint from the community vehicle lingers still in the corners of my fingernails and on the hem of my "Radio Popular de Guatemala" shirt. As an artist, painting this vehicle helps keep me present in the hope that I can do justice to this sense of the radical erotic which moves me to do justice.

"The world will be saved by beauty" was a favorite quotation of Dorothy Day, mother of the Catholic Worker movement. Described by David O'Brien in *Commonweal,* as "the most significant, interesting and influential person in the history of American Catholicism," Dorothy Day was a pacifist activist who was arrested countless times for acts of civil dis-

[6] For the story of Zacchaeus, a tax collector who jeets Jesus and gives away and gives back money he has come by dishonestly, see Luke 19:2–8.

obedience.[7] She is better known for her caustic remark, "all our problems stem from our acceptance of this filthy rotten system," than for her love of beauty. Yet she knew deeply the power of beauty.

The story that best exemplifies Dorothy Day's sense of the salvific nature of beauty was the time she gave to a homeless woman a diamond ring that had come in a donation. When criticized because she did not sell the ring for money to run the house, she defended herself saying, "Do you think the poor do not appreciate beauty?"[8] In this act, like the woman who anointed Jesus, I see the radical erotic expressed, the erotic that Audre Lorde calls power.[9]

> The erotic functions . . . in several ways, and the first is in providing the power which comes from sharing deeply any pursuit with another person. The sharing of joy, whether physical, emotional, psychic or intellectual, forms a bridge between the sharers which can be the basis for understanding much of what is not shared between them, and lessens the threat of their difference.[10]

For me this saving beauty and radical erotic are captured in Jesus' talk of open-table commensality, that joyous feast of the bridegroom, the upside-down kingdom, where beggars eat first. Beauty is free, flowers spring up through cracks in the concrete and babies smile in tenements.[11] But we all know that this is not the case in our culture, where beauty is a signifier of worth and the province of the rich. To paint murals in the inner city and grow gardens on vacant lots is shocking because it conveys that the poor are worthy of what is beautiful, that they are valuable. Part of what I love about the Catholic Worker tradition is its insistence and my

[7] Robert Ellsberg, "Introduction," in *By Little and By Little: The Selected Writings of Dorothy Day,* ed. Robert Ellsberg (New York: Alfred A. Knopf, 1983), xvii.

[8] Ellen Rehg and Mary Dutcher, "Dorothy Day's Aesthetic," *The Round Table* (Spring 1997): 4.

[9] Read the Markan and Matthean versions of this story (Mark 14:3–6 and Matt. 26:7–9); the Lukan and Johannine authors use the story for other purposes. See Elisabeth Schüssler Fiorenza, *In Memory of Her: A Feminist Theological Reconstruction of Christian Origins* (New York: Crossroad, 1985), xvii.

[10] Lorde, "Uses of the Erotic," 56.

[11] I struggle with a satisfactory shorthand for this "new society in the shell of the old"—beloved community, unbrokered kingdom, God's imperial rule—but I generally use Ada Maria Isasi-Díaz's "kin-dom" because it emphasizes the nonhierarchical/family/community and because it sounds like "kingdom," retaining the rich associations of the kingdom parables with their urgency and radicality. See Ada Maria Isasi-Díaz, "Solidarity and Love of Neighbour in the 1980s," in *Feminist Theological Ethics: A Reader,* ed. Lois K. Daly [Philadelphia: Westminster/John Knox Press, 1994], 4).

experience that pleasure is not at odds with ethics.[12] Obviously, the Catholic Workers and Audre Lorde are not unique in this insight. This synthesis of eros/beauty and ethics is captured also by the early labor ballad and Catholic Worker classic "Bread and Roses":

> As we go marching marching in the beauty of the day
> A million darkened kitchens, a thousand mill lofts grey
> Are touched with all the radiance that a sudden sun discloses
> For the people hear us singing: bread and roses, bread and roses!
>
> As we go marching marching, unnumbered women dead
> Go crying thru our singing their ancient call for bread
> Small art and love and beauty their drudging spirits knew
> Yes it is bread we fight for, but we fight for roses too.[13]

In my sexuality I know this beauty as I hesitatingly come to know G*d's/love's abundance. As I come to trust that all parts of me are loved and that I belong, I am less able to reject others. The less I am trapped by the need for "one true love," the more openly I am able to love and the more erotic connections are possible. Because I do not or cannot limit my erotic response to one person, one gender, one activity, but meet it, claim it, act it where it calls me (or I am learning to), then the scent of sweet peas as I work in my grandmother's garden, a child's chalk drawing, a man, a woman, a just society, become my lovers, objects of my desire and actors in my passion play. I delight in Mariana Valverde's description of eroticism as mutual empowerment, and I strive toward it in my loving.[14] The feeling when I open to a lover, that I am as big as the sky, is the same as what happens sometimes when I paint. The best way I can describe it is not that I pray but rather that I am prayed. And I cannot imagine how these experiences are not of G*d. My response to beauty, physically, spiritually, sexually, and politically is joy.

But living in community with the urban poor, living under patriarchy, living in the United States of America, is often not beautiful. It is not beautiful when the toilet overflows again, when a friend steps on a dirty needle in the garden, when a neighbor ODs, when a child is shot. It is not

[12] For a discussion of the social construction of desire and a feminist sexual ethics of resistance, see Mariana Valverde, *Sex, Power and Pleasure* (Toronto: Women's Press, 1985), 203–6.

[13] Verses 1 and 3 of "Bread and Roses," a labor song inspired by a banner in the huge 1912 walkout of textile workers in Lawrence, Massachusetts. See *Rise Up Singing,* ed. Peter Blood Patterson (Bethlehem: Sing Out, 1988), 245.

[14] Valverde, *Sex, Power and Pleasure,* 43–44.

beautiful to know my own capacity for violence, my desire for control, and my willingness to sell out. But my tradition says and my experience confirms that beauty is not an escape from these things nor its opposite. G*d is known in the ugliness of people's lives, and the heart of the story is that salvation is just another homeless baby and resurrection is a community that can't forget.

Eucharist

The House of Bishops of the Church of England stated in 1992 that bisexuality is always wrong; the Episcopal Church of the United States is at best ambivalent in its policies and practices toward gay men and lesbians; and the Catholic Church considers that only celibate men are fit for ordination.[15] These are the churches with which I have the strongest ties. I have been asked and I ask myself, why I don't join a church with a model of priesthood and leadership that is more in line with my own concept of justice and the early church, and whose social teachings and practice around women and queers is less repressive. Why do I retain an association with an organization that persists in harming me and the people I love? Why do I submit to what Robert Goss describes as ecclesial abuse?[16]

My continuing presence in the church is not a sign of the depth of my oppression, and the church is not my abusive partner. I do not give money to churches; I do not excuse their sexism, racism, classism, homophobia; nor do I tolerate them. But I struggle, in community, to make my way on the periphery, an unlicensed practitioner of sorts, in part because of the sacraments. Perhaps strangely for a radical, activist feminist who insists on inclusive language, I love ritual. I am very much an "altar" Christian.[17] It is not simply that I have a deep affection for what is familiar, and I do. But in a way that is utterly sensual and completely spiritual, liturgy and sacrament work for me in a way that worship experiences with a less traditional sacramental focus do not. My eros and spirit meet at the altar.

[15] The bishops' report, "Issues in Human Sexuality," states that bisexuality is always wrong since "it inevitably involves being unfaithful." This report was affirmed by the Anglican Church of Canada in 1992, "Church of England bishops reject actively gay clergy" (*The Anglican Journal* 118 [January 1992]: 1).

[16] Robert Goss, *Jesus Acted Up: A Gay and Lesbian Manifesto* (San Francisco: HarperSanFrancisco, 1993), 115.

[17] Seminarians Interacting, an interfaith dialogue organization, asks Christians to self-identify not as Protestant or Catholic, but rather as "altar" or "pulpit," a division that I find both telling and useful.

Without engaging in long arguments about suffering, sacrifice theology, and soteriology (the meaning of salvation,) I would like to talk a little about the Eucharist as a place where the intersection of my sexuality and my spirituality is revealed. The Eucharist, or communion, is a central rite in many Christian churches, where bread and wine or grape juice are blessed by a clergyperson and consumed by the congregation. Individuals, denominations, and churches attach various meanings—memorial, symbolic, sacramental—to this ritual.

The Eucharist as I experience it is profoundly sensual, appealing to touch, taste, sight, sound, and smell: the fire of the wine, the snap of the wafer, bread that clings to the roof of my mouth, flickering candles, the touch of hands, the smell of incense—or, oftener where I worship, the smell of unwashed bodies pressed close together. It moves me deeply that my tradition retains the knowledge that eating and drinking are sacred acts and the hope that the divine is known in sharing food.

Although my experience of Eucharist is very much a body experience, it is a sensual and spiritual experience that demands justice. I understand my spirituality and my sexuality as socially constructed, and thus they are political, not private, concerns. Historically, there may not have been a Last Supper, but there is ample evidence that Jesus practiced a radical, open-table commensality; that is, he ate with sinners and outcasts.[18] As a Jew, he would have taken part in a Passover celebration each year, the ritual meal reliving his people's history, a history of enslavement where G*d acts on behalf of the oppressed. The phrase "body and blood" in Jesus' time conveyed martyrdom, and political execution, the consequence of living a life opposed to empire, not sacrifice as we have come to understand it. These Jewish roots of the Eucharist, the Christian ritual meal, emphasize the traditions of justice and liberation, which I believe are essential to its practice in the present. The Episcopal Church's eucharistic prayer emphasizes this imperative to action:

> *Deliver us from the presumption of coming to this table for solace only and not for strength; for pardon only and not for renewal.*[19]

I suppose that it is possible to celebrate the Eucharist without having your life be in some way about the work of justice. But I believe that the only "Real Presence" that is possible occurs if we *become* the body of

[18] John Dominic Crossan, *The Historical Jesus: Life of a Mediterranean Jewish Peasant* (San Francisco: HarperSanFrancisco, 1991), 360–61.

[19] *Book of Common Prayer.*

Christ, loving justice in the face of empire, living active resistance to the forces of domination. It is passionate engagement that makes the difference between live and dead ritual, not the credentials, status, gender, or orientation of the celebrants.

Two experiences illustrate some of the beauty, mystery, power, and ambivalence I know in the Eucharist. Mass at Guadalupe House is where I most consistently catch a glimpse of what I think the early Jesus community was like: you don't have to be ordained to preside, we all consecrate the gifts, and the icons and banners are homemade and beautiful.[20] But the two most important things are the prayers and the meal. Almost everyone who comes: addicted people, homeless people, people who hear voices, dirty people, frightened people, people with houses—all these people—feel that our living room is a safe place to speak their prayers. At Guadalupe House, we don't do mass without also doing dinner, a meal for all our guests and neighbors, many of whom live in shelters, in cars, or in the street. Our sacrament is an actual meal that feeds real hungry bodies. Our celebration is far from perfect. It is too male, too white, too leader-oriented, but I catch glimpses of holiness and beauty.

The second experience happened in 1989. I was visiting the village of San Jorge in Guatemala to bring cloth from a family of weavers to their son, a refugee in Mexico. I arrived in the heat of the day, having walked and hitchhiked since early morning. Dirty and with faltering Spanish, I found my way to a two-room house with dirt floors that was home to a family of eight. A child who had never worn shoes and who probably never would was dispatched to the only refrigerator in town, and I was given bread and cheese and Coca-Cola and a bowl of water with which to wash myself. That meal was more real a sacrament than any I have experienced in church.[21]

Jesus

I write this essay identifying as a bisexual Christian. Because of Christian patriarchy, homophobia, heterosexism, anti-Judaism, and racism, it is not especially fashionable for feminists, even Christian feminists, to talk

[20] The original house at the Tacoma Catholic Worker.

[21] In 1991 San Jorge became one of the approximately five hundred villages destroyed and burned by the Guatemalan military since 1954. For a synopsis of U.S. involvement in Guatemala, see Jack Nelson-Pallmeyer, *School of Assassins* (Maryknoll, N.Y.: Orbis, 1997), 10–17.

about Jesus. Although it feels dangerous and risky, I think it is relevant, and possibly even obligatory. But I wonder how I can reduce my passionate faithfulness and equally passionate doubting to just a few pages. I also wonder, What do I have to say that is "uniquely bisexual" about Jesus?

As one schooled in Christian liberation theologies, I see Jesus as someone who deliberately took the part of the systematically marginalized—the poor, the outcast, women—as an illustration of what G*d in the world is. I think, however, it would be a dreadful mistake for us to attempt to formulate a bi-liberation theology or to reclaim a bisexual Jesus, citing perhaps references to his love for Mary Magdalene or John the beloved disciple.

Over the past fifty years the complexion of Christian theology has been changed by theologians who speak for and from marginalized communities, claiming, or rather reclaiming, Christ/Jesus from white malestream Christianity. They/we have "taken back" Jesus by re-membering him with the rejected and hated (denigrated) qualities of that group.[22] Latin American theologians speak of Jesus the *campeseno;* African and African-American theologians speak of the Black Christ; women of Jesus the feminist, or Christa—the feminine Christ-spirit, not related to Jesus' maleness; gay men and lesbian theologians claim the Queer Christ.

> The queer Christ is politically identified with all queers—people who have suffered the murders, assaults, hatecrime activities, campus violence, police abuse, ecclesial exclusion, denial of ordination and the blessing of same sex unions, harassment, discrimination, HIV-related violence, defamation, and denial of civil rights and protections. Jesus the queer Christ is crucified repeatedly by homophobic violence. The aim of God's practice of solidarity and justice-doing and our own queer Christian practice is to bring an end to the crucifixions in this world.[23]

The insights of liberation theologies come from oppressed people reading scripture and identifying with stories like their own. The main reason why I think a bi theology of liberation would be an error is that I do not think that bisexuals are oppressed as bisexuals.

Clearly, inasmuch as we are queer, bis are subject to the violence of homophobia and heterosexism in our culture at large. I do not deny either that bisexual persons have experiences and patterns of experiences with

[22] Elisabeth Schüssler Fiorenza describes a fourfold hermeneutics of suspicion, remembrance, proclamation, and creative actualization (*Bread Not Stone: The Challenge of Feminist Biblical Interpretation* [Boston: Beacon Press, 1995], 15).

[23] Goss, *Jesus Acted Up,* 85.

gay men and lesbians that are painful, violations, and in need of healing (and I absolutely believe that Jesus is about healing). But feminism has taught me how important it is to be careful about language and power structures. Oppression is the systematic abuse of a subordinate group by a dominant group, the unjust exercise of power and authority.[24] I do not believe that bisexuals, with our varying degrees of access to heterosexual privilege are oppressed, are a subordinate group, so I would argue that a bi liberation theology is not appropriate. So called bi-phobia, the fear of and/or bigotry against bisexuals, operates more at the level of prejudice or "horizontal oppression" and functions to keep all of us from the work of our liberation.

I can think of no aspect of gay and lesbian prejudice against bisexuals that is not either the direct result of heterosexism/homophobia or does not spring from the same roots (sexism, sex negativity, dualism, and fear of difference). Bisexuals are called weak, fickle, traitors, and sellouts because straight-seeming behavior is rewarded, no matter why it is chosen. Accusations of infidelity, disease carrying, and immaturity are charges that gays and lesbians have faced for years, deflected onto bis, transpeople, and others because we threaten a precarious and sometimes hard-won security on the edges of straight legitimacy. Moreover, we are a threat because we imply, simply by being, that the world is not made up of paired opposites: boy–girl, straight–gay, right–wrong, black–white, but of infinite variety and goodness.

I believe that to follow Jesus is not to ask, What would Jesus do? but in my own way to try to "live Jesus" today. Of course bisexuality is not closer to Jesus than any other sexuality, but bis do have unique opportunities. We can live and love joyfully and defiantly, like Jesus embracing the glorious ambiguity and refusing to be held by purity codes, gay or straight.

When I study the Jesus stories in the communities where I live and work, again and again I am shocked by the radicality of the call to resist the persistent invitation to cozy up to the powers of domination. Bis can hold fast to a radically inclusive vision of the kin-dom, not simply one that will have us if we behave. And we can guard against the temptation, individual and corporate, to redraw the legitimacy line with ourselves and our friends inside.

This brings me to my second hesitation about a bi liberation theology. I see Jesus as one who was passionate and alive, who lived and loved in

[24] This definition is spliced from Webster's and Random House dictionaries and from my own familiarity with the popular use of the term in various justice-work communities.

defiance of empire. Jesus had a great deal to say about money, taxes, wealth, and power and very little to say about sex, so I am very wary of contributing to the pattern of playing down the political/economic work of Jesus. I am not proud when I go to Pride Marches and I see corporate floats, gays in the military, and the white male precision cell phone drill team. My passion is for something much finer than a piece of the status quo.

For me, to identify and to renounce heterosexual privilege and to strive for radical inclusivity in my thinking and acting have something to do with Jesus, but as a white, educated, North American Christian to dwell on the Christlikeness of my marginalized identity as a bisexual seems ludicrous. It makes much more sense for me as a follower of Jesus to look at my world in terms of empires, powers, and principalities. Who are the pharaohs, Herods, Romes, and Egypts of my day? In the world of savage global capitalism, neoliberal economics, and white supremacist hetero-patriarchy, whose interests do I serve? The spiritual questions are political and economic: What do I have? What has me? What do I stand for and what will I stand against? What will I risk arrest for? And, if this truly is the way of the cross I/we am walking, what will I live and die for?

A Conclusion of Sorts

Elizabeth Reba Weise said that to be a bisexual feminist is to lead an intensely examined life.[25] It is my experience that for a bisexual feminist who is also an activist, artist, and scholar in the radical discipleship movement, this is even more true. Like many bisexual women, I first came out as a lesbian, and then—if you will pardon the pun—I experienced a "second coming out." As I learn to be unashamed of my many loves, I find it is true that "love always brings us out of closets."[26] My tradition says that G*d is love, and I take great delight in the knowledge that, despite what churches may tell me, G*d/love is forever pushing me and pulling me out of the closet and onto the street.

[25] Elizabeth Reba Weise, "Introduction," in *Closer to Home,* xi.

[26] Nina Silver, "Coming Out as Heterosexual," in *Closer to Home,* 45.

I Am Goddess and God, Therefore I Am Bi

PASHTA MARYMOON

I AM, FIRST AND FOREMOST, in love with the Divine, married via the intricate inner twinings of Goddess-God/soul-spirit. Bound to something both rooted in the core of my own being and infused into the beyond. I dance between these indivisible Two—an active point of union between Them. I walk the undulating path of Their creative tension—a singular journey of a humyn life. I am as married to both faces of the Divine within the wholeness of who I AM, as I am married to both of my own hands and feet within the physical world. I am certainly not perfect, nor do I hold perfection as a standard: in Wicca, how one attempts to walk the journey of life is more important than some preconceived goal.

For me, being bi is not just about who I am drawn into relationship with and/or choose to have sex with: it is the fundamental quality of how I understand myself and my world as both/and (rather than either/or). As a Universalist, I can dance with the archetypal gods of many religions as the path of my own life visits the qualities of their particular wisdom stories. But nowhere have I found a spiritual home base that honors the both/and, the polarity of the Divine and Its firstborn child, the Universe, as in Wicca. Certainly one does not have to be bi to be Wiccan, nor Wiccan to be bi, but they have become two sides of the same coin for me personally. Likewise, my own story of discovery follows a both/and path—two parallel streams, weaving in and out of each other.

Growing into MaidenHood

I was raised atheist, but quite early on I chose a spiritual bent, much to the chagrin of my parents. In part, my choice was due to the constant violence within my household and was a response to my yearning for protection. When I was four, my mother, brother, and I escaped this violence by moving to England to live with my uncle. The first thing I saw when I reached my new home was a bright, full moon. From a child's mind, I was convinced that the moon had followed us over from Canada just to watch over me personally. She became symbolic of our freedom, and she became my other Mother.

We returned to Canada eighteen months later, and eventually my mother was manipulated into returning to my father. Being the eldest of the children, I had taken on the role of protecting my younger brother (and eventually a second brother) and even my mother. Shortly afterwards, when I was eight, I was introduced to Christianity. At this point, I developed a strong relationship with this "older brother" called Jesus. I was no longer the eldest, no longer alone in trying to protect the others or understand what was going on. Jesus was my daytime confidant; the moon, my nighttime muse. These relationships grew side by side—not directly connected but with no sense of contradiction.

Maiden to Mother

As an adolescent, I seemed to have less interest in sex than many of my peers, although my romantic interests seemed to be with males. I began my relationship with my husband of ten years when I was only fourteen, but I was always somewhat aware that I was primarily marrying a brother—actually, someone as close to Jesus as I could find, and not a lover. After a couple of years, my sexual interest in the relationship waned almost entirely. We were in an "open marriage," and my sexual interest was there for other male lovers, but only initially. I soon realized that my interest in other lovers was more about building a larger family than it was about sex.

When I was eighteen, I spoke to my doctor about my general lack of interest in sex. She said I was just too young to be interested. I doubted her conclusion. Even at that relatively young age, I suspected that beyond my adult efforts to recover from the terror I knew as childhood, I was mostly asexual.

During these years, I realized that my relationship with Jesus was not of any ordinary Christian type. In adolescence, he transformed for me from older brother to spiritual lover. But I knew that even among the Quaker (Society of Friends) denomination, which I had joined by then, I needed to be careful about how I spoke about my relationship with the Christos, "out of the silence" in a Quaker Meeting for Worship.

Then, in my early twenties, I had a deep experience of identity with the Mother Mary during a reenactment of the Stations of the Cross. I walked with a group of radical Catholic friends and co-workers (Catholic Worker and L'Arche community folk) carrying a life-size cross up the central hill in Seattle. I was one of the first to carry it. When my time was up, I was to pass it on to a fairly young man—younger than my twenty-four years, at any rate. I found it extremely emotionally painful to pass this burden on to him. I felt almost crucified myself in doing so, but I knew that, superficially, my feelings didn't make any sense—I didn't even know the man.

By the time that we had completed the walk, I realized that I was responding to this passing of the cross to him, as if I were the Virgin Mary herself passing it to Jesus for him to carry and suffer under, and ultimately to die on. What mother wouldn't choose, if she could, to take that cross instead of her child? What mother wouldn't herself feel more mortally wounded by having to watch her child go through this, than by going through it herself? When I realized that that was what I was feeling, I realized that I had moved out of the spiritual-lover stage and into the mother-son relationship with Jesus. Again, I was reluctant to speak openly about my particular relationship with the Christos. I couldn't imagine anyone understanding.

At this time in my life I was introduced to Wicca. I quickly realized that my relationship with the moon as Mother was consistent with Wicca, and that my relationship with Jesus had evolved, in correct order, through the mythological stages of the Wiccan god—first as brother of the Maiden, then as lover of the Mother, and finally as adult son of the Crone. While I understood the differences between Wiccan and Christian mythology and theaology, these relationships felt consistent and compatible to me, as they had in simpler images when I was a child.

Even being Wiccan and Quaker is part of the both/and path of my life. These two religions have much in common in terms of fundamental attitudes—equality, social awareness, and so on—and both are forms of practical mysticism. Yet, in terms of worship style, they are extreme opposites. Quakerism is a practice of nonritual, with an extremely simple and direct worship style—silent communal meditation. Wicca, on the other hand, practices one of the most ritualistic and complexly symbolic worship styles—recently termed a "poemagogic religious practice." It is a constant and intricate interweaving of mythic and poetic images and symbolic action.

At the same time that I recognized that my relationship with the figure of Jesus had transformed to that of mother and adult son and became acquainted with Wicca, I fell in love with a womyn. I assumed that my general lack of interest in sex with males was due to being lesbian. "Hallelujah! I finally understand," I thought, although I was still attracted to and involved with men. A later, six-year marriage to another womyn clarified for me that my lack of maintainable interest in sex was not gender based. I had exactly the same problem as I had had in my marriage to my husband, losing interest in sex early in our time together. Further, I recognized that what I really wanted out of the marriage was a sister. After this marriage ended, I decided to be mostly celibate.

The only sexual relationship I have been able to maintain for any length of time was with a bi-gay man. This relationship led me to question whether I was really bisexual or, psychically, bigendered. This relationship seemed to be based on a complex quaternity of relationships—straight womyn (me) to straight man (him); straight man (me) to straight womyn (him); lesbian (me) to lesbian (him); and gay man (me) to gay man (him).

Each of our gender identities shifted and flowed, allowing all of these possibilities to emerge. Sometimes one aspect of our relationship was distinct for a short time, sometimes several aspects were overlapping, and sometimes we only noticed the predominance of an aspect in hindsight. I felt all of my aspects cooperating with one another, as one face would come to the fore at the appropriate time, then release its dominance when another face was required.

While I am quite happy being a womyn, this quaternity of relationships allowed me to explore the masculine aspects of myself in a way I never have before or since. Since childhood, I had been aware of a range of inner personas, some of which were distinctly masculine. Some of these I recognized as being created in compensation for the trauma of my childhood years—who is to say that my "brother Jesus" was not a projected persona, evoked as the needed support to maintain sanity? Others seemed to arise without any specific purpose, or in response to any specific need—sometimes recurring, sometimes only as fleeting glances of a different and more masculine perspective. I had always been fairly comfortable with their existence, but now they had the opportunity to "act" within my life in a fairly safe context.

At that point in my life, this relationship was the only one where I had been able to incorporate all of the different parts of my self. A vivid example of this was that one of the happiest days of my life was spent with him and with a womyn lover, who accepted him in my life and in her own as a brother. It had such an amazing sense of finally not being divided up into acceptable pieces, but being all I am, whole. To know myself as multiple but cooperating faces was to enact the nature of the gods, shifting appropriately between the most required and, therefore, momentarily dominant face, but all within a common, unified purpose.

A long stretch of celibacy helped me become aware of other aspects of my relationship with gender. The first was not new—that I had strong attachments to men that had no sexual component at all. These were, I discovered, like a relationship with an adult son, but, during this period, I began to understand the reason for this. Part of being a womyn for me, is being "womyn" rather than "a womyn"—a residual memory of all wymyn throughout time. As such, every male on the face of this earth and throughout all time, is as one of my sons.

As womyn, I refuse to give up half of my children. There were certainly times, as a feminist, when I was quite prepared to cut off all relationships with men entirely. The mind-set gap between wymyn and men in our culture often feels like an unbridgeable chasm, which I periodically tire of trying to leap. But, my essential love for the God and my sense of being the embodiment of all wymyn always brought me back from that edge.

The second thing that I noticed was that the only time that I had any sexual interest/drive was around Beltaine, a Wiccan holy day on May 1st, focused on the marriage, mating, and procreation of the Goddess and the God. But this rise of energy around Beltaine was not so much about sex as it was an archetypal drive to get pregnant again. Even more literally, I yearned to be ploughed and sown like the fields, which is actually what the mating rite of the Goddess and the God represents. I have enacted that mating ritual as the sacred rite a couple of times, therefore breaking celibacy. In many ways, participating in the rite satisfied my spiritual urge to offer myself up while channeling the Goddess aspect of energy in the most potent way we humyns have for enacting creation itself. Though purely symbolic, I found it to be a totally absorbing and gratifying act.

But each time there was a sense of disappointment too. It was very hard to find a male who was capable of participating fully as the God and not as himself—a man who was capable of putting aside his own identity and ego to totally offer himself up to the God aspect in the rite. Very few people of any gender can actually do this. And if a lover relationship did not already exist between the participants, I found that it was very difficult for men to put aside the element of relatively anonymous sex and maintain the intention and energy of a holy rite between Goddess and God.

Of course, this inability to maintain the intention of the ritual caused a wide range of problems. And, because this particular rite is distinctly heterosexual, specifically representing the reproduction of life, I could not choose a womyn as an option for a mate. I won't say that I will never enact the sacred rite again, but I have certainly learned to be very cautious.

Mother to Crone

Over the past four years, my Beltaine urge has changed its tune. At first, I just noticed that Beltaine would pass and the urge did not arise, or that my fantasies seemed to turn to relationships in the fall, but I assumed that that was just circumstantial. In my forty-fifth year, I got hit hard with the urge for sex in a most unrealistic and inappropriate situation, and, in processing the feelings, I realized that this spiritual urge has firmly shifted to autumn, the time when the Crone face of the Goddess shows herself. I understand now that I am definitely croning—not just in body, but psychically as well.

The urge of the Crone, at least as I experience it, is not to reenact. It is more about a surge of energy to reevaluate one's life and to renew focus and direction. It is accompanied by the adoption of a useful new perspective on life—what I would call a watcher/witness appreciation for the qualities of youth, rather than an actor stance.

There are two distinctly connected and critical features of this Crone urge. The first is to reevaluate the glamours/spell of romance and sexuality and to consider how it has played in your life, leading you blindly into both positive and negative situations full of potential learning. This reflection includes evaluating how the work of the essentially benevolent, but often confusing, trickster god-energy has affected our choices. At this point in our lives, we come to realize that much of the glamour/spell of romance and sex is archetypal and is best left in its own realm—not fully enacted as real life in the mundane world, but through the power of ritual.

The second is to refocus that energy where you are most truly in love, with life itself, with all of earth's children, with your own destiny and work, and with the Divine as both Goddess and the God. Croning, with less focus on doing and more on being, also allows for the multiple sides/aspects of self to become more integrated and to find their fulfillment through witnessing, rather than acting. Such a development allows one a deeper appreciation of all around and within, without having to "live it all out."

I think that it is unlikely that I will choose to enter into a long-term relationship again. I have a chronic illness that allows me only very limited time and energy. There is no question in my mind that my priority goes to my work within Wicca and to interfaith concerns, and not into a personal relationship. I also have no wish ever again to have any responsibility for satisfying someone else's libido. Interestingly, I still fall in love quite often, with members of both genders, but I do not feel the need to enact that love sexually. Finally, while this is not true for all Crones, celibacy seems to be an important and archetypal part of my own croning.

I have considered the possibility of a future relationship, however, and whether I would be more likely to end up with a womyn or a man. To be honest, I just don't know. I see positives and negatives with either, though I believe there is less difference between genders than between different people within each gender. If a relationship were to come into my life, I predict that my choice would depend more on the specific person, not that person's gender, and the circumstances would have to be very unique.

Blessing the Whole

When I was younger, I felt an incredible urge to become a nun, while being quite aware that I was neither Catholic nor Christian, not to mention that at the time I was a committed wife and mother. Only later did I realize that this urge was, at the time, the only way I had of representing the fact that my primary marriage was to the Divine and not to another humyn being. The term *nun* was replaced with *priestess* of the Goddess and the God, and I have come to affirm that my sexual, or more accurately, my romantic, orientation is based more on my religion and the archetypes within it than on a specific sexual orientation. I am in love with both the Goddess and the God, and I can and do extend that love to Their humyn representatives, both femael and male. The act or attraction of sex itself has very little to do with it.

In Wicca, the Divine is understood to be a Whole within Itself—the ultimate whole which is more than the sum of its parts! It expresses, enacts, and represents Itself as polarity, as the extremes of position/potential within the Whole, by being stretched into a tension that demands movement/change and therefore, constant rebalancing. It never becomes absolutely separated. Without this constant rebalancing tension of polarity, no thing could ever be created, or transformed, and one of the primary qualities of the Divine—creativity—would be thwarted.

There is no absolute duality in Wicca. Any potential side is neither evil nor good, in and of itself. The Taoist yin/yang symbol is perhaps the best nonanthropomorphic image of polarity that expresses this, if you see that image as holding the white circle within the black side as a window into what lies behind the black and vice versa, or if you see the white circle within the black side as a focus of white within black and vice versa.

In either case, one is firmly rooted in the other. They are inseparable. They are only biases of potential. It is the tension of these biases that creates the zig-zagging/waving/serpentine movement that itself is the foundation of ex-IS-tense, the ALL that is, stretched out into creative tension.

Polarity has many forms—gatheredness–separateness, context–focus, circumference–center, content–activity, as well as the more common ones, such as black–white, dark–light, cold–hot, and so on. However, humyn beings have shown a need over the centuries to be able to identify the immanence of the Divine directly with themselves, and the clearest polarity between humyn beings is that of gender. Therefore, Wicca reflects a belief with which I agree—that it is easiest for humyns to relate to the polarity of the Divine as Goddess, the aggregate of femael-like qualities and God, the aggregate of male-like qualities.

In Wicca, the Divine is understood to be immanent in all things, animate and inanimate: Wicca questions the qualifications of inanimate, as does quantum physics. Each is an expression of some group of qualities of the Whole. Therefore, each humyn being is also considered to be not just a child of the Gods but a living representation of Them. Witches often formally greet each other with the statements "Thou art Goddess" or "Thou art God."

Even more accurately, in Wicca every living being is both a daughter/expression of the Goddess *and* a son/expression of the God. One could say, each one of us is the living expression of the genes of both Goddess and God, no matter what one's gender appears to be. Reflecting this understanding, many ancient and some contemporary cultures considered hermaphrodites and homosexuals to have a special relationship with, or be a special representation of, the Divine—specifically because it was understood that they held this polarity as equal forces within their own beings.

Personally, while I find the images of Goddess and God useful in expressing the polaric nature of the Divine, I often try to avoid such anthropomorphic gender polarizations—using the term *soul* as Goddess-like and *spirit* as God-like—since in our culture, humyns generally understand themselves to have both soul and spirit but not to have distinctly both femael-like and male-like qualities.

To me, life itself is a constant act of sex—the uniting in common bond to create (ideas, choices, directions, goals) that reaches far beyond a specific sexual act, to the mating of electrons in an atom and the dance of whole galaxies within the universe. Am I asexual or all sexual? Many non-Wiccan spiritual people, married to their own understanding of the Divine, have noted that the two are only the different sides of one choice. Whether or not I ever have physical sex again, or with what gender, is not so much the issue for me, but to live my life and to have all of my relationships with other people be an enactment of the mating of soul and spirit IS.

To love the Divine, then, is to feel the most intimate of bondings, sexually enacted or not, with both the Goddess and God potentials within the Whole. It is to see, and to choose to touch and to intercourse with, both essential expressions of Divinity within our bi gendered world. For me personally, then, how could I not be open to the deepest of intercourses with the soul/spirit, with both gendered forms, with femael and with male?

Blessed Be.

PART 2

Communion with Spirit: Wholeness Is Holy

Lovemaking

Susan Halcomb Craig

Loving God,

Your healing embrace is sealed
in our hearts;
Waters cannot quench
the streams of your love,
nor can the rising floods drown it.

Today be with those
who know twin rivers in our loving,
who sing the whole of your song
in one breath.
Gemini, we thrill to the dual touch
of women and men
in your holy creation;

We see you in images redoubled
and find your shalom
in love's fullness.
Yet others,
misunderstanding and fearful,
would split us from our selves
and diminish us by half,
forcing choices.

Reprinted, with permission, from *More Light Update,* a publication of More Light Presbyterians for Lesbian, Gay, Bisexual, and Transgender Concerns, PO Box 38, New Brunswick, N.J. 08903-0038.

Touch our hearts
and create us anew, O God,
that we may all
freely and faithfully
imagine the glorious realm
of your loving.

Dearest Jesus,

We remember
the Beloved Disciple's head
on your breast,
and the life-giving touching
between you and women.
We know you opened to love freely,
giving without stereotyping
and without counting the cost.
Teach us and touch us
as we cross old boundaries,
rewriting the maps of Love's journey
in our lives.

Beloved Lover and Spirit-friend,

Help us know in ourselves
and welcome in others
the rich possibilities
for loving in the world.
May we drink from your living waters,
and know the everflowing streams
of your love
in our own loving,
with each other and with you.

In your strong name we pray. Amen

Hear, I Pray You, This Dream Which I Have Dreamed

DEBRA KOLODNY

The Wandering Jew

FROM THE SPIRITUAL DESERT of a devoutly atheist upbringing, God called. In my sixteenth year I stood at the Kotel (the Western Wall) facing the site of the fallen Second Temple. For the first time in my life I prayed. I did not believe in prayer at the time, but felt that if ever there was a good time to do it, it was then. My brother was in trouble, going through a horrible time as only eighteen-year-olds can. I prayed for him to be released from his suffering.

Standing at the wall I felt the touch of that which is unknowable. The air heavy, a deep quiet seeped into my soul, as a palpably resonant energy field enveloped me. Time slowed. Separation between me and the world I usually thought of as outside of me evaporated. I knew then, not out of faith, not out of teaching, and not out of dogma, that I was not alone. We are not alone. Something profound and mysterious and so much bigger and more complex than anything humans could create did indeed live. Every muscle, bone, tendon, and nerve ending in my body knew it. I knew why I prayed. And I cried.

When I returned from that trip my brother was a changed man.

I returned from that trip a changed woman.

From the desert I was called.

Though my body and my soul had learned all they needed to know, through the workings of my mind I still wandered. In college I learned for the first time the language of my ancestors—Hebrew. The daughter of a musician, I inherited a good ear and I was a quick study. I wrote to the host family from my high school exchange experience, but took my new proficiency no further. Reading Torah did not occur to me then. Despite my personal contact with the Divine, I was not yet contemplating a structured, ongoing relationship. I still identified my Judaism as a powerful cultural component of my identity, not as a spiritual one.

During law school I took another step forward in my spiritual quest, still wrapped in the security of intellect and reason. I wrote a paper for my jurisprudence class on the reconciliation of immanence and transcendence. Unlearned in religion, unschooled in doctrine, unexposed to "expert" thought, I pondered the question of how we can be *both* material/corporeal beings and also beings of spirit. I decided that any theology which viewed humans as merely corporeal could not be valid. In addition, I held that any belief system calling for arbiters between ourselves and God missed the mark—that God yearns to be with us as we yearn to be with God, and that no clergy or priestess is necessary as a conduit for that connection. My mind cried out to understand the experience of my spirit.

At the very moment I began this quest for understanding, my body and heart shifted too. As I wrote that paper, as I intellectually integrated the notions of holding both immanence and transcendence together as one, as my mind grappled with the wholeness inherent in that prospect, I came out as bisexual. After five years identifying as a lesbian, and as many before as compulsorily heterosexual, I discovered my capacity for loving beyond gender. It seems that embracing both/and (being both immanent and transcendent, loving both men and women) instead of either/or (heterosexual/lesbian; God[dess]/ human) infused body, heart, and mind at once. I was utterly unaware of the remarkable synchronicity of this shift at the time. I only knew that I was scared to be leaving known territory, and that the gifts of this shift, both spiritually and emotionally would be worth any risks.

This spiritual inquiry also birthed my ongoing embrace of the mystical. I read voraciously on metaphysics and shamanism and witchcraft. I experimented with ritual and meditation and healing practice. I found glimpses of my experience at the Kotel and had some success with the healing work. Finally, terribly lonely in my spiritual quest, yearning for companionship, I sought community. I knew that I could not continue to grow in the spirit by myself. I needed support and guidance.

The first place I looked was not the synagogue. While I held fast to my cultural and political identity as a Jew, it didn't occur to me that I could find what I was looking for at *shul.* As I lived the notion of both/and, I saw no reason why a Jew could not worship in other contexts and still be a Jew. I explored several options, and at twenty-eight I joined a Quaker Meeting. The first day I attended Meeting for Worship, for the very first time since the Kotel, I felt the powerful and palpable experience of spirit, this time in the silent joining of a community in prayer.

Though spiritually satisfied by the form of Quaker worship, I began to question my wandering. As universalist as my meeting was, I remained aware of its Christian underpinnings. And while I always felt like a Jew who chose to worship with Quakers, when someone asked me when I had converted to Christianity, I was horrified. The notion that anyone would think I was anything but a Jew was abhorrent to me. I would never reject my proud blood heritage. I was certainly not willing to have my assimilation assumed. But, more importantly, I had to ask myself, Why was I seeking everywhere but home? I was born a Jew. I had my first spiritual experience at a Jewish holy site. It was time to acknowledge what my blood, my soul, had been telling me for over a dozen years. To listen and act on my yearning to come out of the desert.

I started to attend *Shabbat* services at a lay-led independent egalitarian Jewish community named Fabrangen. I liked the people there and really enjoyed the feel of it. I didn't realize just how powerful it would be to worship with people who looked like me and sounded like me. I was warmed by the community and the sense that my values—gender equality, lack of hierarchy, sexual orientation diversity, *tikkun olam* (repair of the world), *tzedakah* (charity), justice, and mercy—were represented in the language, practice, and philosophy of the *chavurah* (community). But my lack of familiarity with the prayers and my loss of what little Hebrew I had learned in college meant that I couldn't follow the bulk of the service. I felt communally connected and at the same time lost and inadequate. I also felt barraged by the verbal prayer and discussion. So little silence—negligible really. Yet silence had always been my gateway to the Divine. First at the Kotel, then in my own meditation, and then in the Quaker silent worship. How could I make my experience in synagogue both immanent (present with the prayer) and transcendent (tangibly relating to the God force)?

After six months of regular attendance, I stopped with a heavy heart. I felt more spiritually adrift than ever. I knew where I wanted to be, but I didn't feel like I belonged. The amount I thought I needed to learn to be spiritually literate as a Jew overwhelmed me.

Several years later I could take the isolation no longer. At thirty-six I began eighteen months of preparation for a ritual acknowledgment of my *bat mitzvah.* This course of study filled more than enough of my literacy gap. Learning and understanding the meaning of the prayers, the meditative nature of the service, the patterns and intention of the liturgy, of the Torah, and of the cycle of holidays lifted the veil between my spirit and my blood.

Despite my age, I experienced the preparations for this day and the day itself as a portal into adulthood. The eighteen months were not just spent learning my Torah portion and learning about Jewish practice; they were filled with searching about how I could better realize my calling and serve in the ways I was meant. Integrating my spirit self into my cultural identity—being a Jew in all senses of the word—marked a profound passage into wholeness. Almost twenty-five years after the fact (one becomes a *bat mitzvah* at thirteen whether or not a ceremony is held) I celebrated with the world that I am a daughter of the Torah.

Three months before my thirty-eighth birthday, I celebrated with family, friends, and community. I led a meditation on holiness during the morning service, and I participated in giving the *d'var torah* (sermon) with the other members of my class. I wore my new *tallit* (prayer shawl), which I had designed so I could wrap myself in sacred presence every time I prayed.[1] The shawl is quilted with representations of the four elements: purple mountains, turquoise river, a dove in flight in the skies, and Yemenite stitchwork aflame on the collar. Embroidered along the front hem in Hebrew are the words *Hineni osah et atzmi, merkava L'Shechina,* "Here I am, transforming myself into a chariot for Divine Presence." But the most significant aspect of the service—the cornerstone of any *bar* or *bat mitzvah* was when I *leyned* (sang) from the Torah. I was so nervous. I felt as if I were going to black out. The honor, the gravity of reading aloud from the holiest of texts touched me in ways I had never been touched before. My voice trembled. A lifetime of love of song poured out of me—as if I was singing something that mattered for the first time. Three hours later I lost my voice for two days—also a first. I guess I had said enough.

I was first aware of God's touch twenty years before—almost to the day. I was finally prepared to take on the responsibility of that blessing.

[1] *Tallisim* are worn only during daytime prayers, except on Kol Nidre, when they are worn also at night. Because I don't attend evening services, the vast majority of my prayer time is during the day. But there are a few occasions when I am praying without wearing this garment.

Now that I am deeply engaged with Judaism I experience that original synchronicitous connection between my bisexuality and my faith magnified manyfold. I find intersections in scripture, in theological principle, and even in the very name we call ourselves.

My people are Ivrim, Hebrews. Some say that the word comes from a root which means boundary crossers, transgressors. Some say that it was a word of contempt, given by masters who saw us as out of control.

As a bisexual feminist I will not, I cannot, live in the boxes created for me by others. I cross the invisible line and say: "I love whomever I love. Regardless of the package they come in, I love all of who they are . . . the softness and the hard, the courage and the fear, the broken and the healed. I love them and that love is good, and that love is honored by God." Every day I hold the whole. Every day I am Ivriyah.

Holding opposition. Both/and. Boundary crosser. Bisexual.

Judaism calls to me for many reasons. The most essential, the most powerful, the most compelling, is that it is alive. And it is alive in a way designed to hold oppositions at once. Judaism is a path that grows and flows and connects the present to the past to the future. Every week of every year, for as long as we live, we read the story of our people. Yesterday is today is tomorrow. Torah is alive. *L'dor v'dor.* From generation to generation we pass down the story, the laws, the frame to hold the people together as we cross into the unknown. Judaism connects the infinite to the finite and the here to the there. There is even a name for the indwelling presence of God–*Shechina.* She is here with us. We are joined as one.

Judaism makes boundaries even as it crosses them. What foods can be eaten, and what foods cannot. What stories to tell and questions to ask at the Passover seder. When to work and when to rest. What is holy and what is not. A dramatic tension created to invite us to explore the holiness in our lives, and to find holiness in ourselves. A tension that provides fodder for discussion, for disagreement, for aliveness. Surely you have heard . . . two Jews, three opinions.

As a bisexual I experience sexual orientation, both attraction and behavior, as fluid–as shifting, as both immutable *and* changing. I am always bisexual, whether my partner is male or female. I am always bisexual, whether in my dream last night I felt passion with a man or a woman. While my identity is constant, my attractions, dreams, and partners have changed over the past fifteen years.

In its aliveness Judaism too is fixed and changing. The givens form the framework, and while observant Jews vary in how they relate to those givens, they are essential to all of us: the Torah, the *mitzvot* (commandments), the cycles of the week (Shabbat—the weekly Sabbath is a day of rest and spiritual devotion), of the month (every new moon, Rosh Chodesh, a new month begins and is celebrated), and of the year (all of the holidays, each one attached to the cycle of the earth), the daily rituals (kissing the *mezuzah* on the doorpost, daily prayers), the tangible ritual objects (*Shabbat* candles, *tallitot, kippot*—head coverings). Both within and beyond those givens exist the doorways to ecstasy, one's relationship with holiness, the invitation to grow ever deeper and higher in awareness of the divine, the possibility for learning ever more powerful lessons and insights from the text, from the ritual, and from life, and ultimately to live one's life in a constant state of transformation.

Holding oppositions. Both/and. Boundary crosser. Jew.

For me, every soul embodies both maleness and femaleness. I am convinced that as matter and spirit intersect within us, we cannot help but transcend gender. It is the unique manner in which the spirit lives within us which creates our destiny, not biology. Genitalia, hormones, and even socialization are far less significant in making someone attractive than is the soul. My belief that we incarnate in this world as both men and women over the course of many existences reinforces my sense that the Spirit lives beyond gender constraints.

In Judaism we are taught that each of us, woman and man, and those who consider themselves in between or beyond such categories, are *all* made in the image of God—*betzelem Elohim.* The only way that this can be true is if our spirits hold the spark of all gender possibilities, just as all of those possibilities exist within *Ha-Shem* (literally, "the Name," a Hebrew name for God). If that is true, whether I love a man or a woman or someone who identifies outside of those categories, I am loving *both* a woman and a man, and I am loving someone created in the image of *Ha-Shem.* If I did not acknowledge this, I would not be accepting all of myself and all of the person whom I am loving beyond the assumptions, constraints, and packaging of his or her gender.

If one looks at kabbalistic thought, one finds profound work on the integration of genders within the Divine. The *Sefirot,* the kabbalistic schema that finds balance and integration in the world through a series of ten principles, has an equal measure of feminine and masculine energy. Once, when reflecting on this integration of male and female energies, a teacher of mine of Kabbala said that God was bisexual. English was his third language—after Hebrew and French. I think the word he was actually looking for was hermaphroditic or intersexed, both male and female. But I was touched to the core. God is bisexual. God is straight and gay and transgendered. Indeed.

Holding oppositions. Both/and. Boundary crosser. Bisexual Jew.

Exploring the Homeland and Finding Myself

One of the ways that Judaism is alive is through the tradition of Midrash, finding the untold stories within the text and reading between the lines to tease out learning. Indeed, this principle of learning more deeply into the text, of finding things you don't necessarily expect, is fundamental. It reinforces to me that both fixedness and fluidity are valued in my faith, but it does something more. It allows for the possibility that I might see myself in our most sacred text. That in delving deep into the texture of Torah, I will find messages that touch upon even the most complex and commonly misunderstood aspects of my bisexual self.

This happened for me as I was preparing for *Shabbat,* December 12, 1998, when I gave a *d'var torah* of the Torah portion: *Vayyashev* (Genesis 37:1–40:23). This particular *parsha* tells much of the story of Joseph. When we meet him he is inciting his brothers' jealousy, sharing prophetic dreams of his lordship over them. When he tells them of his nighttime travels, Joseph says to his brothers, *Shimoo-na hachalom hazeh asher chalamti,* "Hear, I pray you, this dream which I have dreamed" (Genesis 37:5). I was taken by his request. In his youthful enthusiasm, Joseph didn't realize that his brothers, already jealous because he was his father's favorite, would be angered by his dreams of power. He only knew that he had dreamed a truth, and he wished for his truth to be heard. I sat with Joseph's naivete, with his passionate desire to be heard, and I was touched deeply. How often do we have dreams that we wish others would hear, or recognize, or support us in. How often do we need that acknowledgment to have the strength to make our dreams come true? How powerfully did I long for the realization of my dream—to live in a world free from oppression and exploitation and hate. I saw myself in Joseph. But, I saw much, much more.

I launched into the research for my *d'var torah* on the subject of dreams. I planned to speak about Joseph's power in dreaming, about the place of dreams in Judaism, and about prophecy within dreams. What I found instead surprised and delighted me. I started with the general topic of dreams, but ended up finding what could be an answer to one of my own dreams.

In addition to delivering the *d'var torah* that *Shabbat,* I also helped to lead the first part of the service: *Psukey D'zimra* (Songs of Praise). After the morning blessings and my favorite prayer, *Elohai neshama shenatati bi, tehora hi,* "My God, the soul which you have given me is completely pure," I led the community through a chant that I had composed just for this service. Using Joseph's request to his brothers as the *kavanah* (spiritual intention), I invited those gathered to think of a dream that they wanted someone to acknowledge, or maybe even wanted God to acknowledge. Together we chanted, *Shimoo-na hachalom hazeh asher chalamti,* "Hear, I pray you, this dream which I have dreamed." Later in the service we chanted the same melody without the words (a *niggun*) one more time. As a community, in one voice, we invited our dreams to be heard.

What Dreams Have Come

In the context of this collective call, I offered a *drash* that explored the powerful role Joseph played in the history of the Jews. Joseph alone of his siblings possessed the skill, ability, and vision to save the Hebrews and the Egyptians from death by famine. How is it that he was blessed to play this pivotal role? On the face of the story, we know that despite being sold by his brothers into slavery, he possesses a powerful gift—he can dream prophetic dreams, and he can interpret the prophetic dreams of others. Because dreams were recognized in biblical times as vehicles of divine communication, we can be sure that Joseph lived as a powerful conduit to God consciousness.[2] And Joseph wasn't just any dreamer. He is memorialized among Jews in some ways as the greatest dreamer of them all.[3]

I couldn't help but wonder: What in Joseph's background, in his blood line, combined to create this capacity for greatness? And was this something his other siblings lacked? Why did Joseph have this direct line to

[2] Nahum Sarna, *Understanding Genesis: The World of the Bible in the Light of History* (New York: Schocken Books, 1966), 213.

[3] So enduring are his impressive powers that Joseph's dreams are the only ones mentioned during collective prayer. In some synagogues, on certain holy days, worshipers twice recite a prayer concerning dreams. "Master of the universe, I am Thine and my dreams are Thine; I have dreamed a dream, and I do not know what it is?" They continue that if the dreams are "good" dreams, may they be "strengthened and be made firm, fulfilled like the dreams of Joseph." Monford Harris, *Studies in Jewish Dream Interpretation* (Northvale: Jason Aronson, 1994).

God? And, perhaps more importantly, why did Joseph have favor in God's eyes?[4]

The inheritance of his gifts of prophecy, of direct relationship with God, and of favor with God is clear from his earthly lineage. Both of Joseph's great grandparents, Sarah and Abraham, received instruction directly from God and God's angels.[5] In the next generation Rebecca receives direct word from God regarding the ascension of Jacob to carry the blessing and mantle of third-generation patriarch.[6] Finally, Jacob, son of Rachel and Isaac, father of Joseph, is visited by a divinely crafted dream, wrestles with an angel from God, and later receives a message directly from God.[7]

It is not news to any reader of the Hebrew Scriptures that God was in close contact with the "first family" of the Jewish people. But Joseph's siblings share most of this lineage. What distinguishes Joseph? The only obvious difference is that Joseph was the love child of Jacob and Rachel—the first of only two children borne of one of the most passionate couplings we see in the Torah. We don't know of Rachel's own powers in relation to dreaming and receiving messages from God, but we do know that Leah, her elder sister, was described as having weak eyes. Many interpret this to mean that she was not attractive. But perhaps this is a sign to Jacob and to the reader that Leah herself does not hold the gift of sight, of vision, and that her offspring will also not carry it. Perhaps Jacob realizes, either intuitively or deductively, that because he has one parent who is challenged in this area (Isaac, who is often described as not being able to see, and who does not seem to share his wife Rebecca's connection with God), he must choose a partner who will reinforce rather than weaken the prophetic vision of his children.

We know that Rachel and Jacob loved one another dearly, and that Jacob

[4] See Genesis 39:2-3: "And the Lord was with Joseph, and he was a prosperous man; and he was in the house of his master, the Egyptian. And his master saw that the Lord was with him, and that the Lord made all that he did to prosper in his hand." See also Genesis 39:21: "But the Lord was with Joseph, and showed kindness unto him, and gave him favour in the sight of the keeper of the prison." The translation is *The Soncino Chumash,* ed. A. Cohen (New York: Soncino Press, 1983).

[5] See Genesis 12:1–25:8 for dozens of incidents of God speaking with Abraham. Conversations with Sarah are much harder to find. Genesis 18:10–15 describes an incident that can be construed as a conversation with God, but is at minimum a conversation between Sarah and God's angels.

[6] See Genesis 25:23: "And the Lord said unto her: Two nations are in thy womb, And two peoples shall be separated from thy bowels; And the one people shall be stronger than the other people; and the elder shall serve the younger."

[7] See Genesis 28:12–16; 32:25–30; 35:10–12.

had not chosen any of his other three wives. Two came in a package deal as handmaidens and Leah was forced upon him unwittingly by Laban, her father, who refused to marry his youngest daughter before the elder. We know that Jacob was willing to work first seven and then fourteen years in order to actualize his love for Rachel (see Genesis 29:25–28).

Again, I wondered. In addition to pure genetics and to the potential for Rachel's vision to be passed along to Joseph, was his destiny ignited by something more, something beyond genetics? Was he destined to greatness as the child of a passionate *basherte* (divinely intended) coupling? Do partnerships borne out of true love have more power than others to transform the world? Do the partnerships we choose, the partnerships we feel called to embrace, rather than the ones that are chosen for us, hold more power—power for creating greatness, for connecting with God, for *tikkun olam* (repairing the world)? Perhaps in our passionate choosing we are making God-inspired decisions, the ramifications of which cannot be known for centuries to come.

As this question unfolded for me I began to think about the implications of this message for today. Who are the Jacobs and Rachels of today? Who are the people who feel passionately called to one another, only to be told that their love must be subverted to the proper order of things? Who in this day and age would go to such lengths, through such hardship (akin to fourteen years of labor!) to be with the one he or she loves? Or worse yet, who has resigned him- or herself to a life where love must never be realized? Or purged? Or "converted"?

Controversy rages today around the efforts of some right-wing religious extremists to convert people from their naturally occurring same-sex attraction and from the partnering choices they feel passionately drawn to, to a life that meets societally imposed rules on the moral imperative of male–female partnering. Today the story might read, Jacob, you must wed Leah instead of Richard. Is our cultural bias, and in some circles mandate, for heterosexual union any more compelling than marrying off the eldest daughter first was in the time of Rachel, Leah, and Jacob?

Because we started this journey from the perspective of what glory Jacob and Rachel's love had wrought—the critical role that their love-child, Joseph, played in preserving the people of Israel—one might wonder how same-gender love could bear a comparable fruit. What is the link to the Torah? Neither nature nor science has yet shown us a way for same-gender couples to commingle their DNA and create genetic offspring. Yet we know that on both a spiritual and a practical level, any time a family of two or more is created, that joining of hearts and minds and vision and blessing has the capacity to change the world. The fruits of this joining, whether they literally be children (adopted and/or biologically related to one parent) or gifts of the heart, realized through community service, through beauty, through hospitality, through the shattering of myths and the melting of hearts . . . whatever that coupling brings into the world has the capacity to save us all. Who are we to judge the passionate choices of others? Why be Laban and stand in the way of what is meant to be? Of what greatness might we deprive the world if we deny the symbiotic potential of hearts destined for one another regardless of the mere flesh-bound package those hearts come in? What dreamers, what heroes will be lost?

That morning my spiritual community chanted for our dreams to be heard, to be seen, and to be rightly interpreted, so that they may come into being. We explored the text, as we do each week, looking for divine insight and relevance to our own lives. We discussed how this *parsha,* and those preceding it, could help us understand the world-saving potential offered by human choice driven by natural passion in concert with divine intention.

As I find myself mirrored in the patterns, in the principles, and in the practice of my spirit path, is it possible that I also find myself in our most sacred text? Indeed. From the wilderness I came home, and I found that I was already here, waiting for myself . . . I and my dreams.

Holding oppositions. Both/and. Boundary crosser. Bisexual. Feminist. Dreamer/Activist. Jew.

Merging Candles—From Dualism into All

Robin Renee

I made a change on my altar last week. In a brief, solitary ceremony I removed the two candles representing the Goddess and the God and replaced them with one single, white taper. Though I think about and celebrate the deities and call that intangible force by many names—Lord and Lady, Adonis, Quan Yin, Brigid, Artemis—I cannot help but feel the ultimate oneness of them, and us all. When I speak to one, I know that I am somehow communing with The All, the Universe. I cannot ultimately divide a profound, infinite Awareness by gender. Last week, I translated this reality into the symbolism I use to connect with that Source.

I was intrigued once when I read an unfamiliar term in a pagan magazine—Budeo-Pagan. I take to labels with great hesitancy, but for the sake of convenience, I use them. Budeo-Pagan came as close to a succinct description of my spirituality as any term ever had. I was pleased to hear that others were drawing from both Eastern and Western traditions, discovering truths and describing them in ways I have as well. There are other names I call myself: I am bisexual. I am bicultural. I am gender mutable, if not unequivocally bigendered. I am polyamorous.

When I have been less serene, less aware of the Source, I have fallen into the trap of dualism. There were times when all parts of myself seemed separate, and they warred against each other in a slow, fiery frustration. A passage in *Re/Search #13* describes the dismantling of dualistic thinking as the essential task for human growth, and ultimately for our survival:

> This mind/body split is sibling to a host of other dualisms—binary oppositional pairings which are never equal, which always force a hierarchy: man/woman, white/black, straight/gay, primitive/civilized, self/other, new/

old. All dualisms are artificial and must be analyzed as a part of a system of either/or thinking which imposes restrictive categorizations.[1]

I have nearly always asserted my cultural differences outwardly. It has not happened without struggle. There have been many times when I heard the whispered, fearful voice of the dominant paradigm. It told me I must be black-OR-white, masculine-OR-feminine, loving one person-OR-another. Yet, alongside and running deeper than the false dichotomies has always been the true voice, so that I know that I am whole, and there are no divisions.

My life has been a continual adventure of bending labels, breaking out of boxes, of coloring outside the lines. There were years as a child when I felt lesser than—certainly not beautiful. Then there was the gradual realization that being a woman and having dark skin was not ugly and low. It took me a relatively long time to begin to release my shame at not being reflected in American cultural images of beauty or power. It became increasingly important for me to look into my mirror with different eyes. Better yet, to smash the mirror and to simply feel my internal drives, ideas, and voices. It became vital to me that I learn and develop through some kind of internal process. I find sexuality and spirituality to be parts of the same personal evolution.

I came out as a lesbian at age nine, then clearly as bisexual at twelve. Since that time, my bisexuality has been crystal clear, fluid, and essential throughout my life. My inner process, a listening process, actually, began early. It has brought me less to a sense of faith or a belief system per se than it has to a simple sense of knowing. I don't feel the need to believe in the rightness or wrongness of my bisexuality. It simply exists as a peaceful, naturally occurring part of myself. I don't pontificate that it is a conscious external expression of an expanded worldview. But if sexuality and spirituality dovetail for me in a way that nurtures expansion, I am all the more joyful. In some pagan/Wiccan philosophy, to have an awareness of polarity and the flowing nature of gender is key:

> Magic is creative work . . . androgyny is an important component in the creative individual.[2]

The middle is a strong position because it contains both poles. It is where

[1] Andrea Juno and V. Vale, eds., *Re/Search #13: Angry Women* (San Francisco: Re/Search Publications, 1991), 4.

[2] Laurie Cabot with Tom Cowan, *Power of the Witch: The Earth, the Moon, and the Magical Path to Enlightenment* (New York: Delta, 1989), 164.

> we experience the reconciliation of opposite forces, and reconciliation is the gateway to experiencing oneness with all things. Nothing is stronger than that.[3]

I do my best to act according to my truest nature as it presents itself, and myself, to me. It reveals me as the truth emerges from the riddle of a Zen koan.

It is pleasing to have reached a place in my rituals and meditation where separation of the Source into true, separate beings of gender seems an impossibility. It is sometimes powerful and profound to connect with "Goddess," "God," or "the deities." Running through this state of mind, however, is the constant current of an Absolute. The experience of Absolute that I approach here may be divided into many, but is always distinctly unified. It is not a Being with a sex, gender, or even attitudes. It is not a personality that demands worship, but a higher consciousness that is self-evident where all of us may commune. It is a release of our tireless dualisms, where there is no better than/lesser than, no self, or other. We are all IT, and IT evades description. IT is experiential. Since that childhood/young teen awakening, I have called IT the Awareness. Later, from Buddhism, the Void. Brad Blanton, with a secular approach, attempts to describe IT in *Radical Honesty:*

> After about the first four or five months in the womb, we had our first experience of being: a dawning of consciousness. . . . For the first time, we experienced *experience itself*. . . . That is, we were our experience. . . . It is indefinable, unrememberable in any graspable way. *All religions, gods, metaphysics, theologies, philosophies, and teachings of masters of all faiths are attempts to remember these eternal months past, this lost sense of unity.*[4]

So over time my way of seeing has become this: we are distinct, yet clearly one. We can talk about our various aspects and know our wholeness, without contradiction. My experience of sexuality is remarkably the same. Sex models the imagery of separateness remaining separate, becoming one. The act of my making love with a man may be talked about differently than the event of my making love with a woman. There are cultural contexts for lesbianism and for heterosexuality. There are social attitudes that can be pointed out and political implications of each. But when I make love, I do so with my whole self. Whether relating to a

[3] Ibid., 161.

[4] Brad Blanton, *Radical Honesty: How to Transform Your Life by Telling the Truth* (Stanley, Va.: Sparrowhawk Publications, 1994), 32–33.

woman in the moment, or to a man, my openness to both, my bisexual nature is ever present. To be restricted from the possibility of either the emotional potential or the physical reality would be a distortion of my Truth. Impossible. It would feel as bizarre to me as the notion that there is a single correct way to experience a single God, and that all others are misguided. Nothing in my experience brings me to this.

> The great path has no gates,
> Thousands of roads enter it.
> When one passes through this gateless gate,
> He [*sic*] walks freely between heaven and earth.[5]

[5] Mu-mon, "The Gateless Gate," in *Zen Flesh, Zen Bones: A Collection of Zen and Pre-Zen Writings,* ed. Paul Reps (New York: Doubleday, Anchor, 1989), 88.

From Orientation to Orienteering

Ann Schranz

Emptiness embraces all Form as the lost and found Beloved.[1]

ORIENTEERING IS A CROSS-COUNTRY RACE in which each participant uses a map and compass to navigate his or her way between checkpoints along an unfamiliar course. Rather than hold the relationship between my spirituality and my sexual orientation as the static snapshot of a landscape, I prefer to use the metaphor of orienteering—of finding my way through an evolving/shifting/emerging landscape—to capture the ongoing dynamic between these two essential elements of my being.

My life experience is the map I use while orienteering, and my values activate the compass. Other people may arrive at the same checkpoint using very different maps and very different navigational aids. But to those of us sitting around the campfire trading stories, it doesn't matter a bit what the maps or compasses look like. The pleasure of meeting at a checkpoint is the opportunity for reflection, rest, and companionship.

In order to provide background for what follows, here is a thumbnail sketch of my story. I identified as heterosexual through college. Nearly twenty years ago, I began a two-year process of shifting my self-identification from heterosexual to lesbian. I lost my home and the love of my mother when I first came out to her as lesbian. (I was living under her roof at the time.) I became involved in gay and lesbian activism, primarily in the Los Angeles area. Mom and I have since reconciled in that we

[1] Ken Wilber, *A Brief History of Everything* (Boston: Shambhala Publications, 1996), 338.

agree to disagree on the morality of any sexual orientation other than heterosexual.

About seven years ago, I began a year-long process of shifting my self-identification from lesbian to bisexual. I moved to Florida five years ago, where I co-founded the Gainesville Bisexual Alliance, a support group that met monthly for three years. I also served for a year as a BiNet USA regional organizer for the southeastern United States. As an "out" bisexual, I was not welcome in some lesbian circles. I was dismissed as a thrill seeker who would benefit from heterosexual privilege when she was with a male partner, like it or not.

Like a Las Vegas gambler, I have lost more than I have won when playing the game of sexual-orientation identity politics. One day I began considering sexual expression as orienteering instead of orientation. In the spirit of trading stories around a campfire, here are ten ways that my sexual orientation has contributed to my spirituality.

1. Identifying as a member of a sexual minority has meant facing prejudice. That has made me more sensitive to other forms of prejudice. My support of various liberal causes is due in part to my experiences of homophobic and biphobic oppression. I have felt marginalized, and I therefore reach out to others who are marginalized.

2. My family's disapproval of my lesbian sexual orientation was based on the Bible and on their belief that God disapproves of homosexuality. That spurred me to think about whether that interpretation was valid and whether I cared what God thought.

3. The lesbian community's disapproval of my bisexuality felt more painful than my family's disapproval of me. In an effort to deal with my pain, I was drawn into learning forgiveness or "letting go" sooner and more deeply than I otherwise would have learned.

4. As a bisexual, I choose both/and instead of either/or. I find it natural to honor all the wisdom traditions of the world, and I find it unnatural to think that anyone has a monopoly on truth. I find Unitarian Universalism suits this both/and perspective.

5. Choosing to come out as lesbian was a deep honoring of my body and sexual desire, and so was coming out as bisexual. Because of that experience, I can only participate in a spiritual community that is not body-negative or sex-negative.

6. My involvement in queer communities has influenced my involvement in my Unitarian Universalist congregation. My experience as a newcomer in various communities is that I go through stages: the initial honeymoon stage, the "after the bloom is off the rose" stage where individual and systemic dysfunction may be apparent, and a stage of commitment to doing what I can to improve the situation. What I learn in queer communities I apply in spiritual communities.

7. The underdeveloped bisexual community made me realize how hard it is to build a community infrastructure and how much a supportive environment helps people grow. Because I recognize the power of community, I am ready to invest energy into building a spiritual community.

8. I learned that identities are not fixed because my sexual-orientation identity has changed over time. I have found that identities are helpful up to a point, after which they cease to be helpful. If I had remained straight, I would not have explored spiritual identity and the politics of spiritual identity in this depth. Any spiritual self-identification (God, Goddess, secular humanist, Unitarian Universalist, Christian, pagan, or "none of the above") fails to convey the evolving nature of Spirit.

9. Identifying first as lesbian and later as bisexual led me to explore gender issues. Neither a male "God" nor a female "Goddess" corresponds to any spiritual reality for me.

10. Being on what some might call one leading edge of social change with bisexual activism, I have experienced the thrill of knowing that "all the good stuff" hasn't been done yet. It is still possible to make a contribution in society. I carry that expectation over into my spiritual community. As with my work in the bisexual community/movement, I am not so much a caretaker of what others have created in the Unitarian Universalist community as I am a cocreator of it.

Although my bisexuality has influenced my spirituality, my spirituality has also influenced the expression of my bisexuality. My approach to spirituality is to follow no one and to watch how my mind works. This independence, rejection of external authority, and emphasis on self-knowledge have enhanced my personal development as a bisexual who is not afraid to be a sexual minority. Following no one has also led me to explore polyamory in the face of pro-monogamy pressures inside and outside queer communities. In contrast, during many of the years that I identified as lesbian, I was a follower, distorting my sexuality to fit in with expectations of the lesbian community.

I have experienced a profound spiritual sense of being a co-creator of what is. Because I see myself as co-creator, I am not inclined to accept that the way things are is the way they necessarily should be. In this way, my spiritual understanding has led me to bisexual activism. It is not enough for me to find a partner or partners and settle down behind a white picket fence. As co-creator, I feel an imperative toward activism.

At times, my spirituality has wobbled between being very inward focused (contemplation) and being very outward focused (social activism.) The writings of transpersonal theorist Ken Wilber have put my wobbliness into perspective. He writes that the unfolding of Spirit has four facets: the individual's realization of Self, Self embraced in culture, Self embodied in nature, and Self embedded in social institutions. In other words, the Spirit evolves within and through the individual, nature, culture, and social institutions.[2]

What this means for me is that, while I am Ann Schranz, I am also evolving Spirit. To the extent that I am evolving Spirit, I look for ways to include and transcend current reality in each of the four quadrants (individual self, nature, culture, and social institutions.) To anchor the abstraction in the relatively narrow topic of my bisexuality, it is therefore not in the best interest of all concerned that I remain a "closet" bisexual, blending in with the mainstream whenever I leave the house.

That course of action fails to provide the momentum and the mechanism for evolution of Spirit. The short-changed entities include culture, society, myself as an individual, and the natural world of which I am a part. Culture (what Wilber calls the "depth dimension" of people in groups) is short-changed because it loses an opportunity to witness a particular interpersonal and intrapersonal relationship fluidity. Society (the "surface dimension" of people in groups) is short-changed because institutional sexism and compulsory monosexuality go unchallenged. The natural world of which I am a part (the "surface dimension" of the individual) is short-changed because I repeat past behavior though the conditions in which I live may have changed. Finally, as a "closet" bisexual, I

[2] Ibid.

am short-changed because my own depth dimension with its complexities remains unexplored.

All this talk of evolution may seem to fall into the old Western spiritual trap of emphasizing transcendence at the expense of immanence. Using shorthand definitions, by "transcendence" I mean spirit beyond or outside us. By "immanence" I mean spirit within us. In my occasional direct experience as the Spirit, transcendence and immanence are not two separate movements.

I feel an affinity both for transcendence and for immanence, and I decline to choose between them. In the same manner, I am attracted to both men and women, and I decline to choose between them. I am not suggesting that a bisexual orientation is better than any other orientation because I believe that all orientations are valid. It is just that, for me, the experience of nonduality in one context makes it more likely that I will see nonduality in other contexts.

When we generalize about men and women, we are often talking about male and female gender and gender roles. Gender might be defined as how someone with a given body expresses himself or herself relative to expectations. You might have seen the bumper sticker that says, "The Moral Majority is neither." My spiritual understanding about nonduality has helped me make sense of this bumper sticker: "The opposite sex is neither." What we refer to by "sex" in the phrase "opposite sex" is most often the social construct of gender, not biological sex differences. Describing men and women as "opposite" gives us a handy excuse to avoid expanding both male and female gender roles to the point where all things human are celebrated uniformly, whether expressed by men or by women.

Here is a description of the interplay between gender, sexual orientation, and spirituality that rings true for me. The words are from Starhawk, who identifies as bisexual and who is an influential voice in contemporary paganism. She writes:

> I would no longer describe the essential quality of the erotic energy flow that sustains the universe as one of female/male polarity. To do so enshrines heterosexual human relationships as the basic pattern of all being, relegating other sorts of attraction and desire to the position of deviant. That description not only makes invisible the realities of lesbians, gay men, and bisexual people; it also cuts all of us off, whatever our sexual preference, from the intricate dance of energy and attraction we might share with trees, flowers, stones, the ocean, a good book or a painting, a sonnet or a sonata, a close friend or a faraway star. . . . If we could, instead, take the whole as the model for the part, then whomever or whatever we chose to love, even if it

> is ourselves in our solitude, all our acts of love and pleasure could reflect the union of leaf and sun, the wheeling dance of galaxies, or the slow swelling of bud to fruit.[3]

As Starhawk so eloquently points out, the erotic energy flow that sustains the universe is much more interesting and complex than that represented by relationships between humans of any gender or sexual orientation.

Yet concepts of gender lie at the heart of negative attitudes toward gays, lesbians, and bisexuals. After all, the thing that is "wrong" with us is that the men don't act like men, and the women don't act like women. I will bet the farm that if we were not confined by gender expectations, we would not particularly care about the sexual orientation of ourselves or the orientation of others. Without fully exploring gender expectations, I doubt that the real and true and healthy multiplicity of paths and the marvelous unexpected turns of those paths will ever be fully accepted by those uncomfortable with winding roads. What is life if not the opportunity to explore an unknown landscape? The path, quite beyond unknown, is unknowable, because we create the landscape as we go.

[3] Starhawk, *The Spiral Dance: A Rebirth of the Ancient Religions of the Great Goddess* (San Francisco: HarperSanFrancisco, 1989), 9.

Harlot for the Queen of Heaven

SHERRY MARTS

> Sing, feast, dance, make music and love, all in My presence, for Mine is the ecstasy of the spirit and Mine is also joy on earth. For My law is love unto all beings. . . . Let My worship be in the heart that rejoices, for behold—all acts of love and pleasure are my rituals.[1]

The Harlot Finds Her Voice

IN SEPTEMBER 1993 I HAD a life-altering experience. I learned that a woman who had attended one of our local monthly gatherings for Goddess women had objected to some joking about sex that had accompanied our usual introductions and check-in. She objected to the jokes because she believed that talk about sex wasn't appropriate at a spiritual gathering. I responded to her objection by facilitating a discussion on sex and spirituality at the next monthly gathering. Preparing for the discussion forced me clarify my own thinking about the link between sex and spirituality. The discussion inspired me to pursue the topic further, in my personal life and by presenting workshops at women's festivals and pagan gatherings.

I've now been thinking, writing, talking, and teaching about the sacredness of sexuality and the sexual nature of spirituality for more than five years. My personal work has included participating in a group that

Portions of this essay originally appeared in the May Day 1998 issue of *Of a Like Mind* [Madison, Wisconsin] and are reprinted with permission.

[1] Excerpt from "The Charge of the Goddess," traditional ritual invocation adapted by Starhawk in *The Spiral Dance: A Rebirth of the Ancient Religions of the Great Goddess* (San Francisco: Harper & Row, 1979), 90–91.

explored the practice of sacred sex in ritual, participating in workshops with sex educators Clara Griffin and Kim Jack, and exploring what it means to be responsibly nonmonogamous. Reclaiming the sacredness of my sexuality, and of my body and its seemingly infinite capacity for pleasure, is at the root of my own healing and now forms the basis of my work facilitating healing for others.

The History of a Harlot

I am a witch. My religious practice has its roots in the pre-Christian tribal practices and beliefs of northern Europe. My religion is based in the sacredness of nature, and so acknowledges and honors seasonal and life cycles. I am a polytheist. In my practice I call on goddesses and gods who both embody and symbolize the sacred. At the same time, I refer to all I hold sacred as "Goddess," whole, entire, and infinite. My experience of Goddess challenges the false dichotomy between the physical and the spiritual, the sacred and the profane. The Goddess is immanent, present in me and in the world around me in Her infinite entirety. Our bodies and all of our bodily functions are sacred, just as the earth and all that lives in and on the earth is sacred. Witches honor and celebrate the body and all of its functions, including sexuality. Rather than holding sexuality in opposition to spirituality, we celebrate sex as a potent form of communication and as an expression of each person's divine nature. Sex is a sacred wellspring of power and inspiration.

The culture in which I was raised values control and domination—power over—above all, resulting in the disconnection of men and women from their own bodies, from each other, and from the natural world, including sexuality. In her book *Dreaming the Dark,* Starhawk calls this the "culture of estrangement" and outlines the historical process that brought it about.[2] Our alienation from our bodies begins with the assumption that mind, body, and spirit are separate and distinct. Added to that is the assumption that mind is superior to body (and emotions, which are rooted in the body) and spirit is superior to mind. These assumptions were made by the philosophers of classical Greece, who regarded physical needs and earthly activities as separate from and inferior to mental and spiritual activity. (Hence the ideals of the "platonic" relationship, a mental and spiritual communion that rises above physical desire.) They led to

[2] Starhawk, *Dreaming the Dark: Magic, Sex, and Politics* (Boston: Beacon Press, 1982).

the belief that achieving the ultimate goal of acquiring as much power-over as possible begins with establishing control and domination over one's own body. Emotions and bodies are disorderly, demanding, and inconvenient. They must be controlled, disciplined, brought into line. Reason and rationality must rule over emotion and bodily needs.

In this system of thought, women are seen as unable to rise very far above their physical natures due to menstruation, childbearing, and lactation. Women are therefore regarded as inherently inferior and unable to achieve the spiritual purity aspired to by men. Christianity combined this body/spirit dichotomy with beliefs in a transcendent deity and in eternal reward or punishment in the afterlife. This further facilitated the denigration of nature and the body, and thus of women, while focusing on the need for salvation from sin. As Marilyn French observes,

> Earlier dichotomies had diminished nature and the flesh as inferior to man and reason. . . . Christianity added another dimension to this duality: nature and flesh and women constituted a threat to man's eternal soul.[3]

French points out that of the basic physical needs—food, water, shelter, and sex—the need for sex is the one most amenable to conscious control, hence our culture's fixation on the shamefulness of the body and the evils of sexuality.

This forced separation of body and spirit prevents us from becoming fully erotic, from knowing and working from the rooted wholeness in which we are born. When we deepen our awareness of body/spirit unity, we deepen our awareness of the unity of earth and spirit, and we experience the immanence of Goddess in the earth, in our physical surrounding, and in our selves. Sex is one way to experience the nonseparateness of body and spirit. Other ways include ritual, ecstatic dancing, drumming, vocalizing, and meditating. The methods, tools, and techniques of deepening sexual experience are the same ones we use for deepening spiritual experience: breathing, relaxation, focus, opening the heart, being fully present in the body and fully aware of what is happening in the moment, and letting go of judgments and assessments in order to just be.

The challenges I face in my spiritual development are the challenges of becoming fully erotic; to know the unity of spirit, mind, and body. It is a challenge for me to remain fully present in my body. It is a challenge to be completely clear about who I am, what I want, and how I want to obtain or achieve what I want. It is a challenge to communicate my truth to my

[3] Marilyn French, *Beyond Power* (New York: Summit Books, 1985), 520.

partners and to remain open and honest and willing to hear their truths. The work of becoming fully erotic involves the movement and exchange of energy; truth telling and hearing; and healing that happens on the personal level, in interpersonal interaction, and in community.

The Harlot Meets the Goddess in the Mirror

Meeting the challenge of becoming fully erotic has included my coming out as bisexual and my being truthful to my primary partner about my desire for a nonmonogamous relationship. What a relief, after years of trying first to pass as heterosexual, then as lesbian, finally to say "This is what I am. I love men and I love women. This is the true nature of desire as I experience it." What freedom, after years of struggling unsuccessfully to stay monogamous, finally to say, "This is what I am. I am capable of loving more than one person at the same time, and I want to find ways to act on my desires that honor and respect all of my partners." What a joy finally to know, with all my many ways of knowing, that sex is a sacrament, a holy act. What a homecoming, to worship an immanent Goddess who tells me "all acts of love and pleasure are My rituals."

In becoming fully erotic I defy the gender restrictions our culture has created. Witchcraft offers me a Goddess with more faces and names than I can hope to learn in this lifetime. She defies all categories, including gender. At my initiation I dedicated myself to Brighid, the Irish Triple Goddess of poetry, smithcraft, and healing. Brighid at her forge is a Butch Goddess, muscled and sweating, who hammers and shapes, tempers and creates things of beauty and usefulness. Brighid at her pen is a sweet-tongued bard whose words create the world. Brighid at her well is a nurturing Mother Goddess who tends the sick and wounded and cradles the dying. In ritual I have encountered fierce Warrior Goddesses, scarred and hardened; gentle Maiden Goddesses, tender and yielding; wise Crones who question deeply and answer my questions with riddles. They defy the categories like "masculine" and "feminine," and they all dwell within me.

Within me also dwells a gender-bending God of a thousand faces and names. I know him as a God of sensuous delight, gentle, playful, laughing, and loving, a joyful sissy-boy who delights in His own beauty because it is a reflection of Goddess. He is also the Green Man, rooted in the earth, whose face appears in the vegetation and the trees, whose presence is in the plants that are sacrificed at harvest and reborn in spring. He is the wild

Stag God, the Hunter with the Sun's face, the God of unleashed passion whose desire and love ever draw him back to the Goddess, in love.

Becoming fully erotic means I accept myself as beautiful, just as I am —the image of the Goddess. The Goddess comes in all sizes and shapes, all beautiful and all equally deserving of honor and desire. As with most women in our culture, much of my alienation from my body manifests itself as dissatisfaction with my size and my appearance. I have dieted and exercised, painted and primped, shampooed, cut, and styled, waxed, shaved, and plucked, cleansed, toned, and moisturized, all to assuage the fear that how I look just isn't good enough. Now I hold images of a Goddess who is sometimes slender and muscled, sometimes wide-hipped and large-breasted, and always beautiful. She eats and drinks what she pleases, and she primps, paints, and decorates herself when it suits her. The Goddess has sex with whom and when she pleases. She is the coy maiden whose lovers catch her when she decides to be caught. And she is the ancient Cailleach, the hag whose desire for sex is not dimmed by age. Loving Her, I am learning to love myself more and more completely.

As I become more fully erotic, I am better able to sense and move sexual energy. Sexual energy is highly charged physical-emotional-spiritual energy that, in addition to pleasure, can bring healing and release. I have found that the key to unleashing sexual energy is to have mindless sex, in the literal sense—to damp down the rational, thinking mind and let instinct and passion lead. To simply be in the body, noticing and reacting but not thinking, is a powerful erotic act that deepens the experience and brings me to a glimpse of the mystery that I am Goddess, that my lover is Goddess, that together we are Goddess.

The Harlot's Practice

The meditation that follows is an act of sacred sex that can be experienced as a trance journey, as a masturbation fantasy, or as a setting for ritual sex with a partner. (My personal desire is to someday enact the meditation, complete with a soak in a hot tub, dressing in costume, and entering a suitably decorated space, while still in light trance.) The title of the meditation is a reclaiming of the word "harlot" from its contemporary definition of a woman who exchanges sex for money, to the ancient and returning image of a Priestess, the Quedishtu, who performs acts of sexual healing, in service to the Goddess. ("Queen of Heaven" is in less need of reclaiming, as it has always referred to a Goddess, albeit in a different guises over time.)

I wrote this meditation to bring participants to a deeper understanding of the Quedishtu than would result from a ten-minute lecture and to allow participants to experience what it is to be the Quedishtu, to be the object of ritual adoration and a practitioner of sexual healing. I open the workshop with this meditation, then bring the participants out of the meditative state while they are still in the temple. We do one or more exercises that may explore body image, sex phobia, intimacy, touch, and what "sex" is. Then we return to the meditative state to complete the meditation and leave the temple. The meditation works for women and men, for the service of the Quedishtu was and is still performed by both sexes.

When I guide the meditation in workshops, I do not describe the seeker who awaits the participant-as-Quedishtu, nor do I describe what happens in the temple. I do this to make the meditation appealing to participants of all sexual orientations—the seeker could be male, female, transgender, androgynous, hermaphroditic—and to make what happens in the temple feel safe for each participant, regardless of where she is on the path of healing and reclaiming the sacredness of her body and her sexuality.

Meditation: The Temple of the Quedishtu[4]

[*A note on the transcription: During workshops, I lead the group through a grounding, centering, and relaxation exercise before beginning the visualization, and I end the meditation by returning them to waking awareness very gradually. I've left those details out for the sake of brevity, so use whatever method works for you. The lengths of the pauses are determined by intuition—make them as long or as short as feels right for you.*]

Ground, center, relax into a light trance or meditative state.

You are about to take a journey to the temple of the Quedishtu, the sacred prostitute. You are in complete control of what happens on this journey. If you find that what happens is different from what is described here, don't become concerned, just follow the way that is right for you. And know that

[4] Thanks to Deena Metzger for inspiration on this meditation. See Deen Metzger, "Re-Vamping the World: On the Return of the Sacred Prostitute," in *Enlightened Sexuality: Essays on Body-Positive Spirituality,* ed. Georg Feurstein (Freedom, Calif.: Crossing Press, 1989), 72–77.

at any time during this journey, you can return to your normal waking awareness simply by opening your eyes. You are in control.

Go to a safe place, a place of your own making, a place of power and protection. Now in your safe place you see a path. Begin to walk along that path. Gradually the path widens, smooths, becomes a road. As you walk, you see a city up ahead, and you begin to pass buildings, homes, and shops. As you enter the city, the buildings are closer together, and the streets are wide and lined with trees. Walk through the streets until you come to the Sacred Way, the street lined with temples. Walk past several temples and arrive in front of your destination, the temple of the Quedishtu. Look at the building. Is it small or large? What is it made of? Stone? Wood? Is it plain or decorated? Painted or carved? Approach the entrance to the temple and knock at the door. The door opens silently. Enter the temple. Take some time to look around. Notice the sights, smells, sounds, textures of this place.

Brief pause

Turn to your left and enter a room that contains a large, steaming bath, fragrant with herbs and oils. There is a clothes rack along one wall and a pile of fluffy towels in the corner. Take off your clothes, hand them to the waiting attendant, and step into the bath. The water and herbs wash away your fears, apprehensions, anxieties, concerns. When you feel cleansed, inside and out, step out of the bath, wrap up in the warm fluffy towel that the attendant hands you, and enter the next room.

Pause

This is the robing room. It contains racks and shelves of beautiful gowns, robes, lingerie, scarves, jewels. Select your favorite outfit and put it on. There is a table and mirror in the corner, where you brush your hair, and, if you wish, put on makeup and scent.

Pause

Now you are ready to begin your time of service to the Queen of Heaven. Before you is the entry into the main room of the temple. Pause before the doorway and take a deep breath. As you exhale, let go of any remaining fear or concern. As you enter this sacred space, know that you are to become, for a time, the Goddess herself, healer, teacher, wise and deep. As you step through the doorway, what do you see, hear, smell? Are there others in the temple, or are you alone? Walk into the room and stand before the altar, on which there is an image of the Queen of Heaven. Pause before the altar, and prepare to begin your work.

Brief pause

As you turn away from the altar, before you stands a Seeker, one who has come to the temple for blessing or healing, or both. The Seeker speaks the ritual invocation:

> Bless me, Quedishtu, Undefiled One
> You are Hathor, Ishtar, Anath, Astarte, Asherah
> I am humbled before you, who embody She Who is Queen of All the Wise.
> Your body is the gateway to Her
> Your body is the conduit to the Divine
> I ask this blessing of you,
> That in touching you, I will touch Her
> Loving you, I will love Her
> Entering you, I will enter Her
> Uniting with you I will be one with Her
> Blessed art thou among women
> Holy Quedishtu
> Blessed are all who come to thee
> Blessed art thou, Holy Quedishtu
> Whose touch gives life.

And you reply:

> Blessed art thou, Seeker
> Your desire for Her draws Her here,
> Into me and through me into you
> As we enter into in love, know that what you seek lies within you.

Reach out and take the Seeker's hand. What happens now is up to you.

Long pause

When you have finished, the Seeker speaks again:

Bless me, Quedishtu, Undefiled One
You are Hathor, Ishtar, Anath, Astarte, Asherah
Your body is the gateway to Her
Your body is the conduit to the Divine
Touching you, I touched Her
Loving you, I loved Her
Entering you, I entered Her
Uniting with you I was one with Her
Blessed art thou among women
Holy Quedishtu
You have blessed me, for you filled my senses with the
presence of She Who Gives Life
May all that you give return to you many-fold.

And you reply:

Blessed art thou, Seeker
Your desire for Her drew Her here,
Into me and through me into you
Touching me, you touched Her
Entering me, you entered Her
Uniting with me, you became one with Her
Loving me, you loved Her
And Her love pours out for you still.
Go now in love, knowing that what you seek lies within.

The Seeker departs.

Now it is time to leave your service to the Goddess, until the next time. Stop again before the altar of the Queen of Heaven, and thank Her for the opportunity to serve Her. Walk from the main temple into the robing room, where you take off your temple garb. Step once more into the bath, letting the hot water and fragrance soak away your weariness. Dress in your everyday clothing and leave the bath room and walk up to the door. Step through the door into the entryway, shading your eyes from the light. Move through the entryway and into the street. Follow the street back to the road and finally to the path to your safe place.

Pause

Return slowly to your normal waking awareness, ground and center.

An Invitation to Harlotry

If an army of lovers cannot fail, then surely an army of harlots is unstoppable. To become fully erotic, to move completely into these bodies we inhabit, is to know the mystery that we are all Goddess, that we are children of the sacred earth, and that any act of destruction is perpetrated on ourselves. Becoming a feminist witch led me to acknowledge that I am bisexual and that I am polyamorous, and that what I am is as it should be. Practicing the craft has drawn me deeper into my sacred sexual self than I imagined possible. The more fully erotic I become, the more I am aware that I am sacred, the Goddess embodied. The false distinction between body and spirit melts away in the heat of my passion for my lovers, for my self, and for Her.

All acts of love and pleasure are Her rituals—whenever we reach out to each other in lust and love, we are harlots for the Queen of Heaven. Welcome to the temple.

Excerpts from Capacity to Enter: A Solo Performance

CANYON SAM

Vital Energy

THAY: [*A Zen Buddhist master, foreign-born, with accent. Bows.*] It is crucial to preserve our three vital energies—the breath, the spirit, and the sexual energy. The third vital energy is what I want to talk about today—the sexual energy.

I will tell a story. One day a Zen master and his disciple were walking, far from home. They came to a temple. "Brother, can we get a drink of water here?" asked the disciple to an old man sitting outside the gate. The old man looked at him with eyes like muddy puddles. His skin was dry and rough, his hair thin, matted. "Master, he doesn't understand, he is too old," said the disciple. The master said, "He is not old. This is a man who has spent his sexual energy like a river overruns a dam, heedlessly, recklessly. This man is but fifty years old."

This is related to the third precept: Aware of the suffering caused by sexual misconduct, I vow to engage in sexual relations only when there is love and commitment. I changed this precept this year, because my Western students say, "Thay, I had commitment . . . for the whole weekend." So I have added the word "long-term." I vow to engage in sexual relations only when there is love and long-term commitment. [*Bell.*]

Universal Language

I went to therapy. The Iris Project, in a big yellow Victorian on Valencia Street, a feminist therapy collective. I saw Fern, a redheaded therapist. [*Angst-ridden, in shock and disbelief.*]

What's happening?! This isn't happening. Wake me, shake me, tell me it's not happening. Who me? No, I'm not scared. I'm freaked out! The worst part? . . . I . . . I enjoyed it. I liked it. Don't you think it's bizarre that I have great heterosexual sex now? Now?! I'm gay! All this work coming out, and I'm going straight! Five years as a gay activist, gone!

It's abnormal! It's unnatural. I'm going straight. I'm not? How do you know?

Fern told me about the Kinsey scale. The sex study where they found that sexuality falls on a continuum of one to six. One is a straight arrow, straight ahead, heterosexual, attracted to the opposite sex their entire lives, exclusively. Six is a stone homosexual. Never an urge or an inkling toward anyone except the same sex. Womb to the grave: queer.

Everyone else in between—five, four, three, two—at some time in their lives—could be puberty, or later in life, had a dalliance, had a crush, slept once with their best friend, flowed over the borders: attracted to the same sex, the opposite sex. The opposite sex, same sex.

What Fern said calmed me down. Still, I worried. I was raised the old fashioned way . . . as a radical lesbian feminist separatist.

Web of Desire

THAY: [*Bows.*] People have asked me to speak more about the third precept. The third precept is a caution not to lose your mindfulness . . . in Desire. It is practice to be mindful about getting caught in the web of Desire. When you practice the third precept, you check the impulse to bow to the power of Lust. You hold back sexual energy till the stability of the relationship is established. So sexual expression is the fruit, the fulfillment, of a relationship, not the impulse for it. [*Bell.*]

Untitled

I don't know. How do you meet straight men? Go to the Hard Rock Cafe and cruise around the bar? Pretend to admire the Oldsmobiles sticking out of the walls? Besides, even if I were willing, where would I meet a man who'd want to be in a long-term, committed relationship with a radical lesbian feminist ex-separatist?

I meet Russell at the Berkeley Rep. Every time I look up, he's there. Asks intelligent questions about the play. We have coffee afterwards. Then he shows up at a reading I do three days later in Berkeley. I find him so astute, thoughtful, supportive, unobtrusive, so . . . young. I don't think he's clear of his twenties.

For the next few days, I can't believe I'm toying with the idea of going out with a straight white *man*. Not even MAN, he's . . . he's barely post-Watergate. My friend says, "We fought the last thirty years so we wouldn't be judged on the basis of our sex, our sexual orientation, our race, our age. Wouldn't it be ironic to turn around now and dismiss someone on those grounds?"

Russell and I get together one night for dinner at a Vietnamese restaurant. Russell wears blue jeans, a denim overshirt, a crewneck T-shirt underneath.

RUSSELL: [*In response to her question.*] Weeelllll, I spent most of the day organizing my notes from the summer. I spent August in Maine with my grandmother, recording family history. We've done it for four summers. Oh, very close. In fact, I call her mother.

Actually, I went to therapy this afternoon and when I talked about my grandmother, I started crying. I feel sad cuz she's getting old, she lives so far away, she's all alone . . . I love her so much.

CANYON: [*Aside.*] I sipped my spicy beef noodle soup and listened. There was this hair popping out the top of his collar.

RUSSELL: Then I talked with my best friend, Trish, she's a poet . . . she had a great idea: my grandmother's also a poet, she thought I should include some of my grandmother's poetry in the family history. . . . Well, yes, actually, a lot of my close friends are women. Trish and I were lovers for five years, now we're best friends.

CANYON: [*Aside.*] Wow, he goes to therapy, he cries, he loves women. Look at that hair . . . hazel-colored and furry. Where does it go? What does it feels like? You never see that on women. The landscape, the vegetation is totally different.

Afterwards we walk around 24th Street. In his field of doctoral study they study politics, religion, education . . . class, race, gender. He has a way of asking questions that really draws out my thinking. He's smart, but completely unpretentious. I feel . . . relaxed . . . comfortable.

Near Bell Market, I run into this good friend of mine. [*Banters with friend.*] Oh, um . . . Sue, this is Russell. This is Sue, Carol, Dion, Billie.

[*Aside.*] They're all lesbian lawyers, drive lavender Saturns. Sue, I've known over twenty years, she's the second Asian lesbian I ever met, at a time when there were just a handful of us. [*Resumes banter with friends.*] Russell was standing by this tree. At one point I thought, Oh, oh, maybe they can see that there's something going on! But is there something going on?! No, nothing's going on. Is there something going on?!

Back at my place, I was really getting kind of tired, but I didn't want him to think I was just going to turn him out.

CANYON: You want to come in for a cup of tea? [*Aside to audience.*] Not too long, I thought.

So we had some tea. And he stayed. And we chatted. He stayed and we chatted. And he stayed. I was really getting tired. I don't know how to tell somebody, "I'm tired, I'm forty, I need to go to sleep." Finally, at some point, he was gonna leave and he sort of leaned into me. Yeah, okay, I like you, we can hug goodbye. Then he started kissing me. Yeah, this is okay, relax, just try to relax. At one point he leaned his head into my shoulder, and he started sliding. This guy's maybe 5'9", 5'10", but he was slumped way down in the sofa, in my armpit. I have no idea what's going on: Is he shy, is he sleepy, is it some heterosexual signal?

Aiyaaaaaa!

Mother–Redux

[*In her mother's kitchen.*]

CANYON: Mom I have something important to talk to you about. Why don't you sit down? . . . Mom I don't want this to come as a shock, but this way if I bring someone home it wouldn't take you by surprise. [*Awkward pause.*]

I've started dating men. [*Beat.*] Mom?

CHINESE AMERICAN MOTHER: You know, your dad and I had lunch yesterday with Betty Dong at Denny's . . . you know that $2.95 cheeseburger is quite good, a big portion, free Coke, not too greasy. . . . Did you have lunch, dear? Well, I have a crab sandwich, do you want a crab sandwich? [Moves swiftly to refrigerator, with her back to her daughter. She prepares a sandwich.]

CANYON: Mom, uh . . . did you hear what I said?

MOTHER: Mayonnaise or ranch dressing?

CANYON: Mom, uh . . . what do you think? You know, about what I said?

MOTHER: [*Pregnant pause.*] Lettuce? Well, dear, you're almost forty, you can decide these things on your own. You know . . . Denny's is not bad . . . on a Tuesday afternoon . . . not busy at all.

CANYON: Mom, I thought it'd make you happy. I mean, all these years you . . . rather . . . resisted my being gay.

MOTHER: I never said that! . . . Tomato? It's from Lorraine's garden. . . . I just want you to be happy that's all, I just . . . but how can . . . ? I don't understand . . . I mean people . . . Your father and I have done our best to be educated and informed . . . and they said it's all determined by the age of five. And now, you're . . . I mean people don't just stop in the middle of . . . tea drinkers don't switch to coffee . . . and coffee drinkers don't switch to tea . . . at the age of forty.

CANYON: Mom, it's not that simple. I mean . . . there's this Kinsey scale. There's this spectrum, this continuum of sexuality over a person's entire lifetime. . . . You're a nurse, you know this!

MOTHER: Aiya! . . . [*She finishes the sandwich, turns and serves it to her daughter.*] Whatever makes you happy, dear . . . But does this mean . . . grandchildren?

Triathlon

Vonne

CANYON: My friend Doc was working at Land of Medicine Buddha, a center for Eastern healing arts, when a Feng Shui master came through. "The power point for relationships is the far right-hand corner as you walk into a home. In this corner, you put plants, goldfish, beautiful flowers. Symbols of nature. But the main thing is to have something red. The magnetizing color, the lucky color, the power color is red." Ping, the director of the center even hung a red scarf, Doc told me, and within twenty-four hours got a call from a colleague, from eleven years ago, back east. He had a revelation. He flew out, two years later, they were married.

[*A day later.*]
Superstition, I thought. Coincidence. Nevertheless, that night, before I go to bed I look through my drawers and shelves. . . . I don't have anything red, I don't wear red, I have nothing except this faded cotton sock. [*Gingerly hangs it in right corner.*] I hang it on a picture hook, above my file cabinet.

The next morning, there was a knock on the door. It was my neighbor Cheryl; she had a New Year's party last week.

CHERYL: Canyon, hi. Yvonne Hunt called me. She saw you at my party, she said she'd like to meet you.

CANYON: Yvonne Hunt?! Yvonne Hunt is this celebrated writer, activist, social critic. She is brilliant, fiery. I've seen her electrify whole auditoriums of people with her incantative poetry about race and gender politics and radical polemics.

Are you sure she was talking about me, Cheryl?

CHERYL: Described you to a tee. You were the only Asian woman at my party, Canyon. Here's her number. Call, she really wants to meet you.

CANYON: She wants to meet me. What does that mean? Meet me for what? Our first meeting, she drove over the bridge in a blinding rainstorm, sheets of pelting rain, torrential winds, to meet me for dinner.

YVONNE: [*Wiry, mixed-race woman, speaks in sometimes hip-hop, sometimes Ivy League accent. She is rushed, checks watch.*] Jeez, I'm jammin, I need to leave at 7:30, my schedule's like impossible.

You didn't try to call me over the weekend, did you?

I was in L.A. Gave a convocation speech. [*Moody and perturbed.*] No, shit, it was a bummer. I talked about Jeremy Rifkin's theory of technocracy. I said, you're wasting your time. There won't be any jobs. By the time the freshman class graduates there won't be any jobs. This is where the global economy and downsizing's headed. They didn't barely clap. [*Imitates their weak applause.*] Like dat. Ah ooh know. 't sucked.

CANYON: When we walked back to her car, a sleek black Lexus, she stood there in the pouring rain, said . . .

YVONNE: [*Abruptly.*] I'd like to see your work.

CANYON: I didn't think the evening went too well, she didn't seem happy to meet me or anything—but I thought about how she stood there in the pouring rain, said: "I'd like to see your work." [*She ponders this awhile, then makes a decision.*]

So, I sent her an audio tape of my show. [*Writes a note.*] "I know you're wildly busy, but maybe in a . . . month . . . when you have time. . . .

[*Near giddy with excitement.*] Three days later, I get a letter! She'd listened to it twice! . . . looked up Tibet on the map, called bookstores, special-ordered books on Tibet.

She writes me long letters on gray vellum stationery with midnight blue ink from a fountain pen, ablaze with questions . . . about Tibet, about my life, about Buddhism.

I write back, tell her about my spiritual practice. About my slightly confused sexual orientation. About school, about writing, about Russell.

Rosella

CANYON: I meet Rosella at a Buddhist retreat in Santa Rosa. She's Italian from Bologna. A winemaker in Napa. Third day I'm there, we're on a cooking team together in the kitchen. She looks up from chopping tomatoes, puts her face close to mine.

ROSELLA: A tall robust blonde, thick Italian accent. Uh, Canyon, the furst timme I seenn you, whenn you walk ennto the dormiTORy that nnightah, I zinking: She is viz whorman. Just . . . [*A flash of knowing*] . . . she is viz whorman. Tell mme . . . es true?

CANYON: She makes a pizza that night. It's the lightest pizza with just a whisper of a crust and the most delicate, luscious sauce. The kalamata olives, the fresh mozzarella, the vine-ripened tomatoes all ring together in your mouth. Everybody raves!

ROSELLA: Ah, eet's nozhing, you should go to ETaly!

CANYON: As I get up from the table, I brush my hand across her soft alpaca sweater, her shoulders are so solid, so broad. She grew up near the Italian Alps, she tells us, ran up and down the Dolomites. We take long walks up the winding backroads of the Sonoma Mountains.

ROSELLA: Canyonn, I am liking jawst thees dreemm to have a small refugeh in the m*ou*ntainns. To leave thees making MONNey, making wine, always whorking so much-a. To have only a smmal-a hoouse in the m*ou*ntains. To leavve how I was grroowing up-a: baking bread-a, growing veg e ta bles, chopping zhe wood. Theees is the thing, eesn't eat?

CANYON: I love her big warm hand around mine, her long loping stride, her broad chest. She is all food, earth, heart. In the crease of her forehead I see all the pulling in her. The price she pays.

ROSELLA: Just me and my belooved, in the mountains. And to have cheeldren. . . . Canyon, do you want have cheeldren?

CANYON: Not from this body. I think we should turn back now, Rosella, my hip's getting sore.

ROSELLA: I make MAssage-a you, at homme-a. No, I can, I like, I make. I make MAssage-a you, Eet is my Hawpiness-a.

Russell

CANYON: Russell and I get together pretty regularly. We buy a burrito, rent a video, go dutch on everything. It is so spare, yet so sturdy an arrangement. Sometimes he wants us to socialize with his friends or go away for the weekend, but I pass.

RUSSELL: I'll put some water on. Oh, how'd your support group go yesterday?

CANYON: Well, I told them. They didn't say much, except this one woman. She said, "Well, Canyon, I don't think you're a lesbian." I told them in Buddhism you want to shed your ideas, your perceptions. Otherwise, one day you might get trapped . . . in your own labels. I told them I started feeling differently about men after my year in Asia. They're in the mix, you know, as sentient beings, what are you going to do?

RUSSELL: What kind of tea would you like? You think you're going to stay friends with them?

CANYON: Tension Tamer. I don't know. It's like my parents; when I came out, their attitude was, "That's fine, just don't bring any women home." With certain friends, it'll be, I love ya kid, but I don't want to meet the guy. . . .

RUSSELL: Oh, no! Shoved into the closet . . . and me with you!

CANYON: [*Laughs*] Yeah, betcha never been there. Then we talked about butch/femme. I said I don't relate to either. Twenty years ago we were trying to dismantle sex roles, not celebrate them. Now it's another language. "Femme bottom switch seeks soft stone butch top." What does that mean?! Where is the glossary?! Remember when we were all just . . . What was it? . . . Polymorphously perverse? Ginsberg. Remember?

RUSSELL: [*Shakes his head, shrugs.*] 'fraid not, honey. Before my time . . . I only remember stuff after 1978.

Vonne

CANYON: Vonne writes me long letters, in a fluid, almost manic style. Sends me books of poetry, gift-wrapped.

If we go to a busy restaurant, she can talk to the maître'd, and even though it's packed, he shows us a table right away. It's like she has a kind of magic with people.

She has bad moods though. One time, she got in a long row with the woman in front of us in the movie line, said she didn't like how the woman used the word capitalism, and it ruined the whole evening. All through the movie she was slumped down, arms crossed, jaw set, eyes burning, a tight spindle of fury.

Rosella

CANYON: [*Pecks Rosella on the side of the lips.*] Okay, there . . .

ROSELLA: Uh huh. [*With a curling finger, commands Canyon to kiss her full on the lips.*]

CANYON: Rosella, what do you think about the third precept? The third precept. Love and long-term commitment. Actually my friend who's good at relationships says she always waits for the third date. Third date, third precept, get it? Let's take it slow, uh?

ROSELLA: [*Provocatively.*] Why?

CANYON: Tuesday, Valentines Day is a marathon. A triathalon. I am torn, afraid to hurt anyone's feelings. Pulled in all directions. Early dinner with this one, late dinner with that one, overnight with this other one. Crab dinner, pasta dinner, champagne and cheesecake. Berkeley, Oakland, Marin.

I'm seeing a twenty-something, a sixty-year-old, a forty-something. Men, women. One's gay, one's straight, one's bi. The woman is male-identified, the man is woman-identified. All different races. I'm all over the map! Now I know why they have arranged marriage in China. Just get a savvy outsider to look it over, and DECIDE.

I want devotion, but I want freedom. I want motion, but I want stillness. I want romance, but I want sincerity, equality. I can be attracted to men, but I have no tolerance for the male ego. My natural affinity, my political identity, my personal history is with women. My friend says I'm afraid of commitment. My teacher says, no sexual relationship without it.

I'm dazed. Spinning. Like being lost in a snowfield at night and finding each pine tree around you identical to the one you carefully marked to return to. Looking back and seeing your own ski tracks in the powdery snow crossing and recrossing themselves like a scrawl, a manically drawn star. No markers, there are no markers.

The North Star

THAY: [*Bows.*] The precepts are like a guide, something that offers you direction. If you are lost in the night, you are tired, you are very scared, you are CONfused, you look up, and find the North Star. Then you know the way to go, you know your direction.

The precepts are simply mindfulness practice in daily life. If you practice them, you have happiness right away. If you cannot practice them perfectly . . . please do not worry. I know my French students have trouble to give up the wine. The Scan-dan-avians have trouble to give up the CIGarettes. What's most important is progress, not perfection.

Let the precepts guide you. Like the North Star. Because the real meaning of the practice, of being awake, is simply the capacity to enter . . . into the freshness of the present moment, every wonderful moment.

[*Bell.*]

End of Play

Aphrodite Urania: Blurring Lines, Crossing Boundaries

Raven Kaldera

The Bearded Love Goddess

My friend Anne (not her real name) called up the other night, asking me to put on my clergy-person hat. Her husband Cooper was on the other extension, and I could hear Zoe calling in the background. Zoe is Anne's lover. I could also hear Anne's and Zoe's children playing together, fighting over toys as preschoolers often do.

Some years before, my wife had performed a handfasting (a non-legal commitment ceremony) for Anne and Cooper in our house. I'd bound their hands with a braided cord in order to symbolize their union, while my nine-year-old daughter held their year-old baby girl. They were both bisexual activists, committed to love over social convention. Now they'd called to discuss another option: could they do a second ceremony, one that would handfast Zoe to them as well? Anne explained that she loved Zoe, and that she wanted this relationship to have the same community and religious recognition as the one she had with Cooper. He explained that they were all one family now, a family that deserved to be blessed.

Of course I said yes, but I knew I'd have to think a bit after getting off the phone. As clergy members of the neo-pagan Hearthgrove Church of the Gods and Goddesses, my wife Bella and I have performed ceremonies for quite a few couples, men and women and both and neither, but this was the first time we'd been faced with a threesome. The situation itself wasn't unfamiliar, as Bella and I are also bisexual and polyamorous, as well as being transgendered. It was just a matter of how to structure the ritual, and what sources of spirit to call on.

After some thought, I decided that the proper patron deity for the occasion had to be Aphrodite Urania. Aphrodite, the Greek goddess of love, has many forms and aspects: Aphrodite Genetrix, patron of procreative sex; Aphrodite Porne, patron of sex workers; and so forth. But one form in particular is most near and dear to me: Aphrodite Urania, who wears a beard on her lovely, feminine face and is the patron of all those whose love crosses boundaries that the surrounding society considers inappropriate—love between different ages, races, social classes; love that leaps cultural obstacles with light-footed ease and little care. The Bearded Aphrodite is, of course, the official patron of queer sex, so much so that the nineteenth-century German term for effeminate gay men and butch lesbians was *Urnings*. But she holds an even more special place in the lives of bisexual and transgendered people. The Bearded Aphrodite betrays us for the "unacceptables" that we are, through her nontraditional gender expression. It is said that she assumed the bearded form to lie with the (himself androgynous) wandering trickster god Hermes, who supposedly preferred men. Their child was Hermaphroditus.

> I am the builder of bridges,
> The slender line of love across the deepest of abysses.
> When you leap off that cliff,
> Holding your breath,
> Knowing nothing is certain but your feelings,
> You find yourself not tumbling terror-stricken
> As you had feared,
> But walking safely on the great span of my heart
> Where you meet each other on the sacred middle ground
> And cross to a more joyous land.
>
> —From the "Hymn to Aphrodite Urania," Hearthgrove Church liturgy

Sexes and Genders: How Many Can We Love?

We wrote the ritual for Aphrodite Urania, my beloved Bella and myself, in honor of her mysteries and the many surprising couplings we've seen her inspire. We also wrote it because neither of us is what most people expect to see when they look for a clergy person to perform their wedding ceremony. My wife and I are both transgendered: she's a male-to-female transwoman and I'm an intersexed female-to-male transman. Together, we are what some people refer to as a "reverse couple" or "cross-couple," the latter of which is surprisingly reminiscent of the Bearded One's sacred ability. Which of us is Aphrodite Urania—she with her XY chromosomes and electrolysis-smooth face, or me with my (presumably) XX chromosomes and newly grown beard? Does it matter? Either way, when we stand before our friends and call Her (or Hir), Aphrodite Urania will lend us her presence. Our mere presence mirrors the tradition in India where members of the transgendered sect known as hijras are considered lucky to have at a wedding. We are the living embodiments of the Two-In-One, and as such we symbolize on a physical level what a marrying couple is trying to achieve on an emotional one.

I think bisexuality is more of an intense issue for transpeople than for traditionally gendered individuals. For us, the issues of identity created by having both straight-appearing and gay-appearing relationships are more likely to plague our partners than ourselves. "If you do it with me," I tell people, "you're bisexual." This limits my sexual encounters to those who are either already bisexual-identified, or willing to struggle with suddenly finding themselves in that space. Bella and I have stood up in the midst of bi-bashing sessions when we hear the claim that there "are no real bisexual relationships, just straight and gay ones held by the same people," and challenged them with our existence, our marriage, our love-most-obviously-bisexual. When we speak up, we, and bisexuality as a category, become real to people, not just a theoretical possibility. This is not to say that one has to be bigendered, or with someone bigendered, in order to have a bisexual relationship. But our presence together in the public eye can be the necessary explosion that silences disbelievers and brings them a step further toward acknowledging other relationships between bisexuals.

Sometimes, when faced with that peculiar uneasiness in a prospective single-gendered lover's eyes as they realize just how different I am anatomically, I find it useful to tell them that they are in the presence of the sacred androgyne every time they touch me. I have come to recognize that indrawn breath of sudden understanding, sudden awe. Making love to one of us is, truly, like a visitation from Shiva, Lilith, Agdistis, Zurvan, Dionysus, Baphomet, the Hermaphrodeity. We are the sacred two-in-one, even when we don't wish to be or don't see ourselves that way.

In a sense, our polyamorous transgendered existence is not only the most extreme and obvious form of bisexuality, it is also the herald of its death knell. "Bi" means two, and the idea that there are only two sexes is breaking down rapidly in the minds of many individuals. Sooner or later, the term "bisexual" is going to have to give way to "pansexual" or some other more inclusive and less numerical term.

Tying the Knots and Unsnarling the Red Tape

Marriage is both a personal and a political act, a public acknowledgment of an intensely private decision. As such, it has no use if it cannot be made to reflect all the endless permutations of humanity's ability to love. Marriage between only two people, even if we get to the point where the letters M or F on their driver's licenses are irrelevant (and assuming that we are eventually allowed more than just two letters), does not cover the full spectrum of passion and possibility. And, interestingly, the closer we get to legalizing gay marriage—and the more the queer community protests that we're "just like all the straight couples"—the less appropriate Aphrodite Urania appears to be to the vanguard of the queer rights movement.

This may or may not be a mixed blessing. There is nothing fun about having to fight for your relationships to be recognized, but part of the reason it's taken so long for the "B" (Bisexual) in "LGBT" (Lesbian, Gay, Bisexual, and Transgender) to get there (not to mention the caustic infighting over the presence of the "T") is because both bisexuals and transgenders are often two or more steps away from "normal." We blur boundaries. We dance back and forth over drawn lines as if they didn't exist, enraging those who have staked their worldviews on the existence of those lines.

We bisexuals (and pansexuals) are often accused of constant infidelity, as if being able to love more than one sex or gender precluded the ability to make a commitment. As a practicing ethical polyamorist, I know that I am (on the surface at least) likely to resemble the bogeyman of the unfaithful bisexual more than most. And although polyamory isn't any more common among bisexuals than among hetero- or homosexuals, I know that it is bisexuals whom the average monogamous person thinks of when the word comes up. So here I am, guilty on many counts. My wife, my boyfriend, my friends that I'm occasionally sexual with . . . it's the stuff of hedonistic fantasy on the surface. No one sees the hours and hours of negotiating, communication, and processing that make the glittering edifice stand. Our four-page contract and our constant monitoring of emotional tides seem grubbily unromantic and certainly not particularly spiritual.

What most people don't see about polyamory is that it takes a huge amount of faith and trust to say to someone, "I believe that you will not knowingly leave or hurt me, and that you will think of my feelings first," or "I accept your say over what other people I sleep with say, because I believe that you consider my need equally with yours." There is a great deal of serenity in knowing that your relationship is that strong, that it need not succumb to the demons of jealousy or martyrdom because you are both watchful and considerate and willing to work hard for that peace.

It is not easily achieved; all parties must be skilled at negotiations and reasonably honest and self-aware. But more and more people all the time are choosing to create relationship—and even marital—bonds that include more than one person, possibly in nonheterosexual groupings. It doesn't help the case of queer marriage advocates who claim that we "only want the same things as straight couples," but here we are and we cannot be denied. I am not willing to wait for a day when loving groups like Cooper, Anne, and Zoe are able to make their unions legal; I am going to help them cement those vows in the eyes of what really counts, the Spirit that speaks to all of us, and do it now. There's not enough love in the world as it is. Those who can generate more than the usual amount should be rewarded, not punished.

Putting Faces on Divinity

In the same way that the term "bisexual" may eventually become an outdated piece in the game of identity politics, replaced by the notion of pansexuality, the concept of deity is in need of an overhaul. It is almost a cliché that God the Male has reigned alone long enough, and that Goddess is being rediscovered by women and men all across the country. But when many people speak of a God/dess, they are not talking about a two-in-one but a sexless, sexed-less, sexuality-less (and often abstract and faceless) neuter deity. To me, speaking of God/dess depersonalizes the deity. Perhaps this is because the idea of a deity that is androgynous yet intensely personal, individual, sexual, is practically inconceivable to most people. Yet if Goddess is reflected, as women's spirituality claims, in the faces of individual women (and by extension male deity in individual men), then we two-in-ones must reflect some personalized hermaphrodeity that is anything but abstract and distant. We are God/desses who live uncomfortably close to other people's skins. The more visible we are, the more our faces will begin to fill out other people's concepts of the divine. It is imperative that we be seen, and be seen in spiritual concepts.

Not all religious traditions promote or make use of the concept of a personalized deity, certainly. I concede that for many an impersonal deity may be more useful. However, I strongly feel that this material plane, our world of consciousness and reality, is as sacred and no more profane than any internal or external "spiritual plane." If this is so, it requires that we accept the human experience, including all human variation, as sacred. Consciously personalizing deity—deliberately choosing images that expand our minds as well as those which create psychological comfort—is a way to recall the intrinsic holiness of one's own human-ness. If we can remember that on some level we are ourselves connected to divinity, perhaps we can start to behave as if we believe it.

In the neo-pagan religion that I practice it is acceptable to conceive of deity in erotic terms, as a lover-god who embodies the best of what you seek in romantic partners. It is not out of the question to visualize a divine lover, nor later to call an internal, transcendent union with such a vision a compelling experience of the sacred. Yet for bisexuals, the myths are somewhat lacking. There are far too few archetypes that actually depict my friends Cooper, Anne, and Zoe and their family; and even fewer that portray myself, my wife, and my FTM boyfriend. We need to find or create pictures of deity that actually describe us. For myself, the perfect love deity might well be a divine androgyne, like Aphrodite Urania, someone whose male and female sides I could relate to simultaneously, who could give me an inspirational relationship that resembled my actual ones.

I wonder how many single-gendered bisexuals might find Hir (and other divine androgynes with real faces) useful in the same context. Clearly, bisexuals, polyamorists, transgendered folk, and practitioners of radical spirituality are allies by nature, whether in practice or not. We all "go too far," according to those who would prefer to split the world into an either/or dichotomy: man–woman, husband–wife, gay–straight, God–Goddess, monotheistic–polytheistic. We knock over those fences; sometimes even evaporate them by sheer accident as we blunder toward other human beings with our arms held open in welcome.

Sacred Fencesitting

After reading the fine anthology of African American women writers entitled *This Bridge Called My Back*[1], I am sometimes tempted to write something called *This Fence Called My Butt*. It seems that wherever I sit down, that is where the fence is. No matter how hard I try to belong to a group,

[1] Cherrie Moraga and Gloria Anzaldua, eds., *This Bridge Called My Back: Writings by Radical Women of Color* (New York: Kitchen Table Women of Color Press, 1981).

sooner or later someone draws a line and it inevitably ends up going right through my body, my desire, my soul, my gods. "One thing or the other!" is their rallying cry. I refuse to choose one or the other, no matter where they'd like to split me. I choose both, again and again, every time, because I truly believe that this is the only real choice, the one that my God/dess would make if S/he were Me.

Cooper, Anne, and Zoe will have their handfasting ceremony in August. Their children will tie all their hands together with a braided silk cord as part of the ritual, symbolizing their bond—and they are having fun trying to train the four-year-old and the six-year-old to tie knots together. By performing their ceremony, Bella and I will be out on a limb once again, sitting on a fence, crossing a boundary that others may shy away from. Most clergy, even those willing to perform commitment ceremonies for gay men or lesbians, wouldn't be willing to publicly support a three-way bisexual polyamorous relationship. By stepping forward and wholeheartedly supporting them, we are pioneering the path that will teach organized religion that in the end, it will always be in the best interests of a spiritual structure to celebrate love in all its resilient, exuberant manifestations.

Living in the Margins

DANNY KLOPOVIC

biologically–male,
physically–deaf . . .

socially–working class;
politically–anarchist,

religiously–anabaptist,[1]
philosophically–postmodern;[2]
sexually–bisexual. . . .

THAT THERE IS A SYMBIOTIC RELATIONSHIP between all the above categories, I am convinced. Yet even if I were to offer a near comprehensive listing of categories, it would still only open onto myself a partial window. These categories illuminate rather than circumscribe who I am as

[1] The Anabaptist tradition is not a branch of mainline Christianity (Orthodox, Protestant, or Catholic) but is a tradition in its own right, having a different understanding of Christianity. Other designations for it include free church, believers' church, gathered church, or the Radical Reformation wing of Christianity. The radical tradition includes the range from the first Anabaptists to their spiritual descendants–Mennonites, Hutterians, possibly Quakers, Moravians, River Brethren, Amish, and the First World radical Christian movement. For an exposition of the Anabaptist tradition, see John Howard Yoder, *The Priestly Kingdom* (Notre Dame, Ind.: University of Notre Dame Press, 1984); and idem, *The Royal Priesthood: Essays Ecclesiological and Ecumenical* (Grand Rapids: Wm. B. Eerdmans, 1994).

[2] Postmodern is not altogether an accurate self-description. I prefer the closely related currents described as "communitarian" or "perspectivist," but these terms are less familiar. For literature providing a Christian appreciation and critique of postmodernism, see Stanley J. Grenz, *A Primer on Postmodernism* (Grand Rapids: Wm. B. Eerdmans, 1996); and J. Richard Middleton and Brian J. Walsh, *Truth Is Stranger Than It Used to Be: Biblical Faith in a Postmodern Age* (Downers Grove, Ill.: InterVarsity Press, 1995).

a person. The intrinsic mystery of who and what this or any other person is ultimately resists capture.

I am a thirty-two-year-old white male, born partially deaf, a middle child with two sisters, of working-class background. I grew up in a nominally Catholic Croatian family—except for devout paternal grandparents. There were only seven of us, all other family members residing overseas.

My first experience of difference was being the only deaf child in a "normal" school with no peers to relate to. I was acutely aware of my being "other" and resented the reminders both at school and at home of my difference as a deaf child. That early experience shaped my sense of being an outsider. Adding to this was the alienation from my ancestral culture from an early age. My parents' well-intentioned decision not to teach Croatian at home was due to both my deafness and their general distaste for engaging in cultural activities. The absence of an extended family and nonattendance at the Croatian Catholic Church also contributed to my sense of alienation.

At an early age I rebelled against my grandparents' strict Catholicism by privately declaring atheism. At the age of sixteen I adopted Zen Buddhism as my spiritual path. It was a congenial move, as Zen allowed for both my theoretical atheism and a growing desire for a disciplined intellectual and moral life. To this day, I have retained the practice of meditation, and the Buddhist ideal of detachment remains central in my life, albeit transmuted into the Anabaptist Christian notion of *Gelassenheit.*[3]

At the age of twenty I converted to evangelical Christianity. I was drawn by the consistency of evangelical argument and driven by a need for the appealing certainties that it provided. At the age of twenty-three my acceptance of Anabaptism provided the impetus to commit myself as a Christian in the act of baptism.[4] It was during this same period that I became aware for the first time of the fact of my bisexuality.[5]

[3] *Gelassenheit* is a difficult word to translate. It is a term coined by Meister Eckhart, a thirteenth-century Dominican mystic; it describes that state in which a Christian is completely and wholly yielded to God. Anabaptist *Gelassenheit* is akin to Zen detachment, the difference being that in our letting go of the all, we receive fully the All who is God, thus deifying the believer. An excellent book that illumines *Gelassenheit* is Matthew Fox, *Breakthrough: Meister Eckhart's Creation Spirituality in New Translation* (New York: Doubleday, 1980).

[4] My conversion to Anabaptism was due to the revelatory impact of Art Gish's book *Living in Christian Community* (Sutherland, NSW, Australia: Albatross Press, 1979), a useful "primer" on the Anabaptist way of faith.

[5] For literature on bisexuality, see Martin S. Weinberg et al., *Dual Attraction: Understanding Bisexuality* (New York: Oxford University Press, 1994); and Marjorie B. Garber, *Vice Versa: Bisexuality and the Eroticism of Everyday Life* (New York: Simon & Schuster, 1996).

I do not think it coincidental that my conversion to Anabaptism meshed with a growing awareness of my bisexuality. There is at the heart of Anabaptist faith a radical questioning stance that destabilizes and destroys the orthodoxies that one can take for granted. It thus clears the way for lives of integrity and faith that can flourish in a world that is fundamentally out of control. These orthodoxies, whether they be social, cultural, political, economic, religious, or sexual, have been classed under the catchall phrase "Constantinianism" in Anabaptist parlance. Crudely put, Constantinianism justifies a reading of history in terms of uniformity, control, and manipulation. The more usual term for Constantinianism is the religiopolitical unity termed "Christendom." In modern terminology it refers to the various permutations described under the rubric of church–state union.

It has been my experience that many people live in horror of the radical contingency of existence and thus throw themselves into the search for an unshakable foundation. That search may express itself in the certainties of religious dogma—as it did for me for the time I embraced evangelicalism. Alternatively, it can be a drive to ensure personal security by accumulating possessions or by pursuing vicarious immortality through one's children.

The underlying postmodern and anarchic quality of the Anabaptist way instead affirms the reality of contingency. For this reason it is skeptical of all attempts to ensure stabilities, suspicious of defining orthodoxies, and resistant to the idolatrous compulsion of ideologies, whether religious or secular. This form of spirituality can be bewildering and chaotic, lacking in all the supports deemed necessary for human existence. Nonetheless, I find it profoundly sustaining. The support that it gives me is not the support of standing on the land, but that of floating upon the sea.

I believe that my spiritual experience within Anabaptism was an essential precondition for the recognition of my bisexuality. In my early twenties, when I became aware of my bisexuality, I remember well the ambiguity of my feelings. I oscillated between what I erroneously believed were the fixed alternatives of heterosexuality and homosexuality. Given the legacy of evangelical Christian belief, I believed that homosexuality was morally perverse. Hence, my attractions and sexual experience with men caused me great anguish. Similarly, any violation of the precept that heterosexuality was the norm, to be expressed only within marriage, was equally distressing. Then, in a moment of synchronicity, I reconciled being bisexual and Christian. This moment included embracing Anabaptism, a preexisting friendship with a lesbian Christian couple, and the experience of falling in love with a man and a woman at the same time.

Anabaptism assumes that the speech and the lives of fellow Christians (and anyone or anything else) can be the occasion for a Word of God which requires a discerning response. At this moment, this particular Word expressed itself in the faithful life and friendship of this lesbian Christian couple. This Word was a matter of simple, timely presence in startlingly clear contradiction to the accepted orthodox belief which I shared: one was either a Christian or a homosexual/bisexual, but one could not be both. A common assumption then, as now, in both straight and gay cultures is that these are mutually exclusive options. My friends' life together, however, was and is a living demonstration of a contrary reality that overturns this popular shibboleth.

Yet, while I remained evangelical, that Word remained invisible to my sight. Anabaptism gave me the fresh vision that enabled me to recognize the witness of my friends and to create in me the openness toward falling in love.

Simultaneously, bisexuality was the catalyst that destroyed for me the basic certainties that many Christians take for granted and that I took for granted while I was still an evangelical Christian. Most importantly, I am now skeptical about being able to know and access the "Truth." This skepticism enables a willingness in me to expand the definition of what constitutes faithful Christian discipleship. My bisexuality, with its inherent smashing of finite boundaries, set the stage for this skepticism. Concurrently, my journey into Anabaptism complemented this process of questioning and dissolving earlier certainties. Over time, as I familiarize myself with Anabaptism by way of theological study, spiritual practice, and involvement in network groups, I realize that I have found a Christian tradition that encourages and enables its participants to engage in the lifelong and necessary task of criticism.

Bisexuality possesses an inherent anarchic quality in that it leads one to reject either/or thinking in favor of both/and. As I cannot insulate my religious beliefs from the impact of my bisexuality and vice versa, there is a resonance between my bisexuality and being drawn to those strands of Christianity that emphasize both/and thinking.[6] If Anabaptism had not

[6] I do not wish to use the popular shibboleths of dualistic thinking versus holistic thinking. Dualistic modes of reasoning are problematic. Yet I am unconvinced that holistic modes of thought are significantly better. Holism all too often gives the impression of leav-

been a spirituality that is inherently radical and subversive, I doubt I could have committed to it. Bisexuality as a marginal sexuality found a reinforcing echo in the marginality of Anabaptism.

Of course, Anabaptism is not the only tradition where this both/and thinking occurs. For example, I have found pagan spiritualities such as Wicca to have a powerful and intuitive appeal. It is even possible that I would have been Wiccan had I not first come across Anabaptism.[7]

My bisexual identity challenges the thinking of others, as well as my own thinking on many issues. This is most obvious within the arena of sexual desire and choice, yet I find that it arises in many other contexts. Bisexuality has acted as a critical tool that enables me to reject as inadequate a life that separates one's sexuality from other facets of one's personality. Indeed, it is only through being bisexual that I have come to appreciate the partial truth of the feminist insight: the personal is political. Naturally there are "secular" consequences that flow from this stance of both/and thinking in my life. First and foremost, bisexuality contradicts the dichotomies in which straight and gay/lesbian people have vested themselves. Bisexuality creates conflicts with straight and gay/lesbian people when these people have an interest in maintaining an either/or distinction for whatever reason.

I suggest that bisexuality is problematic for some because it violates boundaries.[8] It is easier for straights to define gays as the "other" and vice versa, for it allows for an "us" and "them" stance. The problem arises because bisexuality dissolves the concept of the "other"—hence the discomfort on both sides of the fence. People rely on the concept of the "other" in order to define and reinforce their personal and group identity. In itself, this is proper and necessary, for no one can exist apart from "categories." The real question is whether we, as persons and as groups, allow categories to be windows into the lives of "others" and thus allow for relationship. Do we instead employ categories as a weapon against the

---

ing out uncomfortable facts and ideas that do not fit a preconceived holistic grand scheme. At least with "both/and" one can allow for discontinuities and disagreements to coexist, even if that means living with tensions.

[7] On Wiccan (witchcraft) spirituality, see the excellent books by Starhawk: *Dreaming the Dark: Magic, Sex and Politics* (Boston: Beacon Press, 1982) and *The Spiral Dance: A Rebirth of the Ancient Religion of the Great Goddess* (San Francisco: HarperSanFrancisco, 1989).

[8] Persons who are either intersexual (hermaphrodite), transsexual, transvestite, transgender, or some combination thereof also breach boundaries even more radically as they overturn gender definitions. Of course, sexual orientation will be a further potent factor in influencing individual and social perceptions.

"other"? Too often, though, the category of bisexuality is a weapon used by straights and gays/lesbians.

Equally problematic is the labeling of straight/gay/lesbian people as "monosexuals," as the polar opposite to bisexuals. Perhaps my resistance to all of these definitions stems from my belief that categories are inevitably partial. The truth that they reveal is also at the same time a lie.

Furthermore, in the area of sexuality, some people appear to elude all three "categories." For instance, I would argue celibacy (asexuals?) to be a sexual "category" in its own right and not merely a subset of straight/gay/bi/whatever by virtue of its alleged sexlessness.[9] To complicate matters, where do hermaphrodites (intersexuals), transsexuals, transvestites, and transgenders fit in?

Fundamentally, I would say that these are political questions, inasmuch as politics is a process that defines the shape of our bodies, both personal and social. Where politics (as a way of being in the world) can go astray is if it accepts the faulty premise that one's identity commits one to a particular ideological practice that is exclusionary. The kind of politics that my bisexual identity leads me to support (accented by Anabaptist beliefs) is one that promotes communities with porous boundaries, rather than drawing sharp boundaries to include some and exclude others.

It is at this point that my anarchist sensibilities kick in, for as I understand it, anarchism as political practice is inherently communitarian and antihierarchical.[10] Thus it espouses the most radical form of community possible, one where all find a place, where the common-unity rests on the preciousness and uniqueness of difference rather than the collectivist attempts toward uniformity. This may appear utopian and impractical. I would argue, however, that the truth of such a vision is embodied in the "beloved community" proclaimed by Martin Luther King and carried forward by black Christians and supporters. In such a community no member is infallible—no adversary is disposable—and all are invited to share.[11]

So how do the personal and the political intersect in my life? My politics come out of an understanding of my identity. That identity develops

[9] For example, see Sally Cline, *Women, Celibacy and Passion* (London: Andre Deutsch, 1993), for an illuminating, albeit uneven, discussion along these lines.

[10] See Jacques Ellul, *Anarchy and Christianity* (Grand Rapids: Wm. B. Eerdmans, 1991).

[11] More compelling than any theoretical exposition of this "beloved community" is the living embodiment of such communities. There is an excellent fictional portrayal of such a community given in Starhawk's book *The Fifth Sacred Thing* (New York: Doubleday, 1996).

in the context of a network of relationships, namely, the community or communities I have been in, am in, and will be in.

What does it mean for me to be bisexual? I am not happy with the notion of bisexuality being the midpoint on a continuum between heterosexuality and homosexuality à la Kinsey, for it too easily collapses into the dichotomy of straight/gay.[12] It also renders bisexuality invisible. As one who assumes Christian understandings on monogamy and the sexual virtues, then at the surface level I am either straight or gay depending on the sex of my partner. However, this emphatically does not mean that I switch between being gay or straight—I am always bisexual.

Many have asked, Does having a male partner make you gay? The short answer is no. In this I remember a witty comment I once read on a T-shirt: "I'm not gay but I think my boyfriend is." How is this possible? I define bisexuality as the "potential to be sexually and/or romantically involved with either men and/or women."

I have wondered whether the ideal would be a four-way relationship consisting of two men and two women, justified along the lines of polygamous union. Yet the time and emotional energy required to maintain such an arrangement would, I think, be exhausting. It would, however, render bisexuality visible in a literal sense. Perhaps problematic from an Anabaptist stance is the likelihood that such arrangements do not endure in the long term. I do point out that I lack direct experience of such bisexual arrangements, and doubtless there are permanent arrangements along these lines. Of course, this begs the question, which I leave aside at this point, of whether Christianity necessarily requires permanence as a criterion for sexual relationships.[13]

I am fortunate that my gay male partner does not have the misconceptions that so many have about bisexuals. Prior to partnering with him, those I dated were uncomfortable with, if not hostile to, bisexuality. Gay men were afraid that I would leave them for a woman, and straight women believed that I would cheat with a man behind their back. I ran into any number of myths from both gay and straight dates. The varied responses I get when I discuss my sexuality illustrate a number of earlier points made about the use of categories. Here are a few samples:

[12] I should note that this is a criticism directed at common misconceptions of Kinsey's work.

[13] See Elizabeth Stuart, *Just Good Friends: Towards a Lesbian and Gay Theology of Relationships* (New York: Mowbray, 1995).

- My best friend (who is straight and female) had an easier time affirming me as gay than bisexual. Her unreflective view was that bisexuals are promiscuous, that we cannot cope with being gay (or lesbian) and that it is a confused sexuality. She had a hard time accepting that the mythology on bisexuality was wrong. However, she no longer views bisexuals negatively, a development grounded in our long and rich friendship and her knowledge of me as a bisexual person.
- A lesbian friend who finds the whole notion of bisexuality uncomfortable—but for reasons that I can only guess at. The topic is invariably side-stepped in discussion.
- A gay friend who is convinced that I must be in denial about being gay.
- A bisexual friend in a lesbian relationship who understands bisexuality differently from myself—which is why I'm wary of too precise a definition. She will find a man attractive, among other things, by virtue of his being a man, and similarly for women. By contrast, I find the actual gender to be irrelevant. She illustrates how bisexuality differs from person to person.
- A straight male friend who I think partially understands me in this area. Nevertheless, I think he prefers to see me in a "straight" relationship.

These responses highlight my experience of being an outsider. My history and my faith have also taught me a perspective that allows me to judge, imagine, love, and live in ways differing from the expectations that one takes for granted.

Having experienced what it is like to be the "other" in a number of contexts, I find my bisexuality essential in those areas in my life where I am not the "other." I can only reflect on my life as a white male in trying to appreciate the very real differences in the experiences of other marginalized people. Yet as bisexual and as deaf, I can partially apprehend the reality of discrimination and thus make connections to other marginalized groups struggling for liberation.

The question that now confronts me is whether I will exercise the choice of living in the margins.

The most difficult act that a person can undertake is to make choices.

A process that I'm still working through, albeit imperfectly, is moving from being peripherally marginal to being intentionally marginal. I was first placed at the margins involuntarily as a deaf child. A central life question has been (and still is) whether I will resign to fate or creatively respond by shaping a destiny as a bisexual Christian. This choice between fate and destiny is a hard choice.

A life that accepts fate is secure, but it is also soul-destroying. The shaping of destiny is an insecure and risky enterprise, but it is the requirement for a life that is truly and fully human. Life is a dialectic between these two poles, and I struggle to continuously choose the latter. I have attempted so far to make choices that place me outside of the center. I do this in the hope that I can, like other marginal people, cast my voice from the margins to critique the center in whatever context I find myself.

In this, I find my experience as bisexual underscoring the Anabaptist emphasis on the liberation of the oppressed. This is both sustaining and liberating. Yet ironically it is also a source of guilt and bondage inasmuch as I realize how inadequate my commitments to liberation can be.

Anabaptism is a prophetic discipleship spirituality that is not afraid to do the hard work of "plucking up, pulling down, destroying and overthrowing, building, and planting."[14] This is also true of the impact of bisexuality on my understandings and life, and it forms the subtext of bisexual liberationist movements.[15]

Anabaptism is also a radically incarnational spirituality. Where prophetic spirituality readily discriminates between the "holy" and the "unholy" and draws absolute lines, an incarnational spirituality runs the risk of blasphemy by bridging the divide between the sacred and the profane in paradoxical love. One may wonder at how these divergent strands coexist? The answer is "with difficulty." The perennial temptation is to favor one strand and hence lapse into the extremes of fundamentalism or indifferent quietism.

Sexuality is also intrinsically incarnational; however, the temptation is always present that we (whether we are bisexual, heterosexual, or homosexual) will deny and repress this incarnational drive. As nonheterosexuals are constantly reminded, whether by their own experience or the reductionist messages of the wider society that equate us with our sexual

[14] An allusion to Jeremiah 1:10.

[15] For varied responses along these lines, see Naomi Tucker, ed., *Bisexual Politics: Theories, Queries & Visions* (Binghamton, N.Y.: Harrington Park Press, 1995).

acts, the body is a grounding and source of truth. It is my experience that bisexuality also runs the risk, akin to blasphemy, of treason in attempting to bridge the ancient split between body and spirit.

Bisexuality is open-ended and rich in possibilities. It is many things for me:

- It is not merely a way of being sexual.
- It is not merely finding that gender is irrelevant to one's sexual preference.
- It can be political as it can allow one to relate to other minority groups.
- It is potentially a powerful resource that subverts the comfortable dualisms that we structure our lives around.
- It underscores and throws into sharp relief the prophetic and incarnational aspects of my Anabaptist faith.

Bisexuality stands in a symbiotic relationship with my politics, my religion, and my philosophy. Each strand complements as well as criticizes the other. I recognize that these four elements are not discrete entities with clear and distinct meanings apart from their ongoing relevance and shaping of the complex web of acts and insights that is my life.

Movie Mecca: Confessions of an Amphibian Life Form

KELLY M. CRESAP

. . . and though I was only seven
I discovered heaven at the RKO.
—"Larger Than Life," from *My Favorite Year*

THE LIFE OF A SECRET AMPHIBIAN: a man discovering that going to the movies has everything to do with being bisexual; but more than this, bi-devotional, bi-spiritual, bi-experiential . . . bi-what-have-you.

The sensual power of movies can never be fully measured or explained. Despite being a mass art form, cinema is capable of stirring up the most intensely personal of responses. For some of us, moviegoing amounts to an abiding passion, bordering on obsession. As a kid I used to pore over the entertainment section of the paper, mentally rehearsing the last movie I saw, dreaming about the next one. Like a lot of other queer kids, I had an almost physiological need to lose myself in movie reverie from time to time. It's not a need one simply outgrows.

Movies have ways of getting past our usual defense systems, of awakening impulses and sympathies that may take us askance in the ordinary light of day, as if we'd been drugged or hypnotized. Films obviously serve a strong wish-fulfillment function, but they can also introduce a viewer to wishes not previously entertained—wishes that may be irresponsible, altruistic, childish, laughable, or violent. Usually such wishes are assuaged vicariously in the dark, and dissipate like a half-remembered dream. Occasionally, though, they can divert the course of a person's life.

Ever since I can remember, movies have spoken to me in ways that bordered on the divine.[1] They've uncovered feelings I barely knew I had,

[1] Divine—adj. 2. given or inspired by God; holy; sacred. 3. devoted to God; religious; sacrosanct. 5. supremely great, good, etc. 6. [Colloq.] very pleasing, attractive, etc.—vt. 1. to

solaced and sustained me in moments of crisis, acted as a private confessional, a companion, guide, muse. I cherish them for the internal poetry they give me, for the secrets they pry loose, for all the heightened states they leave me in—sweet-sublime, pensive, sensual, compassionate, giddy to the point of tears, stirred to a righteous anger, charged with a sense of possibility.

I would wager that something in my genetic makeup has rendered me unusually susceptible to the effects of film. My earliest memory is of turning on the TV one day and witnessing a scene midway through a horror film. A fish monster with bulging eyes, walking upright on webbed feet, was creeping up behind a beautiful woman standing on a dock. I turned the set off before seeing what happened next. That night the scene played again in my dreams, and I ran from my bedroom screaming, crying, inconsolable, waking up the whole family at 3 A.M.

Is it any wonder that that three-year-old boy would one day become a film critic? There must be an element of primal therapy for me, fueling my will to review films: revisiting early trauma, talking it out of my system, using tough language to reveal how soft and impressionable I am. Reviewing has allowed me to delve fully into my responses to movies, to reenact and rearticulate them, to search for a dialect equal to the images and sensations flowing at the rate of twenty-four frames per second.

But it is far more than the need for catharsis that draws me to film. By now I've come to recognize that for me, filmgoing is a form of spiritual and sensual devotion. Beyond the reviews lies a very personal story of how film has been counsel to me in the realms of both eros and the sacred.

Eros

In a collection wittily entitled *Reeling,* the incomparable film critic Pauline Kael celebrates the overwhelming sensual power of cinema:

> Movies—which arouse special, hidden feelings—have always had an erotic potential that was stronger than that of the live theater. Enlarged so that they seem totally ours, movie actors are more purely objects of contemplation than people who are physically present. Since they're not actually there on the stage, speaking, rushing off to change a costume, we can fantasize about them with impunity; by etherealizing the actors, film removes the con-

prophesy. 2. to guess; conjecture. 3. to find out by intuition. —vi. 1. to engage in divination. *Webster's New World Dictionary,* Third College Edition, 1994.

> straints on our imaginations. This was obviously a factor in the early disapproval of movies, even if it wasn't consciously formulated. Probably movies weren't culturally respectable for a long time because they are so sheerly enjoyable; in a country with a Puritan background, the sensuality of movies was bound to be suspect.[2]

Conversely, I think that for many of us, the sheer enjoyment of movies provided our first impetus for being suspicious about our Puritan background. A recent *New Yorker* cartoon has a child asking his parents, after seeing *The Wizard of Oz* on TV, "Why did Dorothy want to go back to where they only had black and white?"

The sensuality Kael describes might be discussed as a series of minute neurophysiological changes that steal over the receptive filmgoer, taking her or him unawares. The movie theater is a place of pure desire, a domain where physical stasis opens up channels of spiritual kinesis. The transition from ordinary to cinematic experience involves a kind of amphibian movement to which human organisms are uniquely adapted.[3] We take this movement for granted, but at the advent of motion pictures, audiences reacted with naïveté and fear to see people and objects enlarged beyond their normal scale, suddenly disappearing and reappearing on a screen. We might think of "film sense" as an evolutionary threshold, profoundly influential to the ways we grasp and process the world around us.

The movie-going "amphibian" reacts intuitively to the womblike space created by the movie house. Captivated by flickering images in a dark, cavelike theater, the psyche finds respite from its usual occupations, relinquishes other concerns, and enters a place where familiar class barriers and inequalities (of appearance, manner, wealth, education, ethnicity) can be suspended. The cinema grants multiple forms of repose to the human frame—eyes and ears acclimate to a different mode of stimuli; the sensibility adjusts to a new geography of image and sound. The body's sensation of physical release is mirrored in the consciousness—brain functions alternate and regroup; new sensitivities emerge; a kind of migration occurs as certain nerve endings become reexposed, newly alerted.

In this mildly altered state, the moviegoer is able to feel pleasures, try out roles, entertain affinities and affections that may not be permissible under normal conditions. Recent scholarship has shown how those affini-

[2] Pauline Kael, *Reeling* (New York: Warner, 1976), 13.

[3] *Amphibious* is an adjective from Greek *amphibios,* "living a double life." It can refer to living both on land and in water or to having two natures or qualities, that is, of a mixed nature.

ties do not precisely correspond with a viewer's espoused convictions, or with an artifact's presumed content or meaning.[4] Viewers are unpredictable—they find their own uses for what's presented to them; they "misunderstand" what was intended, reading haphazardly and against the grain, identifying across established demarcations of age, class, race, gender, and sexual orientation.

My own history has given me a keen interest in this last category. How much is sexual orientation influenced by popular culture? Personally, I've never been able to separate my sexual proclivities from the kinds of sparks set off for me at the movies. I located the courage to come out during the same week that I saw two pioneering gay-themed films, *Taxi Zum Klo* (Taxi to the John) and *Making Love.* In April 1982 I was home for spring break during my last semester at college. I'd been questioning my sexual nature over the past year, suspecting that I was gay but not wanting any unexamined expectations—mine or anyone else's—getting in the way as I explored my feelings on the matter. I think I'd have come out when I did anyway, but the films gave me an extra nudge, added ballast to a decision that had had a long preamble.

Given my age and upbringing, it's no surprise that I latched onto Hollywood's vanilla concoction *Making Love,* instead of the more scabrous film from Germany. I was a straight-A WASP kid from a serene neighborhood in southeast Portland, Oregon: studious, introverted, intensely middle-class, still a virgin at twenty-two. I know that *Making Love* has settled officially at about a two-and-a-half-star rating, but I recall that my sensors went off the scales the night I saw it: the thought of it!—two men pursuing an amorous relationship, declaring feelings for each other, kissing on the big screen. I sat there transfixed, unable either to resist or to credit the contradictions I sensed: it's impossible for this film to have been made, and equally impossible for me to be watching it at a public venue . . . and yet there it is, and here I am, and what a mind-bender!

Early in my coming-out experience, I remember telling people that even though I was gay, I still felt strongly attracted to certain leading actresses—at the time, it was Mariel Hemingway (in *Manhattan* and *Personal Best*) and Kelly McGillis (in *Witness* and *Reuben, Reuben*). I think this caveat made the news of my orientation easier for some people to hear; it

[4] See, for instance, John Fiske, *Understanding Popular Culture* (Boston: Unwin Hyman, 1989); Michel de Certeau, *The Practice of Everyday Life* (Berkeley: University of California Press, 1984); Constance Penley, "Feminism, Psychoanalysis and the Study of Popular Culture," in *Cultural Studies,* ed. Lawrence Grossberg et al. (New York: Routledge, 1991).

also satisfied my penchant for nonconformity. Readers of this anthology may wonder why, given this early indication, it took me until age thirty-three to recognize bisexuality as an option.

What interests me now is that I discovered that aspect of myself at the movies. Film provided early clues about a sexual nature that was too nuanced and fine-tuned for me to grasp all at once. My attraction to women was like a competing frequency on a radio transmission, not easily detectable in the din of the main broadcast. Movie sequences and icons validated shifts and undercurrents in my sexual inclinations before I myself was willing to validate them. The amphibian nature of filmgoing itself helped substantiate this transition. A side of me that I wasn't able during my twenties either to decipher psychologically or to integrate socially still got to come out and play when I was at the movies.

Can there be any filmgoer who is wholly immune to this form of play? Are we not all secretly bisexual at the movies, tantalized by ideal renderings of both the male and female form? Granted, we are well-accustomed to the sovereign rule of traditional heterosexual coupling in movie plots. The matinee hero and heroine wend their inevitable way toward an unexamined, ever-after monogamous union by the final fade. What else are sunsets for? But moviegoers, true to their amphibian nature, are more devious than that: by exercising fluctuating attractions to the man and woman in question, each audience member tacitly turns this time-worn scenario into a kinky three-way.

Spirit

Is this kind of playfulness at the movies ever fully distinguishable from what might be called, for lack of a better word, *worship?*

Moviegoing, sexuality, and the realm of the divine have been mysteriously conjoined for me as far back as I can remember. In this regard, amphibianism can be viewed not as a binary alternation between natures that are entirely known, but rather as an ongoing metamorphosis involving complex and unpredictable variables. Another way of stating this is to say that the medium of film has been a *divining* presence in my life: it has prompted changes in my self-understanding, given me intimations about myself and charted transitions even before I was prepared to make them.[5]

[5] Appropriately enough, Divine is also the name of an actor. See Eve Kosofsky Sedgwick and Michael Moon, "Divinity: A Dossier, a Performance Piece, a Little-Understood Emo-

One such transition occurred in the very realm of religious belief. Cinema acted as a guide to me during a tumultuous period in which I was losing my capacity for more traditional forms of worship. Midway through college, I acquired an interest in mysticism at a time when my Christian faith was being shaken to its foundations. One evening I saw Stanley Kubrick's film *2001: A Space Odyssey* and left the theater in a state of visionary exaltation. The cosmic star-child appearing in the final moments had a beauty beyond my fathoming. My mind circled and circled around this literally fecund image—a human fetus suspended inside a solar corona, gazing out trusting and serene across eons of space. The film's ending seemed to turn orthodox Christian theology upside down, yet did so while conveying profound reverence for the possibility of birth and creation, the fragility of life. Mystical experience can never be adequately described, but it is no less real for being incommunicable. What words will suffice for what I felt that evening? For a few moments I had a sense of unspeakable happiness and clarity, mingled with fear and awe, as if a hand had reached out to me through the darkness.

To speak this way about one motion picture and one moment in my life (albeit an influential one), however, is to neglect more vexing issues raised by the overlap of cinema and worship. I know that I'm speaking in unusually lofty terms of the realm of popular culture—a realm not ordinarily mobilized around art and the pursuit of sublime truth but around escapism, pandering, market demographics, mega-deals, and the triumph of image over content. I know that movie stars are objects of blind adulation, and that entire industries are committed to fostering such adulation. Perhaps instead of amphibians I should be speaking of . . . chameleons? parasites?

In his book *Within the Context of No Context,* George W. S. Trow examines the pervasive and insidious consequences of the postwar media and the culture of celebrity. What we really crave, he asserts, is protection from our fears; and in the dance of celebrities we find relief in what he calls "mirages of pseudo-intimacy."[6] How, we might ask, could anything sacred emerge from a medium as irredeemably commercial and artificial as film, with its endless audience con-games and puerile ready-made

---

tion," an essay on the films of John Waters and Divine, in *Tendencies* (Durham: Duke University Press, 1993).

[6] George W. S. Trow, *Within the Context of No Context* (Boston: Little, Brown, 1981), 19.

themes? I hearken to a statement Rebecca Johnson makes in an essay about gardening and the sacred: "If I worship at all, it is at the compost pile."[7] *Taxi zum klo* indeed!

I realize that moviegoing sometimes resembles neither worship nor play. Like other viewers, I've sat through films that left me feeling cheapened, demoralized, cynically manipulated, pummeled. However, I don't want to sound sanctimonious. I would much rather watch lively or provocative trash than sit through an art-house offering strangled by its own pious intentions. For example, I felt instant regret upon seeing Steven Spielberg's *Amistad* earlier this year, but some part of me still hasn't fully recovered from the stunningly odd experience of Paul Verhoeven's *Starship Troopers. Amistad,* a courtroom drama about the rights of slaves, seemed to falter under the weight of its high-mindedness. *Troopers,* a sci-fi flick about giant-insect warfare, had a lowbrow vitality that I found nothing short of enthralling.[8]

Whereas *Amistad* acquires the congratulatory air of a civics lecture, *Starship Troopers* has the audacious appeal of a midnight cult shocker, where half the fun lies in daring yourself to stay seated and remain calm. Watching it was like having an out-of-body experience, invigorating partly because of the degree of disbelief involved. (This is not real! This is not me!) My film-buff friends are divided over whether *Starship Troopers* is a straight action flick or a spoof. Some of the training-camp scenes have the feel of a fascist youth rally as filmed by the makers of *Thunderbirds,* the old TV marionette show. I would have a hard time defending the movie—or my enjoyment of it—on political grounds, but it still catapults me to pop heaven whenever I think about it.

When I apply the term "worship," however, it's with a different kind of film and effect in mind. This kind of film tends to be one that is finely crafted in spite of its modest budget, and its special effects have more to do with radiant screen presence than with industrial light and magic. Every so often there appears a marvelous small film—*Vanya on 42nd Street,*

[7] Rebecca Johnson, "New Moon Over Roxbury: Reflections on Urban Life and the Land," in *Ecofeminism and the Sacred,* ed. Carol J. Adams (New York: Continuum, 1993), 252.

[8] In terms of film orientation, these directors' careers seem to have passed in the middle: Spielberg found his footing in the pop terrain of *Jaws* and *E.T.,* and now has shifted toward prestige historical pictures; the Dutch-born Verhoeven rose to acclaim with art-house fare such as *Soldier of Orange* and *The Fourth Man* and now works on projects like *Showgirls* and *Robocop.*

The Whole Wide World, and *Great Expectations* come to mind as recent examples—whose artistry reveals the extraordinary intimacy of which cinema is capable. The sheer reverence with which such films are made can extend over me like a benediction, leaving me in a state of grace.

I watched Alfonse Cuaron's *Great Expectations* in an almost trancelike condition, not knowing what was more lovely—the presence of Ethan Hawke as the awkward hero, or of Gwyneth Paltrow as the heartbreaking siren, or the caressingly filmed interaction between them. I went to see it only reluctantly, on the advice of a trusted filmgoing friend who knows my stubborn allegiance to the Dickens novel. (I postponed seeing the 1940s David Lean film adaptation for many years, preferring to imagine Pip, Estella, and Miss Havisham for myself, and knowing that even a brilliant film rendering would fall short of the mark.) I regretted the absence of certain plot elements from Cuaron's modernized version, but I could hardly begrudge a film that conveyed Dickens's themes with such illuminating pathos and delicacy. The film, like the book, got me right where I live. It seemed to tell my own secrets—to know what life path I should take, to provide me with a compass, to reassure and forgive me even as it reassured and forgave its hero. Afterward, flooded with emotion, I went for a long walk through the streets, basking in the film's interior life, perplexed that critics and audiences had failed to see its merits . . . but even that failure seemed part of the film's rueful, hard-won knowledge about aspiration and loss. I kept walking that night, without direction, reluctant to break the film's spell by facing the drive home.

That evening walk is as much a part of my spiritual life as my formal baptism in childhood, or the Pentecostal prayer meeting I went to in lieu of attending my high school prom—a prayer meeting in which, unprecedentedly, not a word was spoken, but where everyone who attended had the sense that something extraordinary was occurring.

As I think about it, there's a constellation of such moments stretching back over years of moviegoing—moments of reverie, of amazement in the presence of the miraculous. The films *The Ballad of Narayama, A Year of the Quiet Sun,* and *The Elephant Man* all got to me in this way. The seventy-year-old matriarch in Shohei Imamura's film displays a baffling obstinacy as she insists that her son carry her to Narayama, where, by village decree, she must wait until she dies. Witnessing their journey up the mountain, I felt that if I were fully able to grasp the woman's state of mind, I would have solved one of life's greatest enigmas. The Polish heroine in Krzysztof Zanussi's *A Year of the Quiet Sun* imagines dancing with her lover in the open desert of Monument Valley, New Mexico. This vision appears to have sustained her through years of separation from the man she loves, but it is also, mysteriously and tragically, what prevents her from going to meet him in America when the chance arises.[9]

Such film sequences continue to serve as articles of faith to me—talismans, greatly cherished, mentally revisited, reimagined, as if they held the answer to a basic conundrum of human existence. Reflecting on them can carry me through a day; but beyond that, they seem to drive away the forces of evil and unknowing, making all the rest of what has to be endured in this lifetime more endurable.

I confess I can be a snob about such things. For years I used David Lynch's *Elephant Man* as a social litmus test: there must be something wrong with you if you can't respond to this movie. My attachment to the film grew with repeated viewings—it became like an annual pilgrimage in the mid-eighties. I thought nothing in the world could be more marvelous or affecting. I savored the film's achievements in sound, lighting, editing; its unerring sense of cinematic rhythm, composition, point of view; the consummate ensemble work of the actors; the psychological intrigue of John Merrick and Dr. Treves, and of their interaction; Victorian London recreated in richly textured black and white; the use of music, particularly the Adagio for Strings; the extraordinary suggestiveness of certain symbols and passages— I built up a sort of theology around the movie, arranging its montages and themes into a personal creed. Behind it all, I think, was my sense that the film offered me a kind of absolution from the burdens of growing up queer. Merrick's having to insist that he is a human being, not an animal, carries resonance for anyone who has been treated like, and at times felt like, a freak. Near the end, Merrick's wanting to sleep on his back, as other humans do, even though this will cause self-asphyxiation, impresses me as one of the most poignant expressions of desire ever recorded on film.

No wonder my devotion translated into a rejection of anyone heathen enough to belittle or denigrate the film. It was an aesthetic form of evangelism: my own private inquisition.

There are other symptoms of my devotion to sacred moments of

[9] Other such moments come to mind: the bank teller, *Top Hat,* and title musical sequences in Herbert Ross's *Pennies from Heaven;* the son's departure at the end of Todd Haynes's *Poison;* the exhibition roundup in *Babe;* H.I.'s dream into the future at the end of *Raising Arizona.*

cinema. As you might have gathered by now, I'm a pretty lousy movie date. I tend to go into an ascetic mode once I get to a theater: I consistently avoid the concession stand; I refuse to enter a film after it's started; I don't make any more than cursory contact (visual or verbal) with companions during the show; and I wait around until the credits are done.

Sensual fullness pursued with monastic dedication.

The real difficulties, though, set in after the credits are finished: navigating my way back to the surface while wanting to linger below. Pauline Kael has observed that two people's responses to a movie can be strong enough to form the basis of a friendship—or the demise of a relationship. The complications can increase exponentially if one of the people is bisexual. A few scenarios:

> You come out of a film stimulated and dazed and needing to revise your position on the Kinsey scale, but your date is only interested in finding dessert . . .
>
> You discover weeks after seeing a film that your gay boyfriend feels threatened by your enthusiasm for a certain leading lady—any leading lady, in fact . . .
>
> You're so smitten with an actor that even your partner's sexual advances cannot drive the thought of him from your mind . . .
>
> Your interest in a straight woman fades as she goes on at length about a leading man you thought was a washout; this man becomes emblematic of everything that separates the two of you . . .
>
> It's enough to make you want to see movies all by yourself!

I used to think I'd outgrow the desire to watch films unchaperoned. Walker Percy's novel *The Moviegoer* follows a young man from his solitary moviegoing habits to his breakthrough into the messier realm of human relationships. I wondered for a time whether the novel had me pegged—one day I'd realize with chagrin how ingrown I'd become from going to movies alone. Now I'm of a different mind: I think of it as a luxury. There are just times when I don't want to filter my initial reactions to a film through any form of language or decorum. Later on, I'll talk about the movie for longer than it took to watch. But at the moment of impact, the task of playing simultaneous translator—from my sensibility to another's—is sometimes too cumbersome to bear.

Mecca

The solitude issue hasn't always been a matter of choice. Films have come through for me at times when companionship was unavailable and I needed a touchstone, contact with something palpable and sane and endearing. Films helped sustain me through moments of crisis I encountered at the beginning and end of six months of independent travel in Asia. During the initial flight across the Pacific, I developed an acute case of cabin distress, an intolerable anxiety that I still can't fully account for. Instead of anticipating the months ahead, I felt like I was hurtling into a void. The need for some form of relief, something to focus on, became all-consuming. I remember the in-flight movie—a thriller, *No Way Out*— came as an enormous solace, calmed my nerves even as it caught me up in its tense narrative intrigue. Afterwards I wondered how I might have otherwise gotten through the experience. It was a complete blessing—in spite of what anyone might say about the formal qualities (or homophobic content) of the film in question.

Near the end of my Asian travels, I was stranded in Kathmandu for several weeks during the rainy season, waiting for a prearranged flight to Burma. I passed time by dragging myself from one part of town to another. Far from feeling *bi*sexual, I was hard-pressed to remember a time when I felt sexual, period. Loneliness was my constant companion after nearly half-a-year of travel, and no powers of self-humor could pitch me out of it. Amphibianism implies flexibility and movement, and here I felt as immobile psychologically as I was geographically. I went to considerable lengths one day to secure a private screening room at the city's French cultural center, and to rent a copy of *Merry Christmas, Mr. Lawrence*—which, as it turned out, provided a vivid analogy for my sense of external and internal exile. Perhaps, in that screening room, I was less like an amphibian than a tortoise being coaxed out of its shell.

The film recounts harsh conditions of life in a World War II Japanese internment camp on Java; it aroused feelings of compassion that also released me from an otherwise engulfing sense of helplessness. My heart lurched when the British prisoner played by David Bowie kissed the commanding Japanese officer in full view of the assembled camp. For the soldier it was a moment of daring self-sacrifice and an acknowledgment of true lines of affinity at the camp. For me it was a moment of queer reenchantment, a temporary reprieve from the family-values mentality surrounding me in the culture of Western Asia.

When I reached Burma a week later, I discovered on seeing the vast ancient ruins of Pagan that I was prone not only to homesickness but also agoraphobia. Guiding myself among a series of crumbling, bell-shaped Buddhist shrines dotting the horizon left me with an unshakable case of the jitters. Pagan brought me near to the true impetus behind my decision to travel—a longing to take myself to the ends of the world, wherever it might lead me. Here was one of the most strange and remote locales I'd ever seen . . . and once I got there, I wasn't up for the experience. The day tour threw all my sense of perspective, of right proportion, out of kilter. Which monuments was I to visit, given that they extended as far as I could see? How long was I to keep at it, given that I was unlikely ever to return here? I wandered among them with a growing, and ominous, sense of bereavement, feeling like one of the walking wounded.

On this occasion, relief came in an unexpected form. That evening as I walked through the tiny adjoining village, I found the entire local population huddled together on benches under a thatched hut, mesmerized by an old James Bond movie, *On Her Majesty's Secret Service,* shown on a reel-to-reel projector. I joined them in watching, and sat there nursing a sweetly distracted sense of the absurd. I can hardly describe what a treat that evening turned out to be: discovering big-screen entertainment in a small enclave, seeing narrative again in a brisk form, elements of wit, sexiness, panache—everything the day had lacked until then. Surrounded by Burmese spectators, I felt like a *National Geographic* reporter uncertain whether he was on duty or off. Here was a postmodern tale out of the *Arabian Nights,* entertainment of a kind I could never have devised on my own. It wasn't *love* I found amid the ruins; it was long-lost friends: Miss Moneypenny! Blofeld! Shaken, not stirred! Keeping the British end up! All the accouterments of Western decadence! It seemed to me, at that moment, more durable than the vast Eastern decay that lay outside the hut. As the only native English speaker present, I caught some of the jokes that were otherwise lost in the subtitles, and it amused me to hear the sound of my laughter percolating the assembly.

In spite of all this, I know that movies can't do everything, can't go everywhere. I accept the fact that a lot of great things will never be adequately filmed: certain novels and plays, all of my favorite poems, not to mention roller-coasters, architecture, landscapes, and other ineffable elements of grace.

Still, I'm hard-pressed to find equivalents for certain moviegoing events of my life, and the feelings they've kindled—feelings of wooziness, fright, sadness, redemption, hallucinogenic clarity, high silliness, rage. Does it ultimately matter whether these experiences are more sensual or spiritual in nature? I only know that movies are a renewable and cherishable resource in my life. Recurrently they provide the impetus for shifting to another mode of consciousness, from which the point of departure is shown in a more enhanced light:

The secret life of an amphibian.

Your Love Amazes Me

DIANE PASTA

SOMETHING TUGS AT ME ALL DAY LONG, reminding me that my heart yearns to dwell in that love, pestering me to spend every moment adoring the one who loves me. I enjoy teaching, my supportive colleagues, and our irreplaceable middle school students, yet only this love, standing in the background, makes it possible for me to give my heart and soul to my profession. Although many do not know how it colors my personality, how each interaction is framed by it, this love lives in the essence of my identity. Even the music I listen to is shaped by my desire to hear of that idealized love. Country music often captures the combination of praise and worship, adoration and devotion of which I speak.

> You give me hope; you give me reason,
> You give me something to believe in,
> Forever, faithfully.
> Your love amazes me.[1]

Paradox

My heart is thus ensnared by my intimate relationships with God and my wife. In fact, John Berry's song, quoted above, was the one Lexanne and I chose for our wedding. When I sing "Your Love Amazes Me," I celebrate both God's love and hers at once. As Quakers, we believe in "that of God

[1] "Your Love Amazes Me," the song written by Amanda R. Hunt and Charles Harmon Jones, is sung by John Berry on the release *John Berry* (BMI work # 1807680).

in each person," so when I told her early in our dating that I have to prioritize my love for the Divine over my human love for her, she laughed: "It's the same love." Lexanne uncovered in this comment the most fundamental of paradoxes which frame my life—that sexuality and spirituality, that divine and human love are all integral to my essence and cannot be separated within me. My wife understands that my faith life is an integral part of my love for her, not something that competes for my time and affection. We both believe that if I were not a person of faith, I could not love her as unconditionally as I do.

This paradox or tension between my sexuality and my spirituality enriches both. Feeling, believing, or being two things, instead of either one or the other, continues to be enlightening. As a bisexual, this has played out in some interesting ways. I have spent much of my life asserting that I am both/and: both lesbian and straight. And yet I am always an "outsider" in both the gay community and the straight world.

Bisexuality has some intrinsic challenges, but each of these has enhanced my spiritual maturity. My refusal to choose between dating a man or woman reminded me that gender is less important to me than a person's spiritual gifts. Twice I chose to marry and commit to one person, and one gender. By embracing such a commitment, knowing that it expresses only part of myself, I have matured. Committing to a single choice is humbling. It helped me find the benefits and accept the losses involved in other dichotomous decisions. Externally, I have been constantly confronted with assumptions by others that I am gay or straight, depending upon the community and the situation. As a result, I have matured in my ability to observe others without assuming that what I am seeing in the moment is the only expression of their nature. I sometimes stand up and say, "I know this goes against everything I've said before, but now I think differently!" This would have been embarrassing in the past, but I have learned to be unashamed of my contradictions and changes. What a relief not to have to pretend to be a perfectly unified personality! The fluid nature of my sexuality thus develops my spiritual maturity.

On an even deeper level, my bisexuality enhances my delightful communion with God, and I am a better lover of people because of my spiritual journey. When I accept God's love of my contradictory parts, I learn to accept the contradictions in others. I become less frustrated when people are inconsistent or change their minds or hearts. I can accept their incongruous desires, even when logic tells me they are irreconcilable. I recognize their expressions as different parts of themselves and accept that both are sincere. Similarly, my appreciation of God's forgiveness of my errors and my indecision teaches me to forgive others and love them less conditionally. The complexities of my spiritual journey have matured my self-love, which has made it easier for me to love others.

Ultimately, though, my bisexuality taught me to find a new integrated truth out of apparent paradox, to create intimately honest community, and to find unconditional love. This can be illustrated by an example. Years ago I was not invited to a baby shower for a lesbian couple because I was married to a man, though I was a participant in the community's sexual minorities group. I called the couple hosting the shower, then the parents-to-be, and, finally, the couple who had sent out the invitations, to confront the omission. My efforts were met as an opportunity for honest exploration of my desire to be identified as a sexual minority with the others. The outcome was that I was accepted. And, when bisexual women were included in this community, some of our old hurts from previous rejections by lesbians were healed. Finally, we were not required to "prove" we belonged by choosing or pretending to be lesbian. Later, a transgender person let me know that my assertiveness made the community safe enough for him to come out and expect to be included too. From that point, our community worked on making our gatherings safe for all of the sexual minorities, and our ability to love unconditionally increased.

I gradually applied this experience to other forms of community. Time after time intimate inclusion occurred in response to my honesty and my request to be included "as is." I, and others, learned that there is no need to emphasize nor fix natural differences; that we all still have a God-given place in community.

Claiming My Own Paradoxical Nature

With that lesson, I learned to claim other both/ands. I am both introverted and bold, both poor and rich, both religious and tolerant. Why try to separate any of these, even if some find them inconsistent? Instead, I embrace these apparent paradoxes, which have led to several of the enlightening experiences in my spiritual life. For example, I had worked in my adolescence to become invisible, because of being introverted, but then learned that I needed to be bold to get what I wanted. Though some people know me as an introvert, others laugh when they hear me described that way, for they have seen me be bold. Am I introverted or bold? I delight in being both my naturally shy self when I can, and also the shamelessly bold version when I must. I am also both poor and rich. When Lexanne first met me, she knew how little I earned, how often I did not have the cash to pay for needed services such as gardening. She even asked her housemate whether I could live with them if I lost my house. Her perspective has changed: I own our home, have relatives to lend us money when needed and have had the advantages of a good education. I am rich (in assets) and poor (in income); we accept them both as true. It is a spiritual gift to be in the midst of worry about this month's bills and still feel rich!

None of my life's paradoxes confronted me as strikingly as the way the world changed in January of 1982. It was then that I enjoyed the amazing experience of birthing a human being—my perfect-looking child with her tiny fingers and toes—even as she died in my arms moments after birth. When I recognized that she was both perfect and imperfect, and understood that there was no conflict between these, I saw how life and death were a single whole. I also came to appreciate each aspect of living as something she would never have. From then on, the colors of a sunset would stun me with their palette and bring me to tears. The world had changed, become more vividly sensuous. My ability to embrace this incongruity may well have been precipitated by my experience of paradox in my own nature, that of being straight and gay, and understanding them to be a single reality within me.

Paradox as a Spiritual Discipline

This moment, when I learned to hold the full cycle of life and death, began my conscious spiritual journey. The first thing my husband had done when our daughter died was to turn to his religion, but I had no such support system. My husband was a Zen Buddhist priest and an active Quaker in the Religious Society of Friends, and I had often worried that his deep faith would separate us, because I was not a person of faith. I had heard him say that life and death were a single whole, but I had not understood it until now. Now that I understood that truth, I was ready to find what other truths religion might offer me, and I began actively attending Quaker Meeting. I began as a curious seeker, feeling safe in the silent worship, grateful that I did not need to embrace any creed. As I became more involved in this supportive community, I gradually grew in my ability to resolve other spiritual dilemmas by finding a new level of truth that embraced both of two paradoxical experiences. The discipline of embracing two contradictory feelings or thoughts became a spiritual practice.

I did not believe, for example, that I could accept my disability as a gift as well as a burden. I have Charcot-Marie-Tooth syndrome, a hereditary disease with muscular atrophy, whose burden often feels unfair. However, in a moment of insight, I transformed my complaints on managing life as a disabled person into a litany about how God permeates my life. I now associate some sort of prayer with each of the acts of self-care that have become a sometimes burdensome habit. Both disability and prayer permeate my life, each supporting the other.

My litany: I wake up and immediately put on my support stockings. *Dear God: thank you for supporting my work and efforts this day, in each moment from waking to sleep. Give me the energy this day to do my share of your work.* I take the first batch of my round-the-clock medication. *Dear God, give me the freedom from distractions and energy drains—whether they be pain and fatigue or more mundane clutter in my life. I live to do your will.* Then I feed the dogs and let them out—the dogs that are being trained as service dogs, to protect and fetch things for me. *Thank you God for surrounding me with companions, human as well as canine, to extend your help and protection in my times of need. Allow me to serve their needs too.* I swim, the one form of exercise I can get. *Thank you for the strengths and miracles of the human body.* I revel in the movement, the flow of the breath, the sensation of the water. I stretch some. *Dear God, keep me flexible this day. And help me keep my sense of humor too; I know I'll need it.* I shower using a seat and bar so that I do not fall. *Cleanse me of my fretting about the past and future, wash away my sins and refresh me to face the present; this I cannot do safely without your support, but with it I have no need to fear falling/failing.* I go to school to teach, doing the work I am called to in the way that I can, with accommodations.

Thank you for providing me with the means to perform such a satisfying vocation; guide me as I do this challenging work. Thank you for the flow of creativity that makes the work come joyfully alive and gives rather than drains energy. God, please give me the ability to be fully present to and supportive of each student's needs. I return home to nap for two hours, to replenish my energy, reduce the pain. *Dear God renew me. Help me awaken ready to experience life fully, with new eyes and new ears, fully alive. Thank you for all the comforts that make this easier.*

For the most part, even my volunteer work comes to me or is done by phone, as are friendships, and so on. *Thank you for a loving community that comes to the inviting home provided me. I am grateful for the opportunity to serve and commune easily, in my own home.* If I have complaints about recent expenses in maintaining the home and modifying it (ramps and railings), this too turns into prayer. *Thank you, God, for providing all that is needed, even though I do not earn it.* Once a week I see either my massage/Jin Shin Do specialist or my osteopath. I sense Christ's healing touch flowing through these healers. *Keep me present and receptive to the renewal.* I have an electric toothbrush to deal with my loss of small motor control; Lex does my toenails, fingernails, cooks, and shops and does laundry and housekeeping and all the rest. *Allow us both to experience these services as loving pampering rather than burdensome dependence.*

There is very little about my life that is not affected by the disability. There is very little of my life that is done without being shaped by the awareness of the presence of God. Now all I have to do is remember to pray at each of these moments. *Dear God, remind me, forgive my lapses and remind me again.*

Outsiders' Special Place in God's Community

Each experience of holding paradox prepares me better to embrace the incongruities I find in other situations. This is confirmed by the paradox in the Christian Bible that the outsider (or "the last") is described as being the first in God's reign. The poor, the tax collectors, the widows, and the prostitutes were often the ones to experience Christ most directly in the Gospels. The ability of outsiders to experience directly the God we Christians hold dear seems to have been aided by being different, an outsider to mainstream society. There are numerous examples in the Bible. The first true evangelist may have been a Samaritan woman, a foreigner ostracized as unclean by the Jewish community of which Jesus was part. She and other social outcasts had a special place in Jesus' ministry.

Another example occurs in Luke 23:35–43, where a criminal on the cross recognizes Jesus as the Messiah, while some watch passively and others mock Christ with sour wine and a chorus of taunts. The criminal rebukes the others for their derision of Jesus. The passage ends with Jesus telling the criminal that the criminal will be today in a paradise, called Eden, the "place of the blessed."

Sometimes I perceive God's presence just as the criminal did, reassured, sure enough to rebuke the nonbeliever and be free of fear. This awareness of God-in-the-world has allowed me to experience healing love and has freed me from suffering and fear of my mortality. Likewise, the experience of recognizing that Jesus was there with him made the criminal's faith great enough. How can we recognize when Jesus is at our side? Recognition of Jesus comes from the "being with" experience, such as Jesus being in the same place as the criminal on the cross. "Being with" is not experienced in the crowd of conformers.

Conforming usually means giving up one's separate identity. It creates a crowd which seems homogeneous, but which has simply hidden its differences. My middle school students remind me of the danger in this. They often struggle with their desire to belong by pretending to be something they think is more acceptable. Yet they understand that they are not known for themselves. They fear their fraudulent personality will be pierced and they will not be liked. We all want to be appreciated for our real selves. If we keep those selves hidden, then there can be no true intimacy, and there is no real community. The acceptance of my own differences tune me in to the diversity that others may choose to ignore and allow me to enter the experience of "being with."

In fact, there are ways that I experience the presence of "that of Christ within" those around me particularly clearly when I am an "outsider," subject to taunts or physical pain. Separation, victimization, and suffering are not to be glorified, but in our fear we need God the most, and hence that is where we often recognize God best. I know that this is true for me. Alienation and crises sometimes facilitate mystical experiences for me, and it is there that I, as Jesus promises, come to dwell in a place where there is no fear of suffering and death. One such crisis occurred in 1989.

God's Presence during Crisis

Each year, I set themes for myself. Although I do not always know where I may be led, I keep them in mind and I am often surprised by how much they have influenced my year. My themes for 1989 included emotional integrity—bringing feelings to consciousness, and living with them honestly. That spring I noticed my many emotions, some that I did not like. After the end of a ten-year marriage I was experiencing dating as if for the first time, unhazed by alcohol. I felt foolish, like a giddy teenager. I was more open about my bisexuality and my expectation that I be included in the community of sexual minorities in our Quaker Meeting.

After years of persistence, bisexuals (and even straight people) had been accepted into this community. It had been such an effort to be included when I was in a heterosexual marriage. My bisexual identity was challenged both by those who thought I was denying my lesbian nature and by those who thought I should deny it. One lesbian had even suggested that "you people find your own gathering," separate from the gay and lesbian Quakers of our region. And, just as bisexuals were being fully integrated into the sexual minority community, our general Quaker Meeting became clear that it would embrace sexual minorities. Having felt outside of both communities—gay and straight—for years, I finally found myself a treasured member of them both. This turn of events enabled me to rely on the members of my community when the big crisis came.

After a routine pelvic exam turned up a "lump" on my ovary, fear gripped my heart and body, the fear of death as I faced surgery and anticipated the news of whether or not I had cancer.

Remaining true to my theme for the year, I stayed present to the fear, not running or hiding from it. "Yes, fear: I know you." I came to recognize my posture of fear, the way that I would cross my legs and hunch with my arms across my body, one hand over my mouth. I would find myself in that position during silent Quaker worship, then slowly uncross my legs and arms, straighten up, hands in my lap again, and reopen my heart to God.

And, soon, I would find myself in that posture again. During worship called specifically to support me on the day before my surgery, I stayed centered in an open posture and realized that I had released the fear—I had found the other side of it. I had learned to be fully present to fear, to embrace and know it, then completely release it. I felt blessed, in a state of grace.

I felt blessedly surrounded by God in the form of these Friends. That presence continued as I experienced the miraculous sense of God's love flowing through the care that these faithful people gave me during my recovery. This gift of community flowed in part from my experience of having been an outsider and now feeling included in community. Two surgeries and some healing time later I was cured of cancer. It was the healing of my fear, however, that changed the details of my life. I remained true (in less dramatic ways) to my theme of being present to my emotions. I felt more appreciative of every aspect of human experience—my senses were filled with awareness, attending to details that had passed unnoticed before. Each day was a symphony of praise for life, as I poured forth appreciation for all of creation, especially for the minutiae of human senses.

Once again, colors were more vivid, the scents more intense, the movement of air less subtle, and the depth in the textures of my life's tapestry were more remarkable. My sexuality was particularly awakened, and I risked taking a lover whom I knew to be unlikely to commit. Again, my spirituality and sexuality were intertwined. I could not hold back expressing my joy of life!

My perspective on life was radically changed. Having been through my fear of death, I was now able to accept my mortality. To know that we are to die one day may be a simple matter, but to believe it in our hearts and incorporate this knowing into our living is quite another matter. Our society fights death with our denial, our caution, and our interventions of medicine. Now my spirit called out, "Do not run fearfully from death, but surrender to life!" When I became mortal in my heart, I stopped running instinctively from the reality of death. In accepting my mortality, I overcame my fear-bred caution. I even began to suspect that when my time came, that moment of death would finally fulfill my yearning, my longing for wholeness and reunion with God. As I surrendered to life, I learned to live in the present rather than postpone experiences that could be eliminated by my death. Life-threatening cancer taught me to be fearless and embrace life. For the second time I learned to hold life and death together as one. My dependence bred freedom; my fear generated enthusiasm; and the threat of death taught me to live fully. The paradoxes confronted me and once again proved to be a seamless whole.

Paradox Lost

A new, unbroken perspective is gradually replacing my experiences of paradox. Inconsistencies that used to be dilemmas are now merely opportunities to integrate oppositions into my approach to the world. I am a different person, less confused though not necessarily more congruous. What living do I embrace now? It is the living of an authentic life. I am willing to risk being my true self instead of taking the safe path. I intend to be wakefully alive: body and mind, heart and soul. Released from fear of death or hurts, I have found freedom from overcautious, limited living. I am willing to be "out" in every way. I am open about my bisexuality, but also about my disability, why I do not drink (alcoholism), and what I believe about God, money, and politics. It is easy as a bisexual to deny either one or the other part of myself depending on the dictates of apparent social safety. Instead, I am true to my inner identity. I choose a measured risk in life or love; I live more fully. I have received the gift of being fully present to my emotions, even fears, and releasing them: the gift of being emotionally alive. I have received the further gift of accepting my mortality, which causes me to be more fully alive in other ways too, fearlessly appreciative of my sensations, emotions, and thoughtful awareness. I make different choices now.

What are the new choices? In community, I am willing to risk loving and losing—the fear of the pain of endings is no longer the deciding factor. I give my love to people unlikely to stay around, those unwilling to commit or those with AIDS whose life expectancy is short. I am learning to manifest the same presence to others that I have now experienced in my faith community. I choose to be with them in their suffering, as others were with me in my fear and physical pain. There is no reason to hold back, giving up the best of present life to avoid the future loss of a relationship or present vicarious hurt of a friend in pain. I can risk speaking my truth, even when I suspect I will be a public fool for it. I can face embarrassment as I have faced my fear of death, and I wade into the midst of life instead of observing from the sidelines.

One of the ways that I live my fearlessness is my willingness for my whole self to be known. I am married to a woman, and sometimes confront the assumption that I am a lesbian, just as I confronted the assumption when I was married to a man that I was straight. My insistence on being known creates the foundation for true intimacy.

Being a bisexual enhances my faith life in many ways: by teaching me about finding truth in seeming paradox, about intimately honest community, about finding unconditional love, about authenticity, and about other aspects of God's presence in the world. We can, whether bisexual or not, learn to identify and embrace the paradoxes in our nature, in our lives, and in God's created world. We can, whatever our "differences," insist on being included in our communities of choice, our communities of faith. We can, whether our secrets are about our sexuality or something else, insist on an intimate honesty within our community. We can, whatever our own insider/outsider status, serve the world by being present to the suffering of outsiders, even when we risk our hearts. We can take all these risks and experience that of God in the world. We can embrace the joyous chorus: "Your love amazes me." In doing so we invite the possibility of unconditional love. Then we dwell, however temporarily, in that place where there is no suffering or fear: in heaven.

A Bisexual Feminist Spirituality

BARBARA GIBSON

I AM LOOKING FOR THE STRAND of bisexuality in the woven cloth of my faith. In examining my spirituality, I can see the strands of my childhood religion, of my critical and analytical training, of my life as a poet and playwright, of my history as a radical activist. My bisexuality, which I have recognized for at least thirty years, has been a major part of my life experience, as has spirituality. I know they are tied together.

I have longed to be able to claim a single, specific identity for my sexuality and my spirituality. It is confusing and awkward, at times, to be bisexual. I have wanted to be a full-blown lesbian; I have tried for that. But it is not my inner reality. In a similar way, I have wanted to identify with a particular religious tradition, but it is also not my inner reality or my experience. For whatever reasons, I am destined to be bisexual and ambispiritual. When I embrace that identity fully, I feel joyful and free.

A Spiritual and Ideological History

Does it need to be said that I grew up heterosexual? That was my reality and my conscious orientation, though after I came out, I remember many times when I was attracted to other girls or women. Before, during, and after my twenty-year marriage, sexuality was of major interest to me, and though I was drawn to men, I knew that I was open to a lesbian experience—if only a lesbian would approach me. I had a distorted notion of how woman-to-woman love might come about: I was waiting to be seduced. I had no sexual politics, no sense of the underlying power relationships that inform all prefeminist sexuality.

In 1969, when I was almost forty, I encountered feminism as a movement and a theory. As a result of my first consciousness-raising group experience, I saw that my lifelong resentful envy of men had social and political, not just psychological, roots. I learned about the system of patriarchy, the aim of which was to keep women subordinate and to use them sexually, economically, politically, and socially, and to endow men, especially those of the white upper class, with those kinds of power.

This changed everything for me: I left my marriage, got fired from my job at the university, and took up with a young male lover. Equally important was what changed inside my head: I awakened to an awareness of the deep connections with women which I had denied or ignored. I became aware of my emotional and sexual attractions to women and began to define myself as bisexual.

My spirituality was developing on a parallel track, but less dramatically. After a childhood of attending church and Sunday school at the First Presbyterian Church of Normal, Illinois, I rebelled against what I saw as the weak theology and political hypocrisy of that church community. College and graduate school shaped me into a somewhat arrogant, skeptical atheist. Still, I was fascinated with Zen Buddhism, which I studied in the academic works of D. T. Suzuki and the novels of Jack Kerouac. I found a psychological depth and philosophic complexity lacking in the Christianity I had known.

I had an equal interest in the existentialists, some of whom, like Kierkegaard, had a religious perspective. Sartre, Camus, Kafka, and Dostoyevsky offered a brutal honesty about suffering and the human condition, which sounded rather like the Christian doctrine of original sin. Sartre posed the challenge to humanity of taking the risk to make meaning out of nothing, to create value where no value is given. This appealed to me; it required courage and creativity.

I see now that my own quest for value had roots in a worldview that came from my Protestant background. I valued kindness and compassion for those "less fortunate than ourselves." I had a vision, even after all the years of skepticism, of the kingdom of God on earth. For a few years I tried to embody that vision in a secular form, under the banner of Marxist humanism. My years of radical activism in civil rights, anti-war movements, student freedom movements, feminism, and gay rights—all these were founded on the biblical values of "do unto others" and "love your neighbor as yourself."

I wanted the ethics of my Judeo-Christian heritage without the dogma and the history of oppression that Christianity has perpetrated. I studied

Tibetan Buddhism, a study and practice that are still important to me. I encountered women's spirituality through the works of Z. Budapest and Starhawk, where I met a female divinity and a practice centered in the earth: the change of seasons, phases of the moon, and the inherent sacredness of all beings. At last, in the early 1980s, I rediscovered what I see as the authentic Christian tradition in the work of Christian feminists and the Creation Spirituality movement of Matthew Fox. Creation Spirituality integrates what I hold as the truest teachings of Christianity—the core wisdom of liberation and compassion—and includes ecology, feminism, new science, and the arts.

I choose to use the term *spirituality,* because it is universal, while *religion* tends to be parochial and insular. The kind of spirituality that interests me is based on a partnership relationship between men and women, rather than a dominator model, in Riane Eisler's terms. It does not make judgments about people's worth. It is open to all regardless of race, class, nationality, language, and certainly regardless of sexual orientation. All would be welcome because all would contribute from their own experience, their own values, and their own religious traditions.

I cannot identify as a Christian, because I am horrified by what churches and imperial Christian rulers and armies have done to native people, to women, to homosexuals and bisexuals, to people of other faiths, and to the planet. Identifying as a Buddhist, for a Western person, is somewhat more acceptable, because their history is not in our face. But Buddhists have committed historical atrocities, and Buddhism still treats women and people of alternative sexual orientation as an inferior class, though this is changing. It seems that all religious traditions are tainted by their connections with political power and with dogmatism and fanaticism.

The kinds of spirituality that attract me, on the other hand, follow the mystical and justice teachings within each religion: the core teachings of Jesus (along with mystics like Hildegard of Bingen and Meister Eckhart), the theory and practice of "engaged Buddhism," some of the ritual practices and the ethical tradition of Judaism, and the dances and poetry of the Islamic Sufi tradition. Along with others in the Creation Spirituality community and elsewhere, I am creating a spiritual life that is expansive, inclusive, and relevant to the postmodern age, yet firmly rooted in tradition.

The Feminist Bisexual Dimension

Any authentic spirituality, to me, must be feminist, meaning that it honors women as full partners with men, and that it honors, in some form, a female divinity. Parts of that ideal exist in traditional religions. Judaism includes the powerful female divinities Sophia or Hokmah (the Lady Wisdom figure of the Hebrew Testament) and the Shekinah (the immanent and feminine aspect of God). Mother Mary is the comforting, accessible "goddess" of Christianity. Buddhism has its Tara figures, and the Mother of All Buddhas, Prajnaparamita.

A feminist spirituality must provide an alternative to patriarchal language, liturgies, and teachings. It must include a strong commitment to social justice and peace. The sayings and acts of Jesus, with a few exceptions, meet these standards. The Buddha, too, taught that every human being is precious and has enlightened mind and heart, though these qualities are hidden by ignorance and greed. Everyone is capable of reaching full liberation, no matter what caste, class, or gender.

A feminist bisexual consciousness contributes the spirit and practice of inclusiveness to spirituality and religion. As a bisexual woman, I know about connection and about alienation. I know about inclusion and exclusion. I have experienced all these states because of my sexual identity. I have connected deeply, sexually and spiritually, with both women and men. And I have been alienated from women, because of my bisexuality; I was rejected for being with a man by some lesbians who had been my friends. I have been ignored or scorned by heterosexuals because of my love for women. Having seen firsthand the suffering caused by exclusion, self-righteousness, and ignorance, I want to work for a world and for a spirituality that will be different. I believe that bisexuals have a special role to play in helping create a spirituality which will be available to all people.

I believe that as feminist bisexuals, we have an understanding of what bridging and connecting are about. We have faced intolerance and ignorance from heterosexuals, lesbians, and gay men, and we have suffered internalized oppression from other bisexuals. Yet we have persisted in affirming our identity as lovers of both women and men. We know how to be part of more than one world. We may be more at home in the lesbian or gay world, or we may be more comfortable among heterosexuals, but we are part of both.

Engaging with Men

As a feminist, I have struggled over the years with the question of how to relate to men. I knew that I was attracted to men, that I fell in love with them, that I admired and respected certain men. And yet I didn't much like them as a gender. Men make war, men rape, men abuse women and children, men commit the vast majority of crimes, men run the governments and the mega-corporations that rule the world. It seems that men, through the institutions of patriarchy, had made a mess of things. What, then, could be spiritually significant about them?

I believe that a feminist bisexual spirituality recognizes that the differences and similarities between women and men are sacred, part of the way the universe works. We honor the fact that men are necessary to life; obviously, their sperm is crucial to conception. Even if that biological donation was the only contribution they made (and it sometimes is), it is vital to include men in any universal spirituality. Men are part of the whole. None of us would be here without male energy, male reality. Men are part of the sacred pattern.

Speaking from an archetypal standpoint, I believe that men have a mythical importance, a spiritual role to play. I hold that in the deepest reaches of human wisdom men provide the generative spirit, the spark that starts the fire. Women tend the fire, feed it and use it, but men bring the original flame, the creative moment, the lightning bolt that gets life going.

Too many men, however, are afflicted by the dread "testosterone poisoning," a disease that makes them seem lost in competitiveness and aggression at the worst, and insensitivity and emotional backwardness at the least. And yet I know many "good men"; I was married to one, and I have loved others, respected others, learned from others. Are these men simply an exception to the rule? Perhaps we are creating an enclave of acceptable men, men we consider "different," men who have earned the right to be our friends, mentors, comrades, lovers, and husbands, the fathers of our children, our sons. These "good men" contrast vividly with our common experience of men as dominators, abusers, rapists.

Can we conceive of a spirituality that honors male energy and the essence of maleness without endorsing the horrors of patriarchal oppression that men still benefit from, perpetuate, and use? We have to! We are on a path, looking for and creating a spirituality that unites women and men in a partnership that will literally save our lives and the life of the planet. We must pay attention to the positives: our interactions with the many caring, courageously different, principled men around us. And we must consciously make the leap between our own juicy, complex experiences of love and respect for men and for women, and the spiritual vision that is calling to us.

When Sex and Spirit Connect

It is precisely our unique sexuality that has the potential to make a spiritual contribution. Love-making with women or with men, under the right conditions, for me is a spiritual experience. Although lovemaking can be boring, ordinary, and bland, lustful or romantic, dutiful or angry, deeply intimate or distant, at its best sex stirs up in me a connection not only with my partner but with Spirit, the universe, reality—with the All.

There are some sexual differences in making love with a woman or with a man, but they are not significant to me. The spiritual differences, however, illustrate something about bisexuality that is precious and special. Making love with a woman, for me, implies a spiritual connection that is not always, or usually, acknowledged. Whether we like it or not, whether we know it consciously or not, we are of the same tribe. This tribal connection is spiritual, bigger than any of us.

Our commonality shows itself both in real life and in archetypes. Women have a common task on earth: to create and preserve life. We don't necessarily have to bear children to give birth. It is the metaphor for our deep intrinsic connection with bodies, with the earth, the seasons, with change, with creation. That can translate as having children, writing poetry, community organizing, cooking, scientific invention, political activism, church leadership, counseling, health care, or any of the innumerable ways that we bring something new to life.

I believe that women know, in a deep part of their bodies and their souls, that we are on the planet, alive at this time, placed in these circumstances to care for life—to nurture ourselves, children, the earth, all of creation.

I see this as a collective enterprise. No woman does this work alone. We are not martyrs; we cannot change the world by ourselves. We do what we can. We connect with other women, and I believe it is a spiritual connection. We are indeed sisters, which doesn't always mean being close or liking each other. It does mean recognizing and sharing a certain sameness, an understanding of each other on a gut level and on a heart level. The more we are conscious of this connection, the more we can nurture it—for the benefit of all.

Our connections with men are equally powerful in a different way. Men, at their best, have a new energy to bring to our lives. When I am exclusively with women for a time, I forget about the importance and the joy of male energy. When I encounter it again, I am delighted by how seriously men take ideas, how beautifully they can argue a point, how earnest they are about being right. This quality can be useful in our world, when it is not exaggerated. I appreciate men's objectivity, how they can separate their personal interests and look at a question from a more universal point of view. Men, in my observation, can cooperate with others to carry out a task; they like to achieve; they are productive. Men make a difference in the world, and they take risks. Men stay centered and focused on the matter at hand. They can make sacrifices of their own self-interest to serve the greater good; they can be excellent protectors. They show, too, the strength of independence and of beneficent power. There is much to learn from men.

Of course many women have these qualities too. Again, I am generalizing, trying to see what ideal maleness is, not trying to describe individual men. I want to define the positive qualities that seem to me most archetypally male. We need to know how we can connect with men in a way that helps the planet most, that is most life-sustaining.

We also need to recognize what men are good for, and we need to be honest about why we like men, why we are attracted to them sexually, why we fall in love with them. We don't need to be apologetic about being with men, as I have been in the past. To deny men's goodness is to deny our own sanity and our own goodness, our honest capacity for love.

Women connect with men spiritually, and we need to do that more deeply. The patriarchal religions have sanctioned men's oppressiveness to women, and this chapter is not over yet. Much religious language is still sexist; creeds and theologies still define women as subordinate; institutional religious practices seriously discriminate against women and gay, lesbian, and bisexual people. In the Jewish and Christian traditions, at their worst, women are blamed for everything! How can we overcome this ages-long habit of oppression?

We must continue to critique the religious traditions and to protest when churches and synagogues refuse to acknowledge women as complete and equal members. Women who have stayed within the traditional religions will keep on protesting sexist language, the refusal to ordain women, the preaching of subordination of women in marriage, the discrimination against lesbians and gays that prevails in so many churches and synagogues in America, the rules against self-determination for women in matters of reproductive rights, and the theology of fall and redemption, in which Eve (and by extension all women) is blamed for original sin.

This is a big job; it's no wonder that so many feminists have no interest in organized religion!

For those of us who follow a spiritual or religious path, we must acknowledge that women and men need each other to bring healing to the planet, and peace and justice to the human world. This is a spiritual task, as well as an ideological, economic, political, and cultural one. We don't know if it is possible, but I believe we must work and struggle as if we can succeed. It is our only chance, and our only way of being human, of being hopeful, of keeping the faith, of honoring Spirit. Women cannot do this alone because men are part of the whole; they are members of the dance. Men and women don't need to be sexual partners to make this work—though it can help to be deeply connected in that way. In any case, we do need to be partners in acceptance and understanding.

A Critical Role for Bisexual Women

Bisexual women are in a sensitive and positive position; we have opportunities to make the needed alliances with men and with other women. We can bridge the gaps. In our sexual and social relationships with men and with women, we can bring Spirit to our times together. Spirit is with us, I believe, in every loving and equal sexual encounter. Keeping that awareness with us when we are with men helps us connect with them in a spiritual way, even if we don't talk about it directly. When we love men, when we make love with them, we know they are not the enemy. We know, in fact, that they are needed and valued allies. When we love women we know they are of our tribe. Connection is the key to healing.

Bisexuality informed by feminism unites rather than divides. We are more interested in looking for similarities than in arguing about differences or posing opposites. Our spiritual task as bisexual women is to participate in the creation and extension of the wisdom and compassion movements that provide the freest range for expression of diverse personalities, sexualities, identities. Our role is to honor women and men, while opposing patriarchy, racism, and all forms of oppression. This is our only chance of contributing toward saving this precious existence we have been given. We want to discover and enhance what it is to be truly human, truly mammal, and truly spiritual, on this lovely, and fragile, planet.

A Life of Passion and Compassion

Valerie Tobin

Divinity moves us, handing us body over body into rapture that dissipates into a resonant peace . . . *a moment of sexual union with another woman*. In a hostile world, it is an act of continual re-creation, as though a new life is engendered through our joining, something stronger than ourselves.

Years ago I did not believe that I could feel this power with any man, so I called myself a lesbian. Perhaps, at the time, I could not. I would have been, I suspect, unable to see beyond the artifice of gender to the soul beneath. And isn't this the ultimate faith that is love, to see the spirit within flesh?

Though I was supportive of my bisexual friends, and the woman who became a lover for quite some time, I never considered myself bisexual. I lived a rigid and disciplined life. I was afraid of the lack of boundaries. And though a sexual desire for men slipped in at moments during these years, I would not acknowledge it. I told myself that the work of unveiling our true selves would not be worth the paltry amount of sexual satisfaction I might have found. That deeper emotion might have developed never occurred to me. The home of my spirit was with women. I could not conceive then of exposing myself to a man's expectations of my gender, nor could I envision giving up the love I have for women to be with a man.

Then the dreams began. Erotic and uninvited missives where I was making love to men.

I have always believed that sex, at its finest, is a divine act. We unite, not only with another person but with the elements that continue life, that make the times of doubt and anxiety worth enduring. Sexual union allows us to offer one of the richest pleasures to another person.

When I first felt that withering of isolation through the body of a man, felt the lust rear up and insist that I absolve the rules I had created in times of doubt, I knew that I would never see myself as the same woman. My identity as bisexual did not congeal until I loved him, then left him, then made the realization that I was allowing the decisions of a confused world to become my own. This was the faith that I had to hold: there is something stronger than law and custom. I recognized that something exists independent of the categories we create to describe it. I had never had religion, but I began to have faith. It was simply the trust that over this paradigmless chasm, there would be shelter.

Where was my spiritual home? I had few male friends. Men were from a culture foreign to my own. They were creatures I did not understand and had no wish to. While I had always believed that gender roles inhibit all who fall under their province, I was remarkably disinterested in the experience of men.

Yet to embrace my most true nature, I saw that I had to allow men into my sacred realm. Men are raised with expectations, rules, and beliefs that are different from my own, and which are based on the submission of women to their own neat set of priorities. Like the opposing camps of heterosexual and homosexual, the categories of female and male cease to have relevance unless both parties occupy their appropriate positions. Trusting that I could maintain my self while loving someone who had grown up in a world supporting his will over my own has been a leap into a belief in the ultimate good in the heart of human beings.

When one construct cracks, the others built on it begin to collapse. The architecture of our social roles crumbles as we begin to reveal the assumptions that undergird our values.

Religion sets up a construct of ethics. The Bible holds eloquent morality tales. By many interpretations, the life I live is antithetical to the wisdom presumed in its pages. Where do I turn for guidance now that I have trespassed into unmarked territory? Every day I re-create faith and wisdom. There are less visible rewards for this than there are for living as society dictates. With this choice I trade material security for spiritual maturation. A life without questioning would be a living death; for me this would be the ultimate blasphemy.

I have been a midwife and caught a dead infant, still warm from the body of its mother, in my own hands. Each life is a blessing. A resigned person is a heretic.

I was born a religious bastard. My mother renounced her bonds to Catholicism and my father was an atheist and a Jew. They refused to raise me within a doctrine because in all of their options they saw the reinforcement of misogyny cloaked as divinity. My brother and I could choose our faiths. But the wellspring of ignorance offered nothing from which to choose.

My most intimate life has always existed at the periphery of two worlds: Catholic and Jewish, heterosexual and homosexual. I have matured within the strange spaces where they connect, the gray area between the relevant spheres. Being an outsider, however, has offered me the objectivity of the dispossessed. In religion I see the struggle to define the infinite with only limited faculties at our disposal. I have yet to find a single theology which unifies this dissonance. So I borrow, trespass, and explore. I observe the pivotal to define the essential. What I do have is the will to embrace what I did not conceive. We are inextricably tied to a wisdom we will never penetrate. There is an omnipotence that unites us, whether we name it soul, genetics, God/dess, or chi.

To admit that I had this capacity for love and desire regardless of a gendered body required that I surrender my egocentric belief that I could comfortably mold an ordered existence. My challenge was to find comfort within chaos. Standing between worlds has always been a sacred place. Those of us who do it, in return for our faith, see the unfolding of love unbounded. We have composure amid other's confusion.

My final faith is that I am capable of facing a disapproving, sometimes dangerous, world. I act on my own authority, but I believe that I am advised by a greater will. If I did not, I could not face the challenges that inevitably come to anyone with some magnitude of emotion. To live a life of passion and compassion is a prayer of thanks to the force that brought us to be. Sacrificing one's will to custom violates the gifts of intelligence and emotion. Wrestling with this finite existence is the quality we call life in all its variations.

I have married myself to the conviction that life is only worth living if I can support my deepest desires to create love. Life is brought to be in these moments and is sustained by the connections we have with others. Divinity exists in this promise. Faith rises in my bed when I make love without reservation. It supports me each time I expose my sexual/emotional identity. Ultimately, I believe that I am truly blessed to be able to reach the depths of passion regardless of the gender of my lover. It has offered me the riches of that devotion, as well as a unique peace in the chaos in which we must all find stability.

PART 3

Wrestling with Spirit: Who Defines Holiness?

Untitled

Susan Halcomb Craig

There is no longer Jew or Greek, there is no longer slave or free, there is no longer male and female, for all of you are one in Christ Jesus. Galatians 3:26–28

Spirit of Life,

We are your newest bridge people,
Bisexual women and men in your kingdom
at home in the middle
spanning opposite shores.
Our straight friends ask us to explain ourselves,
Our gay-lesbian friends ask us to defend our ways,
As if our place were no place,
We are pulled apart, belittled, misunderstood.

We pray for your Spirit of Unity.
Help others leave their banks of fear
and join us in our place of oneness.
Heal them from envy, denial, fear of difference,
and enable them to see us, eyes open to our beauty.

We pray for your gifts of love and understanding.

Reprinted, with permission, from *More Light Update,* a publication of More Light Presbyterians for Lesbian, Gay, Bisexual, and Transgender Concerns, PO Box 38, New Brunswick, N.J. 08903-0038.

Help us love ourselves, and the connection we embody.
Neither gay nor straight, both gay and straight.
We are One in our beings and One in you.
Help us know and own and share our gifts
for your name's sake
in your wholeness of your creation.

We pray in your unity,
one in Christ Jesus,
Amen.

If You Do Not Tell the Truth, It Will Strangle You

Gary Bowen

I am a person of Native American descent. I am also bisexual transsexual, disabled, poor, a single parent, and a lot of other things. I am a person of faith. But most important to me is being a Native American traditional dancer. I give testimony to the Creator above every time I dance. Words are simply not equal to the task. This is why Native Americans teach in silence quite a lot. It's also why Native Americans seem incapable of giving a straight answer to an honest question: we have to tell you a story.

But I'm not going to tell you a story, because I suspect that we do not know enough of one another's language for my story to have any meaning to you. Therefore I am going to explain something. Just one thing. But it's going to be a long explanation, because I want to make sure this word enters your vocabulary and that you won't forget it so the next time I want to tell a story, you will understand. I want to tell you about one piece of regalia, about one essential part of the dancer's dress, a thing so important that we wear it all the time, for the most formal and the most casual occasions. I want to tell you about the choker.

This is because you and many other people who are not Native have adopted the choker as an item of personal adornment. You do not know it, but you have endangered your life. And this is why: That necklace you are wearing will strangle you if you do not tell the truth. I see so many people walking around with their neck in a vise and they have no idea of the danger they are in. They think it is a pretty ornament, but it is so much more than that. I know you bought it at a powwow, or maybe you made it. You think something Native American is good and kind and would never ever hurt you. But I'll tell you this—Coyote has a wicked sense of humor. When your necklace strangles you, Coyote will laugh.

Take it off, take it off. See these white beads? They are made of bone. They have stories in them. They have stories in them that go back more than three thousand years. That's how long my people have been making these long, tapered, tubular beads. We made them out of shell at first, then we made them out of bone. Hold it in your hand. This is the bone of a living creature. It ran about on four legs and it ate and it slept and it gave birth and it was slaughtered. It understands death.

These beads, these tapered beads, these are the way we always made them. But in 1890 our religion, our culture, our dress, our hairstyles, our languages all were made illegal. 1890 was the year the Ghostdancers were massacred at Wounded Knee. Remember that. Remember their bodies lying on the frozen earth for three days, the wounded along with the dead. Now rattle the beads together and think how it must have sounded when the frozen bodies were tumbled into the mass grave. These things are never far from our minds, and that is why we call these beads "bones." No matter what they are made of, we call them bones. They are the bones of our dead.

Yours are plastic. This is not right. You should never make necklaces out of plastic. You must always use natural materials, materials that have come from a living creature. Shell, bone, horn—these are the things we make our bones out of today. They lived, and they died. Just as our people have died. One hundred million of our people. We are still dying. We disappear from our reservations and sometimes we are found face down in ditches, with a neat little bullet hole in the back of the head. Ask Annie Mae Aquash.

Rattle her bones in your hand and remember. Remember this too: they didn't fingerprint her body; they cut off her hands and sent them to the lab. She was buried in pieces. These could be her finger bones. Be careful not to drop them.

How many funerals have you attended? Have you attended one for each bone? There are forty bones in this necklace. That's a lot of funerals. That's a lot of dead Indians. Can you stand to be walking around with so many deaths hanging around your neck? These bones will kill you, you know. They are vengeful bones. They demand that you honor them. You must know what happened to them. You must remember.

And you must always tell it true. Because if you do not, they will strangle you to death. That is why these necklaces are called "chokers." When you see Native Americans with bones around their necks, you know that they speak the truth. You know that they are strong enough to carry the dead. They hold up their heads with pride, showing the bones they bear.

I can see that these bones are not so pretty to you now. But this lesson is far from over. This is only part of why we wear the bones. We give ourselves to the bones, and the bones protect us. Drop your bones. Oh, I'm sorry, your plastic is scratched and chipped. Here. Let me drop my bones. See? No mark. Bones are strong, and the neck is weak. The bones protect our necks from knives and fists and other attacks. The bones are armor. They aren't perfect; they won't stop a bullet. But in the day-to-day scuffles, they help us.

But they are more than armor. They are spiritual armor. These bones are haunted. They were once alive, and now their ghost is with us. It guards us from spiritual dangers. It protects us from the spirit drinkers that would consume us. Television, alcohol, despair—these are the relentless onslaught that our bones must protect against. The forces of evil never quit. They erode the mind and weaken the heart, and then the head bows. And the bones pinch, pushing it up again.

You cannot let your head hang in defeat if you wear one of these. They are too stiff, too rigid, too sharp. They are a collar that limits your freedom of movement. You can only do what is right when you wear one of these. You cannot do that which harms your spirit. If your spirit crumbles, your head falls, and the bones pinch. You must stand up straight. You must hold your head up. Pretty soon it becomes a habit, and you will never be weak again. Flip through the old photographs. Look how they stand, with chins raised. It's the bones that make them so. The bones make you lift your eyes. You must look at the sky where the eagles soar. You must look up to Creator. When you wear this necklace, you are praying. You are lifting your face to God. You don't need to speak. He can see the bones around your neck. He can see your promise. Everyone can see it. Everyone knows what you have promised. You cannot fail them. You must keep your word.

The bones are expensive. Horn, shell, bone; they cost money. The gemstones that ornament them—they cost too. The dividers and disks, the leather, the thong. It all costs money. A lot of money. You should not make cheap promises. Cheap promises are easy to break. But if you have faith in your own strength, you will spend as much as you can possibly afford. You will consider the necklace as being more important than food. You will count it as more important than shoes. You will count it more important than almost anything because it is your promise to the world.

You will make it by your own hand, because only you can know exactly what you have promised the Creator. Therefore, only you can make the necklace that is proof of your pledge. You will cut the sinew, string the beads, stitch the leather. You will design it. You will not use anything that is light, or cheap, or weak, or fake. Your promise is heavier, dearer, stronger, and truer than plastic. When you are done you will bow to the seven directions and you will offer smoke and smudge to the Creator. You will lift up your hand to the sky, and you will sing to Grandfather. Only then will you put it on, with eyes upraised, freely placing the choker around your own neck. You will give your life to the Creator. And the Creator will give your life to your people.

These then are the deeds of the people who wear the bones. At powwow, the homeless watched the cooks, not the dancers, and the woman with the bones around her neck saw them and fed them. No one is allowed to go hungry. This is what the man with the bones did: he gave up his forward place and dropped back to help a boy learn to dance. And this is what the young man with the bones did: he pushed an elder in her wheelchair to the center of the arena because she is a veteran. And this is what the judge with the bones did: she gave first prize to the dwarf girl because she had earned it. And this is what all the people with the bones did: they honored everyone for their contributions. The dwarf mother cried and the veterans removed their hats and fireworks dazzled the sky.

But this is what happened to the woman with the plastic bones: she turned invisible. She faded away and was lost on the wind.

This is the lesson of the bones: every member of your tribe is your kin. Every member of every tribe is your kin. You will not discriminate among them. Christian, traditionalist, Muslim, Jew, atheist, Buddhist—they are your people and you will bear witness for them. Black, white, brown, yellow, red; every one is your relative, and you will serve them. Gay, straight, lesbian, bisexual, transgendered, two-spirited, intersexed, every single one of them is your relation. You will defend them all.

You are not above any other person. Humans are not above any other animal. But the Creator is above us all.

This is the truth. If you do not live the truth, the bones will strangle you.

Erotic Spiritualities

LORAINE HUTCHINS

USUALLY WE LEARN AT A VERY EARLY AGE that spirituality and sexuality are opposed, that passion pulls us away from oneness with our Higher Power and that we cannot have spirituality erotically. Religions often teach us that our bodies are "temples of god" but that our desires are to be distrusted and transcended, that it is our nature to act against our best interests unless we are very, very careful—about sex in particular.

Sex is a power to be respected, a power that can hurt. But suppressing sexual vitality and expression does not honor spirit. Erotophobia, the fear of sex and the power of our bodies and life, is deeply embedded—in our culture, and in us. And, as with all healing, recognizing the problem is only the first step. Though we may see how erotophobia limits our capacity for fully loving relationships and feel the negative inhibitions developed in response to messages that sex is distracting and dangerous, incorporating healthier alternatives into our lives is much harder. How do we find or create replacements for the guilt-producing sex-negative beliefs and attitudes most of us have internalized? Especially when recent studies show that sexual dissatisfaction and dysfunction are much more common than we admit, yet kept shamefully hidden?[1]

To reclaim sexual expression and pleasure it is often necessary to create

[1] John Schwartz, "Study Uncovers High Rates of Bedroom Blues: High Rates of Sexual Dysfunction Called 'Significant' Health Concern," *The Washington Post,* February 10, 1999. This front-page story cites the February 10 edition of JAMA [*Journal of the American Medical Association*] and its report on a University of Chicago/Kinsey Institute study, the 1992 National Health and Social Life Survey, involving several thousand Americans who were a representative sample of 97 percent of the nation. The study finds that 40 percent of women and 30 percent of men suffer from sexual dysfunctions and that the rates may be underreported and even higher than this.

new images, new rituals, new experiences that enact new models of wholeness. It is a challenge to reclaim the healing worshipful beauty of sex. In our sex-negative-yet-sex-saturated culture, reclaiming the full power of our integrated sexuality means connecting body and mind and transcending the mind–body split in which most of us were schooled. Healing our mind–body split means changing how we think and feel about both spirituality and sexuality. It also means changing how we experience them. That means living our lives differently, more wholly, finding new ways to be in the world, in our bodies, as we hold spirit present. For the past few years I have helped many small groups of people to reclaim spirituality erotically and to reinfuse sexuality with a spiritual base.[2]

My most intense involvement to date was during 1996–1997, as co-leader of Sacred Flame, a group of Washington, D.C., bisexuals. In our monthly erotic rituals we hoped to contribute to the sexual healing of ourselves, our culture, and the planet. Of course we didn't accomplish all this during the year our group flourished, but we learned that the desire for sexual healing is in itself a sacrament, a desire whose flame each of us still nurtures today. You may benefit from our ideas and practices—whether you choose to apply them in the way we did or to adapt them in ways more suited to your own individual or group's needs.

This is the story of how five bisexual seekers, three women and two men, created a year-long ritual erotic journey together—educating ourselves about sacred sex traditions in various cultures and then bringing our knowledge back home. To understand this adventure, it is important to know a bit about the resources we brought with us: the established sacred sex traditions upon which we drew and against which we reacted.

Intellectual For(e)play

Popular interest in sacred sexuality represents a great hunger in the United States today. Since at least the 1960s, more than a few people have been studying the once-secret techniques and philosophies of sacred sex in order to heal the split between mind and body, between the erotic and the religious by bringing them together through new daily practices and

[2] I have done this as part of my doctoral research in cultural studies. I am focusing on the intersection of the sacred and the sexual in today's society from a queer-friendly and feminist perspective, with particular attention to those who create erotic rituals and call themselves sexual healers and sacred prostitutes.

special ritual experience. The most popular and widespread sacred sex approaches in the United States today are influenced by the Tantric and Taoist traditions of India, Tibet, and China, imported and translated for American consumption.[3] Living in a culture that promotes immediate gratification, we Americans think we can learn a life-changing approach in a weekend workshop, and we often get frustrated with a spiritual practice whose mastery requires daily devotion over years. Nonetheless, in an age when people are often stressed about both sexual performance and sexual violence, these gentle, mindful, sacred sex practices from the East have much appeal. Contemporary Tantric/Taoist practices emphasize whole-body sensuality, gently prolonged touching, breathing deeply, and visualizing oneself and one's lover as divine. In these spirit paths there are also ancient yet living traditions of female deities. The feminine, as well as the masculine, is revered and honored. In these traditions God is not only, or even supremely, "male." For bisexuals, as people attracted to both sexes, it feels quite right to hold both sexes as equally divine.

In addition to these more well known traditions, we found that there is also a variety of European, African, Middle Eastern, and Western Hemisphere earth-based religions where female deities and a more sex-positive, body-positive approach to spirituality are evident. Yet with all of these, even with those that have a more egalitarian deity model, there is almost invariably a heterosexual assumption:

> For a long time I searched for a book that exemplified the spiritual nature of sexuality between women. I have read many Tantric books, but they have all been directed towards the heterosexual experience. The reality of balancing the feminine and the masculine within one gender is never truly accepted. If it was, then the fact that this integration exists in homosexual relationships would be an equally explored avenue of Tantric sexuality.[4]

[3] "Sacred sex" is my preferred term for this discussion, and by it I mean using erotic energy with sacred intent. Another somewhat broader term that many of my colleagues use is "sex magick." Sex magick's roots are in the European occultist tradition. Although there is some overlap between the terms and practitioners, the important distinction is that sacred sex focuses on realizing divinity in oneself and one's lover(s), whereas sex magick uses erotic energy for any number of self-determined aims, focusing the power released through sex to create change in the world. Although its residual homophobia leaves something to be desired, a basic starter book for exploring sex magick is Bonnie L. Johnston and Peter L. Schuerman, *Sex, Magick, and Spirit: Enlightenment through Ecstasy* (St. Paul: Llewellyn Publications, 1998).

[4] Diane Mariechild from her introduction to the book *Lesbian Sacred Sexuality* (Oakland, Calif.: Wingbow Press, 1995).

> I've grown tired of the divine heterosexual couple of contemporary paganism. While I continue to invoke a variety of spirits, both male and female, the emphasis is on linking them to my queerness. I might invoke the Goddess as Sacred Bitch, Dyke Sister or Mother of Faggots. Her relationship to male spirits is anything but "traditional." The God I call on has a variety of names. He is the Rising Pillar of Flesh, the Open Hand, Boyfriend, Lover, and Gate of Pleasure.[5]

In mining the available sacred-sex traditions of various cultures to try to create bi-positive sacred-sex rituals we found that even body-centered, sex-positive, woman-affirming philosophies tended to reinforce gender stereotypes. Without feminist and queer consciousness a lot of sexism gets rationalized through the supposedly "neutral" notion of polarity.

Polarity is certainly a basic concept in many religious systems. It holds that the dance of opposites is what creates life, that opposites, like light and dark, hot and cold, man and woman, are necessary to explain and order all that we know. The rub is that in most spiritual belief systems it is, curiously, male qualities that are deemed mental, active, and strong, while female qualities are considered the opposite, that is, emotional, passive, and weak. These dichotomies exaggerate and distort reality. They help enforce not only male supremacy but white supremacy too. People of color are often assigned the same attributes as women, as are children.

Giving power to this either/or way of seeing human nature tends to erase the vast middle ground where most of us live. And it overtly privileges male/female dyads, not to mention privileging mental processes over emotional ones and whiteness and lightness (or white people) over darkness (read women, queer people, children, people of color, anyone with less power than others).

Bisexuals Do Sacred Sex

> The goal of this group is to weave together three often-separated traditions. . . . the first strand is the re-sanctification of the body. Our desires are sacred inspirations and resources that we can use lovingly for the healing of ourselves, our culture, and ultimately the earth. We look for guidance to spiritual traditions, ancient and modern, which recognize the divine in the immanent as well as the transcendent. The second strand is the celebration

[5] From "On Discovering Queer Archetypes," in *Lavender Pagan* magazine (as reprinted in a 1996 issue of *RFD,* the Radical Faery magazine from Short Mountain, Tennessee).

of diversity. We honor the diverse wisdom of many cultural and spiritual traditions. We value the joyful dance and interplay of the variety of cultures, races, and gender identities, both in the traditions we draw from and in the cultures and people we embrace. The final strand is a radical criticism of patriarchal culture. The desires which are the cores and foundations of our beings have been warped and alienated into forms which serve to replicate existing structures of power, domination, and hatred.

We seek to reclaim or reinvent our desires into forms which affirm life, freedom, diversity and love; and to develop a spiritual practice, and ultimately a way of life, both ecstatic and revolutionary.[6]

In Sacred Flame we asked hard questions as we prepared our rituals:

- Do we really honor Goddess, as full Creator in the same sense as God, not just as his consort?[7]
- Where are our queer Goddesses and Gods, our butch as well as femme divas, our gentle and fierce divinities?
- Are our spiritual images homoerotic as well as heteroerotic, or do we still privilege heterosexuality and name it "superior"?[8]

Living in this culture, the five of us internalized biphobia, homophobia, woman-hatred, racism, erotophobia, ableism, and more, before we were grown. We had been taught to fear sex, or at least to be ashamed of it, to see it as something "in the way" of true spiritual development, not

[6] From "Sacred Flame: A Vision Statement" (January 1996).

[7] Take a look at how many tantric texts speak with the male voice and describe the male gaze: all of them. Feminist women and men scholars are just now beginning to point this out and theorize about what happened to the women tantric masters of old. Why have their teachings not survived in written form? See June Campbell, *Traveller in Space: In Search of Female Identity in Tibetan Buddhism* (New York: George Braziller, 1996); Miranda Shaw, *Passionate Enlightenment: Women in Tantric Buddhism* (Princeton, N.J.: Princeton University Press, 1994); Rita M. Gross, *Buddhism After Patriarchy: A Feminist History, Analysis and Reconstruction of Buddhism* (Albany: SUNY Press, 1993); and Monica Sjoo, *New Age & Armageddon: The Goddess or the gurus? Towards a feminist vision of the future* (London: Women's Press, 1992).

[8] We found that while Eastern sacred-sex traditions "claim" that their goal is to have each devotee embody both female and male, yin/yang, wholly in oneself, that, in reality, men and women seem to cling together, wanting completion from each other, and they are mostly unwilling to grant same-sex couples or same-sex desire equal status. Only the most secure and rare teacher remains unthreatened and open to supporting a diversity of sexual orientations and identities. A good book that illustrates same-sex erotic spiritual imagery is Randy P. Connor's *Blossom of Bone: Reclaiming the Connections Between Homoeroticism and the Sacred* (San Francisco: HarperSanFrancisco, 1993). See also his encyclopedia *Queer Myth, Symbol and Spirit* (London: Cassell, 1997), which he did with his partner and daughter.

a pathway of spirit. And although urgency for safer sex, brought about by the AIDS crisis, had encouraged us to talk more sensitively about our sexual and emotional needs, it had also shut us down, made it harder for us to talk about what we want. Interestingly, AIDS, and the sexual debate it facilitated, has contributed to a reevaluation of penetrative, procreative intercourse and orgasm as lovemaking's sole goal. We and others were developing a more spirit-sensitive and broader approach to sexual communication and intimacy. We found that in part, it was an interest in these alternative, safer models that first led some people to explore sacred-sex techniques (erotic massage, meditation, deep breathing, and so on).

Another avenue of exploration was the group lovemaking experience. It is possible that this experience may lie deep in our collective memories—as agrarian fertility rites enacted to help the crops grow, as fantasies of prenatal bliss and unity with the universe, and as a wish to re-create union with others in our adult everyday lives. In group lovemaking, distinctions of gender and sexual orientation can fade or become irrelevant; no wonder bisexuals are often associated with it, whether we engage in it or not.[9] Also, the bi community has developed a tradition of safer-sex parties. Bisexuals were some of the first organizers of the safer-sex parties that modeled and eroticized the use of latex and other forms of safer-sex practice aimed at minimizing the exchange of bodily fluids, maximizing people's sexual negotiation skills, and teaching everyone that honesty and caring are what lovemaking and community building can and should be about. Safer-sex parties are primarily recreational and celebratory and don't involve casting a circle, invoking deities, or meditating together before "getting down." While sex parties aren't necessarily conducted with sacred intent, there is much to be learned regarding communication, boundary setting, respecting limits, and honoring difference—all values which are the basis for spiritual community building.

With this background we sought to create sacred sexual experiences, to use erotic energy with spiritual intention and focus. Whether done alone with ourselves or with our partner(s) in complete private, or in our group as a whole, we worked to combine safer sex and spiritual rituals with sensitive communication and risk taking.

[9] See Kathy Rudy, "Sex Radical Communities and the Future of Sexual Ethics," in *Lesbian Sex Scandals: Sexual Practices, Identities and Politics,* ed. Dawn Atkins (Binghamton, N.Y.: Harrington Park Press, 1999). She discusses the possibility "that these sex groups are in the process of providing for us a new kind of ethic based not on individuality, but rather on community."

Glimpses of Our Erotic Ritual Practices

The members of Sacred Flame drew upon our experiences and our research to plan rituals aimed at increasing our intimacy and pleasure, unlearning oppressions, and healing the wounds between and within us. We usually followed the Wiccan practice of casting a circle to create sacred space, calling the four directions, invoking deities (Goddess, God), and bringing our awarenesses to our bodies rooted in the earth before raising energy together.[10] Group energy was ignited through dancing and drumming, through breathing and moving rhythmically. Focused interactions opened doors in our hearts and deepened our connections with each other. We gave a lot of thought to interactive exercises we could use to bring us back into our bodies, melt away our shyness, and help us connect lovingly and passionately with each other. The simple exercises presented below are meant for adaptation. If you choose to explore them, and if your religious beliefs and/or sexual orientation differs, take only what works for you. What is important is finding ways to heal the sexual wounds between and within us all.

Making One's Place in the Circle

Our bodies are our temples here on earth; our own sacks of skin and bones, given to us temporarily, in trust, as the miraculous wetware we move spirit through. Given this, any good ritual starts with grounding in our bodies first. One simple grounding is a Self-Blessing Ritual, where we call the directions on our own bodies.

Self Blessing Ritual

Stand in the circle naked together. Join hands one by one, saying "Hand to hand we cast the circle." When all have joined, squeeze hands, drop hands, and go into your own body's awareness. Feel the energy running within and among you. Name the earth, air, fire, and water elements embodied in your

[10] Or the four quarters—east, south, west, and north. Many Native American traditions also call the directions, but it is Wicca that casts a circle to create sacred and magical space "between the worlds." However, European Wicca and Native American traditions in this country are becoming so interwoven in many pagan communities that it is sometimes hard to tell which specific traditions are rooted where.

frame. Shake out a little, touch yourselves, your various parts, with honor and pleasure. Hug yourselves and feel alive with intention and energy for what you are about to begin. We bless our bodies and turn to one another in the circle, saying, "Beloved of my heart, thou art the Divine made manifest here among us. Please bless us and what we create here tonight." Answer each other, "Yes, I am the Divine come through you. You and your creations are wholly blessed tonight."

In many Tantra and other New Age sacred-sex groups there is a strong preference for having people stand "gender-balanced" around the circle so that so-called male/female polarities alternate. One alternative our group tried is to have people stand m/m/f/f/m/m/f/f. Here everyone has someone of the other sex on one side of them and someone of their own sex on the other side—the m/f polarity is still represented but so is the comfort of one's own sex—a perfect bisexual solution.

Variations of this next exercise are used in many group encounter experiences. Our particular goal was to increase the erotic/spiritual energy between us.

Eye-Gazing

Face each other in dyads. If you have an uneven number in your group, you can add an interesting twist with a full-length mirror propped up against a wall.

As the group rotates partners, each "odd person out" gets the mirror for partner, and gazes into their own eyes, seeing their self as the divine lover they seek. You can write various scripts for the leader to guide this exercise. Whatever the text, encourage people to gaze deeply into each other's eyes and gradually increase intimacy and trust. Placing one's hands on one's partner's heart while doing alternate breathing (I breathe out while you breathe in, and vice versa) helps. Visualize each other as divine lovers whose power and wisdom are healing, whose compassionate love arises and strengthens the tribe. Let whatever happens happen.

Again, in many New Age groups these rituals are only done m/f, or if there is an uneven number of m/f dyads, those in same-sex dyads are made to feel second-best, less than ideal. With the bisexual assumption there is no need for this false hierarchy. The mirror addition makes clear that one key love relationship is with oneself, one's own inner lover.[11]

How Does This Body Want to Be Touched?[12]

Groups of four to five people are best for this next exercise, so that everyone can rotate all-on-one massages among the group. If your group is larger, just create subgroups. It is certainly not necessary that everyone be bisexual to do this exercise. Nor is it necessary that people be naked. Nor is it necessary that full body massage be given. You can have amazing experiences with simple foot massages or with facial and shoulder massages.

It helps to start by doing a preliminary hand-charging exercise. Have people sit quietly, centered, and meditate upon their hands and the healing power coming through them. It also helps to build in some "Saying No" touch exercises first, so that participants gain ease in hearing and stating limits lovingly. In an erotic massage, great respect is given to what the recipient asks for. As the giver, ask them what they want if you're unsure. As the receiver, make sure you feel safe enough and welcomed enough to say what you want, and then, if you find out you can get it, to receive it with joy and gratitude. It can be as erotic as you make it, as you and your friends want it to be. The important thing is to agree beforehand what the limits are and what your desires are and how they will be fulfilled.

In Sacred Flame we experimented with using a questionnaire that we filled out before our ritual started. We stated what kinds of limits and desires we were feeling that night and who we were desirous of acting them out with. I'm not sure this worked as well as we wanted it to, but there is no substitute for skillful discussion and negotiation, reaching out and taking risks.

[11] I often find it helpful to emphasize this to heterosexuals when teaching them about the Kinsey and Klein Scales of Sexual Orientation ranges. If they've always considered themselves heterosexual because that's where their sexual experience lies and never thought of themselves as desiring their own sex or being aroused by same-sex, yet have had pleasure masturbating, I tell them, they might want to consider that loving themselves is somewhere on the continuum of same-sex love.

[12] Our sources for this exercise came from passages in *Lesbian Sacred Sexuality* about erotic massage and from the teaching of the Body Electric Erotic Massage School. Located in Oakland, California, The Body Electric School started as a gay men's community and now embraces women and all people. You can reach them on the Internet at http://www.bodyelectric.org

Erotic Massage

Start the erotic massage evening with a circle go round where ground rules are outlined and people introduce themselves or share a simple statement about their day. Arrange people in groups of four, so that each massage recipient has three attendants, and so when people rotate doing each other they can give their full energy and not get too tired. When it is your turn to be massaged ask for what you want. Be as detailed as possible about what feels good and what boundaries/limits you want honored. Massagers should work in balance with long complete strokes, reading your body language for feedback, staying in physical touch with you at all times, even if their other hand reaches for more oil or a towel or to re-position themselves. If you have agreed that genital touching is welcome it is best to start with touching the genitals as part of the body, not isolated from it. When we receive so-called nonsexual massages often our breasts and nipples (if we're women, especially) and our genitals, and sometimes our asses (both sexes) are neglected, not seen as part of us. If you have permission, touch the genitals as you work the person's body, lovingly caress all of them. Then, if all agree, the massagers can touch the receiver with more erotic intent and take direction on how to do that.

Stay with the recipient as he or she comes, witness their pleasure, see if they want to be held or rocked or sprinkled with water or whatever pleases them as they release. If they don't want to come or aren't able to come, give them the same praising, aware attention. There is no right or wrong way. Giving them what they need is the point.

Guided Imagery Meditations

Our group was made up of people raised as Protestants and Jews who had known only a male-gendered, seemingly heterosexual God. We were all taught the biblical creation story. It seems that Adam and Eve were cast out of the Garden of Eden and were made ashamed of their nakedness after they gained knowledge of good and evil. What does this really mean? Why is it wrong, or dangerous, or alienating, for the children of God to have knowledge of erotic, regenerative power?

As bisexuals, and as people interested in fluid gender expressions, we wanted to change how we visualized divinity and how we visualized our origins, the beginnings of life on earth. We chose to do this by creating new stories and using them as guided meditations to bring the group into a new erotic spirit space.

Meeting Your Hermaphroditic Deity
(An Abbreviated Outline)

You walk down a path and into a forest, then out into a clearing where you see a god/dess dancing.

The being's gender is unclear, s/he looks like many genders all enthrallingly woven together.

You are attracted to this hypnotic being and s/he gives you a message you ask for, that you long to hear.

S/he embraces you and merges with you.

After a time, you leave the clearing, fuller and wiser, satisfied that pleasure and desire within you are now one.

A New Creation Story

This guided imagery meditation is taken from personal accounts of paths back to sexual healing and wholeness, and woven from our imaginations of long ago.

Tonight we tell the story of Why Sex Is Sacred
Tonight we remember the ways of making/sacred/sex
Tonight we remember back to a time before life became conscious of itself,
a time when there was no difference between sexuality and spirit, between mind and matter
a time when the creative force was all flame, all matter, all air, all fluids dancing together infinitely as one.
There was no shame then, no sense of self-and-other.
No points of hesitance or separation.
No separate word for orgasm,
Since everything breathed with life.

> There were no words for genitals or separate body parts because we were all one with nature's body—our skin a current for ecstasy as much as our cunts and cocks, our mouths as pleasure-telling as our minds . . .[13]

In the creation story we weave together as a group, our ancestors sit around a village fire telling each other what they remember about the beginnings of life's passion and power and play, the mystery and power of creation and our part in connecting earth and sky and passing on the life-breathe given to us, our own erotic spark.

> "It is the place in my body that pulsates with Her. She is the energy flowing through healing me when I hurt," says one.
>
> "It is the intimacy that makes sex sacred," says another. "It is the intimacy, the incredible tenderness of intimacy I long for."
>
> "I can't remember back to the time when we were powerful and peaceful and without shame. I'm afraid, please help me trust myself and you," says another.
>
> "We will," they answer, "you are part of the Goddess, know yourself."
>
> "When we worship, when we honor Her, when we dance and let our bodies answer the drumming we help open the door, rather than just waiting for the door to open us," says another.
>
> "Making love connects us when we do it right. The universe beckons us to re-unite with her through our bodies' movements and our souls' yearnings. . . . you make sex sacred honoring Her in each other. We make sacred sex welcoming each other home. . . ."

Lessons Learned in Bisexual Sacred Erotic Space

The approaches mentioned above are only a part of what is going on in this country today. There are a number of different groups—in New Age, pagan, queer, feminist, and other cultural and spiritual communities—that are experimenting with and conducting various erotic rituals in sacred space.[14]

[13] From Loraine Hutchins, "Tonight We Gather . . . ," as told to Sacred Flame, with thanks to Lynne Biggerwomon's *The Femaissance* (Berkeley, Calif.: West Coast Print Center, 1979) and to Dolores La Chappelle's *Sacred Land Sacred Sex Rapture of the Deep: Concerning Deep Ecology and Celebrating Life* (Silverton, Colo.: Finn Hill Arts, 1988) for inspirations.

[14] See *The Intimate Explosion,* a small sex/spirit newsletter printed in Connecticut; *Green Egg,* the national magazine of the Church of All Worlds, headquartered in Northern Cali-

I focus here only on what we learned from Sacred Flame.

We met and did monthly rituals together for a year. We rotated responsibility for creating the rituals among us. After each ritual we gathered for evaluative discussions, naming what we liked and what we wanted to do better or differently.

We underestimated our societal conditioning, our shame, our embarrassment, our internalized erotophobia and homophobia, our fears of rejection and inadequacy. "Sure, we're all brave, outrageous sex radicals. We can be naked and screw like bunnies. No problem," we muttered to ourselves. We didn't realize that with our friends, with people we knew well, all our insecurities and mind-chatter could kick in and paralyze the passion. We found that we needed a long time to heal from the sexual abuse we had experienced, that just naming it and asking for help were not enough. And we thought we were safer-sex experts, that we knew it all. We found we were wrong and that it was hard to ask questions or to get clear on actual safer-sex practices among us, especially when they involved our emotions and self-esteem.[15]

We had different, conflicting goals for the group which weren't clear until we were far into the process. Some wanted a sex-positive wiccan-type group, not focused on explicit sex. Others really wanted to have group sex in a ritual, sacred context, and nothing less. Some wanted to build long-term intentional community, while for others, creating and enjoying monthly rituals together was enough. We thought that, since we shared bisexuality and a common commitment to feminism, we were one step ahead. This helped, but we still found that in the actual charged interactions of erotic spiritual practice, gender differences, couple dynamics, and leadership issues all got in the way of our creating beloved community.

We also identified significant areas for further exploration. We wanted to learn from a variety of sacred-sex traditions without misusing or mis-

---

fornia, and Deborah Anapol's Sacred Space Institute, located in San Rafael, California. Many groups are doing group masturbation and self-loving rituals in which they dedicate their orgasms to healing each other and the earth. And they are also doing group erotic massage, teaching men especially to be less focused on their own ejaculations and more on pleasuring women, and/or each other. See Mantak Chia, *The Multi-Orgasmic Man: Sexual Secrets Every Man Should Know* and *Healing Love through the Tao: Cultivating Female Sexual Energy* (Huntington, N.Y.: Healing Tao Books, 1986).

[15] Since oral sex isn't as high risk as anal or vaginal intercourse, does it require barriers? Or are some people more exempt from barriers than others, depending on STD status, frequency of testing, and what they do with partners elsewhere? Should we use barriers in group, even if we don't at home? We struggled with these kinds of questions.

interpreting them. We examined various Western neo-pagan philosophies and practices (from Dianic to Druidic to Gardnerian) as well as the Tantric and Taoist traditions of the East, in order to reinterpret them beyond their historic and current privileging of heterosexuality. We also explored Afro-Caribbean traditions such as Yoruba, Santeria, and Candomble, as well as the sacred intimate (Chuluaqui-Quodoshka) tradition Native American (Cherokee) Harley Swift Deer teaches in his Twisted Hair Metis Society.

We discussed how all these traditions express gender, sexual orientation, and erotic power. We also learned about the dynamics of colonization and syncretization—the process by which one religion superimposes itself over another (as Catholicism has done with Yoruban/West African traditions in the Caribbean, for example, or as New Age American Tantra teachers are doing with imported Hindu and Buddhist traditions here).

We also discussed how people in our culture looking for sacred-sex models often stumble upon the Sacred Marriage, or *hieros gamos,* also called the Great Rite. This ritual ceremony symbolizes the uniting of male and female, God and Goddess, through making love, recreating the world through their polarity dance.[16] But perhaps an even more apt image for some of us was the image of the temple priestess, sacred prostitute, or harlot for the Queen of Heaven, who heals us by making love to us, allowing us to make love with her, and in doing so, gives us back to ourselves.[17] And in giving us back to ourselves she helps us return ourselves to community. This image is more about a self/other polarity than a self-consciously hetero m/f polarity, and it suits us better.

Conclusions

We are left with many of the questions with which we began. How can we change our forms of worship in ways that change our selves and our com-

[16] Although as Jews and Christians we didn't feel we'd been brought up with sex-positive imagery in our religious training we did discover some interesting roots. There is a Jewish *Shabbat* tradition where husband and wife are directed to channel male and female aspects of God into ecstatic sexual union as part of the weekly Sabbath ritual. And some Christian radicals claim that Christianity was originally sex-positive and woman-positive. See Margaret Starbird, *The Goddess in the Gospels: Reclaiming the Sacred Feminine* (Santa Fe: Bear & Co., 1998), for instance, where she argues that Jesus and Mary Magdalene lived in partnership and love and that evidence of it has been suppressed.

[17] We loved Deena Metzger's essay "The Sacred Prostitute," in *Enlightened Sexuality: Essays on Body-Positive Spirituality,* ed. Georg Fuerstein (Freedom, Calif.: Crossing Press, 1989); and Kenneth Ray Stubbs, *Women of the Light: The New Sacred Prostitute* (Larkspur, Calif.: Secret Garden Press, 1994).

munities? Does the gendered way a culture sees divinity become reflected in how different genders are treated? And, if this is where it begins, do we need to worship the Goddess over the God, in a sort of spiritual affirmative action approach, for the next however many years? Is it more useful or possible to visualize a multigendered deity or a nongendered deity? And if we believe that polarity is inherent in life, can we reconceptualize that in a more queer and integrated way?

Must there always be male/female poles and attributes, with women inevitably getting the short stick? What about butch/femme instead? Does that change anything? What about self/other as the ultimate polarity? Is that not perhaps more true?

The members of Sacred Flame were all activists and organizers. We shared common values of feminism, queer liberation, polyamory, anti-racism, progressive social-justice politics and earth-based spiritualities. It was exciting to experiment with creating rituals based on these values and experiences, rituals we'd often longed for and yet not found in our lives.

Of course we took on too much and of course we haven't changed the world (yet) but what we did was amazing!

As one of the women in the group said, "We held hands like little kids facing our terror, jumping free-fall into the abyss, Kali on our shoulders. Ok. We're gonna do it, even if everyone says we're crazy, even if people say it's impossible, even if we are scared!"

We found we were not only scared, but also scarred—and that these words were somehow very close to "sacred." We found that sacred sex and safer sex have more in common than their assonance, that there is profound reason why they are connected—both in our blockages and in understandings about caring for each other. We found that our desires were often overshadowed by our pain and frustration, and that joy and celebration were farther off than we wanted or expected.

But we haven't given up on the dream of making love spiritually, as community, beyond conventional boundaries, either. We know that everyone we talked to about our dream, during that year and since, also carries our dream inside them in their own way, translated into their own needs, imagination, and desires. And, that, as I said at the beginning—even our desire for sexual healing, for body/spirit connection, is itself a sacrament. We persist in this desire/sacrament, giving each other permission to want healing and ecstasy wholly, recreating the lost ancient Garden of Pleasure here on earth.

From Fundamentalism to Freedom

AURORA ROSE WOLF

ALMOST ABOVE ALL ELSE, God has a sense of humor. This I know through personal experience. I am a bisexual, a feminist, a psychic, and a borderline genius. I was born into a fundamentalist Christian family with very limited educational background, in a working-class suburb. My family of origin loves and is completely devoted to me. They also have no idea who "I" truly am anymore, and to reveal such identifiers I am afraid would crush them. I let them live in their world and keep them in the dark about mine. We are all safe that way.

My early childhood was one of sunshine, light, and precocity. My earliest memory is of looking up at the sunlit sky and wondering about the clouds. One fine spring day I was spotted sitting on the roof of my father's toolshed by a neighbor. When asked what I was doing up there I replied "Oh, I am just meditating." Spirituality had no name for me at the time, but it did have a feeling—warmth and love.

My sunshiny skies began to turn to rain as I began to attend church and read, thus learning about sin, shame, evil, and the wicked, wicked ways of the world. I was determined to stay on the side of the Light by donning my holy Christian armor and going from door to door, preaching the Truth as prescribed by my church.

Deep inside me, and despite myself, my hidden spiritual self was developing. Psychic abilities, along with my sexuality, were becoming aroused with the blossoming of my adolescence. After school one day I parked my bicycle under a tree near the railroad tracks, waiting to watch a passing train. Suddenly a friendly, clear, inner voice startled me with the declaration "move your bike and get away from the tree." I did so immediately.

Within seconds, the huge oak, which to outward appearance seemed perfectly sound, fell down with a frightening crackle and BOOM. I was amazed. I also realized that I was absolutely alone with my knowledge of the Voice. Such things as the Voice had a pat explanation in my church—the working of Evil. How could the saving of my life be an evil thing, I wondered? I tried not to think about this contradiction and kept the matter to myself.

I soon found myself attracted to men, and I believe my first crush was on Star Trek's Mr. Spock, at the tender age of ten. Mr. Spock knew how to control his emotions! I began to buy teen magazines with his picture in them. My mother warned me against idolatry and was less than enthusiastic about my interest. Three years later I developed my first crush on a woman. She was my biology teacher, and I will never forget her—her perfume, dark eyes and hair, and lively sense of humor. One day she was helping to chaperone a class outing to the movies. The mere sight of her walking into the auditorium was enough to give me a spontaneous orgasm, without ever touching myself. I knew of no one to discuss these feelings with. So, just as with the Voice, I had no choice but to keep this part of my life secret and unexplored, and certainly NOT to be discussed with others.

Buffeted by the waves of strict guidelines from my fundamentalist religion, I turned to intellectualism as the safe port in the growing storm inside of me. I desperately tried to keep erotic images, both male and female, out of my mind. Masturbation, ruled as evil and a form of self-abuse by the church, became my greatest challenge. Try as I could, I could vanquish my sexual feelings for no more than two weeks. Then I would satisfy myself and feel tainted in the process. This psychologically unhealthy scenario continued until I left my parents house at age eighteen.

The God I was worshiping was an angry, stern, demanding white male, exacting exclusive devotion. He became embedded in my superego, in my conscious awareness of right and wrong. Even today I continue to wrestle with him from time to time over my sexual and spiritual preferences to let me go and be free to be who I truly am. His message is the message of fundamentalism, which demands an overbearing degree of sexual and spiritual servitude to the one concept of God and sexuality, with no freedom for diversity.

Then, to my surprise, I discovered that the key to freedom could be found after a careful inspection of my chains. I began to devour more and more church publications in an effort to resolve everything in my spiritual and sexual life. The writings made many references to secular publications, often refuting the thoughts and theories of many famous thinkers, such as Darwin.

One article made a passing reference to Freud and sexuality which I did not understand. So, on my own I began a study of psychiatry and found myself intrigued by the father of this field. I was allowed to purchase the book *The Interpretation of Dreams* and quickly found myself an enthusiastic student. One day paths of parallel reasoning—Freud and the church dogma—came to a screeching crash. A leading church magazine article quoted and debunked him. Horrified, I looked up the source of discontent. The church had taken his words out of context and twisted their meaning to fit their article—badly. I began researching more of their quotes from other authors and found the same pattern of misuse and distortion. A rude realization came to me. My bullying God had been standing on a house of cards. With even one card removed, the house folded and collapsed upon itself. I was finally free to think for myself.

I tried to enlighten my family as to what I had found, but no one was particularly interested. My mother was hurt by my findings and would not budge on her position. Rather than continue to hurt her, I quietly applied for and was accepted to a distant college. I moved away at age eighteen and only returned home to visit after that.

My college years were a blur of tests, papers, studying, and then, to reduce stress and socialize—sex, marijuana, and alcohol. I became more and more aware of how unhappy I was and how I was not dealing with my inner spiritual self and my inner sexuality, my desire to be with a woman as well as a man. This culminated one night in my standing on a narrow bridge over a deep chasm, deciding whether to jump off into oblivion or not. The angry white male God was very displeased with me. I put one leg up and over the rail, wavering. Then I stopped, for I realized that there was something else inside of me, something soft, comforting, and forgiving. Now I know it as the female God. I felt a moment of peace as her love swept over me, and I left the bridge without a second look back. The next day I went to the university counseling center, and my therapy and healing began.

The healing process was to undertake many a dark turn and blind alley, and in fact, it is still an unfinished project. For between the life of a little girl, filled with love and sunshine from the Divine, to the life of an emerging woman, filled with darkness, self doubt, and suicidal thoughts, is nothing less than what is known as the *abyss*. The *abyss* takes many roads and turns all of its own accord. It is a void of nonbelief, an existential hell of disbelief, in which nothing truly matters, in scientific certitude that we are all winding up as graveyard dust anyway. Morality then becomes a matter of not running too far afoul of the prevailing law. It doesn't matter who you screw or screw over, nothing matters. In this mind-set I went through sexual encounters with many men, but only one woman. I smoked marijuana as if it would vanish the next day. Jaded by this form of sensualism, eventually I was to begin a serious search for the Divine. I felt as if I had been walking though a vast desert. Parched and thirsty, I sought the nearest oasis that would accept me for who I was.

I drifted aimlessly for many years in the *abyss*, ignoring my inner spirituality and sexuality. I concentrated on defining a career for myself. I worked my way through graduate school in a stint at a psychiatric hospital. Even as I was immersed in psychiatry, my life became filled with stress. I studied it in school, worked around disturbed patients, and was in therapy. Despite myself, I fell in love with a female co-worker, also bisexual. She was ambivalent in her response to me, and I disappeared again into the identity of a straight person. I struggled to keep my life straight, and simple, or so I thought. Inside the denial of my self was causing great pain.

At my time of greatest stress working in the locked psychiatric ward, I began to spontaneously make chalk drawings of a multicolored tree. It had thick, distinctly colored branches, which ended in strangely rounded, globular leaves. It always turned out to be beautifully colored and strangely compelling. I could not fully explain it, but it did give me satisfaction and comfort to look at.

In this vulnerable state my apartment caught fire and most of my belongings went up in smoke. I myself narrowly escaped death. A friend at work, a Buddhist, implored me to go to a meeting, and with few possessions to speak of, I felt I was at least in the proper position for an ascetic, at age twenty-nine.

My Buddhist experience was sweet, exhausting, and strange, but allowed me to exit from the *abyss*. This particular sect of Buddhism called for many hours of chanting and prayer daily. It also demanded that I go and proselytize, so once again I found myself a street preacher, this time in a fundamentalist Buddhist sect. I will never forget one spring evening standing in the entranceway of the library of a university campus. With the unthinkably massive ionic pillars of the doorway framing me, a surreal scene emerged as I began telling passersby about Buddhism. Many were interested, and most smiled at me with at least tolerance. I was filled with a sense of sheer and utter joy, a sense that I was doing exactly what I should be doing with my life. My sexuality, accepted by this sect, was not an issue for me. I kept it in the background as I swept together the pieces of my life.

After five years of practice my joy in Buddhism soured, as a very contentious rift appeared between the temple and the lay organization. Harsh, unforgiving words were exchanged between the two groups. I was asked to make a choice between them. My choice was to align with neither one of them. My reasoning was that such dissension was an indicator that enlightenment was far away from either faction.

Concerned about unexplainable heart palpitations I was having, my physician recommended meditation. One evening as I leafed through the local gay/lesbian magazine, my eye spotted an ad for a gay/lesbian potluck introduction to a meditation group. With some trepidation, I decided to attend. What I found was an open, loving, friendly group of mostly men. This pleased me; I had long enjoyed the company of gay men and felt I did not need female energy around as a distraction.

I began meditating every Tuesday night with my group. What began as a therapeutic measure to calm my nerves ended up as the doorway to my very soul. I began to hear inner voices in my meditation. They had words of profound advice for me. I learned to label the voices as my Higher Self. I asked my Higher Self to reveal an image of itself to me on two occasions.

The first occasion a man appeared, looking very much like Jesus Christ. I asked, "Are you the Christ?" The answer was, "I am Immanuel, but you know me better as the Archangel Michael."

And so my relationship with the warrior-angel began. This was a very different relationship than with the angry white male God. Michael is accepting of who I am, sexuality and all, and although directive is not demanding or jealous. Sometime after this meditation I found out that Michael is associated with summer and the hour of midday. I was born at noon in the month of August.

The second occasion I asked my Higher Self to appear, much to my surprise, a young woman in Native American apparel emerged. She did not identify her name, but smiled sweetly at me, and I felt a very kind, nurturing energy from her, which juxtaposed nicely with Michael's more aggressive, directive energy.

After connecting to my Higher Selves, I began to have visions in my meditations. I astounded one member by accurately describing the wallpaper in his bedroom. As if a videotape were playing in my mind, I could see detailed images of the nineteenth century. As a group, we went time traveling together. I and another person both visited the future, and independently of each other, both of us had the same type of experience for a particular year in the future, right down to the medium of exchange—small yellow cards.

During one meditation I asked to be shown my spiritual path. I was answered by the vision of a great winding green river and a feeling of incredible love and power. Following an irresistible urge, I threw myself into the river and was immediately swept away by a surprisingly strong current. I understood that this was the way my life would be from now on, that so long as I surrendered myself to spirit, my life would take many unexpected but positive turns.

After three years I realized that I needed more spiritual training than what the group could offer me, so I began attending services at a Metaphysical church that was gay/lesbian friendly. Not satisfied with being a congregant, I became a ministerial student. Not satisfied with the course offerings, I began to study voraciously on my own. I was drawn to the very things I had been warned about as a fundamentalist Christian so many years ago—everything to do with Wicca, the earth religions, and the Western mystery tradition. The Western mystery tradition embraces the spiritual truths of the ancient religious mystery schools of Egypt and Greece, along with concepts from the Judaic Kabbala, a form of religious mysticism.

I learned about calling the four directions and the four archangels, and found out where Michael fit into this picture. I learned about establishing a sacred space and about the power of intent within that space. I learned about forces, and the existence of the male and female Gods. Most importantly, I learned about ethics, and to use what I had learned only for the greatest good of all, not for my own selfish ends.

It was then that I was able to identify what I had had a vision of so many years ago while working in the psychiatric hospital. I was surprised and exhilarated to discover a full-color illustration of the Tree of Life in one of my books. I recognized it as that very same tree I had kept trying to draw so many years ago, as I was surrounded by my psychiatric patients.

The Tree of Life is a construct taken from the Jewish Kabbala and applied to the Western mystery tradition. It is a symbol, a glyph that represents all the power and knowledge in the universe. To comprehend the Tree of Life is to comprehend All That Is. The Tree has a trunk with two main branches. From these branches come most of the *sephirot,* or emanations, of God. The right branch holds the female qualities of understanding, strength, and glory. The left branch holds the male qualities of wisdom, mercy, and victory. The trunk itself contains the middle way of balance and the qualities of the crown, beauty, foundation, and the kingdom.

Each of the *sephira* has qualities of both male and female. In understanding the Tree, one is taught to visualize a lightning bolt of power zigzagging down the tree from *sephira* to *sephira,* starting from the crown and ending in the foundation. People have spent their entire lives in an effort to comprehend the totality of the Tree.

The Tree speaks to me and my identity as a sexual being. For me, it is a Tree of bisexuality, of both the masculine and feminine Gods. One day I was idly contemplating the Tree as I drove to a work site. Then, as I peered through my windshield at the passing countryside, I was allowed a vision of it. For a split second I saw it, the shining tree, with an eternal lightening bolt flashing through it. To me came an electrifying sense of joy and awe, as just for that split second I could grasp the totality of The All. It was then that I realized that nothing else truly matters. There is no drug, no sexual experience, no relationship, no material object, *nothing* as powerful, joyful, or important as the experience of the Divine. I understood immediately, then, the monks and nuns of all religious stripes who have given up every material and sexual pursuit *gladly* in order to embrace The All. In reality they have given up nothing and gained everything.

It was not long after this vision that I became aware of a grave social cause that needed championing, and I knew I had to heed the call and resign my standing as a student. This was just as I was succeeding in my psychic development to the point of being able to touch others and accurately see their lives and their future. I had also achieved the rank, or Holy Order, of Missionary in the Church. I became very aware of the selfishness of remaining and helping a tiny congregation of a few hundred versus venturing forth to meet the challenges and needs of millions. The vision of the Tree gave me the strength to recognize my calling, and I am off on this noble adventure, until the cause is won.

Now I am also finally able to come to terms with my bisexuality and truly to reach out to other women who can love me as I love them, without a feeling of shame and regret. Once again, this has been a gift of the Tree. Now that I am fully open to love, I find persons of both sexes attracted to and open to me. The dread *abyss* remains now as a distant, unpleasant memory, for it is about spiritual abandonment, and I never feel that I am alone now.

I realize that my life's adventures have all been necessary in order for me to have the strength and understanding to do my work. I see how fundamentalism is greatly misunderstood. It is the beginning primer for spirituality which has been mistaken for the doctoral dissertation. It teaches us about rules, sternness, and literal meaning. When we move on from it, many of those guidelines naturally fall away in new growth and understanding. I thank the fundamentalists for that and wish them peace and enlightenment. Without the fall through the *abyss* and the many twists and turns in the great green river of spirituality, I would have neither the necessary compassion nor understanding to complete my task and my destiny. One day, and it is coming soon, I will be free again to contemplate nothing but the Tree. I will do so with clean hands and a full heart, and a male and female lover by my side. The little girl who smiled in the warmth of the sunshine now touches hands with the adult woman who laughs in the reflected flash of the Tree of Life. I have found the warmth and love of the Divine once again.

A Word We Cannot Yet Speak / A Word We Must Now Speak: Bisexuality and the Presbyterian Church (U.S.A.)

Susan Halcomb Craig

Since the 1970s sexuality has been among the hottest subjects of study by major Protestant mainline denominations in the United States. There is now growing discussion in many quarters regarding denominations splitting apart along orthodox and progressive lines and possibly realigning ecumenically. Dualistic forces are driving the churches' dialogue on sexuality into molds like straight or gay, and hetero- or homosexual, in which the first-named of each pair is considered the "good," morally and even spiritually superior to the second. Later Christian scripture and tradition value the male (reason, intelligence, spirit) over the female (body, nature, emotion), setting in motion patterns of domination that persist today. Psychologies that stereotype "masculine" and "feminine" sides entrench bipolarities. And patriarchy's sexist assumption that gay men are "effeminate" drives a further oppositional wedge between, on the one hand, heterosexual men [the norm] and, on the other, gay men and all women. Even in the queer community, sexism lives on, causing tension between gay men and lesbians and continuing the myth of "twoness" and polar difference.

There have been eras when Protestant leaders were at the forefront of political, intellectual, or moral national discussion—most recently during the movement for racial justice in the United States. Yet when it comes to issues of human sexuality, the church community has become a reluctant follower of societal change. While the secular world has begun to validate bisexual and transgender realities and has ventured into discussing more colorfully nuanced sexuality and gender-based variation, little of this dialogue has infiltrated ecclesiastical debates.

But that is beginning, very slowly, to change. This paper documents the Presbyterian Church (U.S.A.)'s inclusion of the term and concept of bisexuality in its policy and politics, writing and conversation. While I honor the need for others to document transgender and transsexual realities, I will here trace only my own narrative as a bisexual woman. And I write from two convictions: that it is the divine intention that each of us "be who we are" in the deepest way possible; and that our communities of faith and the world will thrive only to the extent that we work to make that possible for each of us.

A Word We Cannot Yet Speak

Background Summary to 1990: Denominational Policies Regarding Homosexuality[1]

To date, the words bisexual and bisexuality don't appear in any Presbyterian policy or polity. It's possible that in a base sense many Presbyterians assume that the word "homosexuality" as used in our documents is inclusive of all but heterosexuality, but that has never been tested. The word "bisexuality" remains a word we cannot yet speak on the official front, and one that many gay and lesbian activists have also been loath to speak until recently. Yet on the subject of homosexuality we've been garrulous! From as early as 1976, the Presbyterian Church has explored the question of whether to ordain "self-affirming" and "practicing" homosexuals. Contrary to the recommendation of its task force on human sexuality, the 1978 General Assembly offered its definitive guidance that "unrepentant homosexual practice does not accord with the requirements for ordination set forth in the Form of Government, Chapter VII, Section 3 (37.03)."[2] This guidance stands to this day, weathering the 1983 merger of the two Presbyterian denominations to form the Presbyterian Church (U.S.A.).

[1] This section is dependent on discussions with denominational activists, on memory, and on an unpublished document by Margaret J. Thomas, "Evolution of Denominational Policies Regarding Homosexuality," prepared for the Presbytery of the Twin Cities, September 12, 1995. For interested readers, I recommend Melinda Valliant McLain, "Riding the Waves of Presbyterian Unrest: A Brief History of the Movement for Full Inclusion of Lesbian, Gay, Bisexual and Transgendered Persons in the Presbyterian Church (USA)"; and Melinda Valliant McLain, "A Brief Introduction to 'Presby-Speak,'" in *Called Out: The Voices and Gifts of Lesbian, Gay, Bisexual and Transgendered Presbyterians,* ed. Jane Adams Spahr, Kathryn Poethig, Selisse Berry, and Melinda V. McLain (Gaithersburg, Md.: Chi Rho Press, 1995).

[2] The General Assembly is the elected ruling body of the Presbyterian Church, meeting annually to set denominational policy and polity.

Unlearning to Not Speak[3]

While official denominational structures remained mum, in the late 1980s bisexuals became visible to activists in Presbyterian lesbian and gay rights struggles. In 1987 and 1988, Kathleen Buckley began her careful coming out process as a bisexual woman.[4] Buckley's partner, Susan Kramer, was a board member of the advocacy group Presbyterians for Lesbian and Gay Concerns (PLGC). Buckley invited discernment and support from these colleagues and began shared conversation.

In 1987 the General Assembly appointed a Special Committee on Human Sexuality, which, over the next three years, produced the paper "Keeping Body and Soul Together: Sexuality, Spirituality and Social Justice," popularly called "The Human Sexuality Report."[5] Hearings were held around the country for people of faith of all sexual expressions to tell their stories and express their hopes and concerns before committee members. Although the topic was *human* sexuality, covered in its many manifestations at length in the finished report, the church press and national media focused on its brief, gay-positive chapter on same-sex sexuality.

The denomination's structure of governance is democratic, fostering robust dialogue on many issues. As our increasingly acrimonious debate "went public," conservative and liberal church members chose sides. Other ecumenical Christians were also studying sexuality, and media coverage broadened to include us all. Indeed, it might be said that the secular press has shown more interest in how religious institutions address sexuality and the body than in anything else we do. One could argue in some situations that bad press is better than no press. But in the end, adverse attention in denominational and in secular presses to same-sex orientation and activity played a significant role in Presbyterians' voting against the human sexuality paper.

Although the subject of bisexuality came up in study and hearings, the writers chose to mention the word only a few times. The most interesting reference is buried in a subsection on "Mutuality," as follows:

[3] From a poem of the same name by Marge Piercy in *Circles on the Water: Selected Poems of Marge Piercy* (New York: Knopf, 1988), 97.

[4] Conversations with Kathleen Buckley, 1995–1997.

[5] This report has been edited and now is published by Distribution Management Services of the PCUSA (#OGA-91-001) and retitled *Presbyterians and Human Sexuality 1991* (Louisville, Ky.: Stated Clerk of the General Assembly, 1991).

. . . research on sexual behavior indicates that very few, if any, of us are either exclusively heterosexual or homosexual. There is a whole spectrum between the two, including the phenomenon of bisexuality. On the whole this report has not dealt with bisexuality and we do not have the space here to do so. It does, however, remind us of the complexity of sexual orientations, and cautions us about being too simplistic when we categorize and label persons as sexual.[6]

Committee member Sylvia Thorson Smith recalls the three-year period of study and writing, but not discussing the term bisexuality or explicitly deciding not to explore it. Instead, the writers chose to focus on same-gender sexual expression, narrowly defined as "homosexual": bisexuality was "not an issue" for them at that time.[7]

In "Sexuality: What We Couldn't Say," John Carey, the chair of the Special Committee on Human Sexuality, identified five serious ethical areas difficult to discuss in "middle-class religious communities," and then four "virtually *impossible* for the church to tackle" (his italics.) The first of these last four was bisexuality. Carey demonstrates his own lack of clarity about bisexuality when he writes:

Discussing how we relate as males and females may be difficult, but it is not impossible. Bisexuality, in contrast, introduces a profound ambiguity about personal identity. It reminds us that we carry certain "masculine" and "feminine" characteristics, and that self-designations as "male" and "female" have to be elastic enough to allow for wide variations. The majority of church persons want their ethical analyses clearly stated, and moral boundaries clearly defined. Bisexuality introduces an ambiguity that is more than they can cope with.[8]

At the same time that official denominational sources were silent on issues of bisexuality, activists and authors outside the churches were active, and the word was getting "out." In the early 1990s there was a veritable explosion of books and articles, organizations and networking.[9]

[6] Ibid., 54.

[7] Conversation with Sylvia Thorson Smith, April 8, 1997.

[8] John Carey, "Sexuality: What We Couldn't Say," *Christianity and Crisis* 51, no. 12 (August 19, 1991): 259.

[9] Some of the more important offerings: *Bisexuality: A Reader and Sourcebook,* ed. Thomas Geller (Hadley, Mass.: Times Change Press, 1991); *Bi Any Other Name: Bisexual People Speak Out,* ed. Loraine Hutchins and Lani Kaahumanu (Boston: Alyson Publications, 1991); *Redefining Sexual Ethics: A Sourcebook of Essays, Stories and Poems,* ed. Susan E. Davies and Eleanor H. Haney (Cleveland: Pilgrim Press, 1991). Although all three were in the secular press, they represented a critical mass and soon found their ways to seminary bookstores as

Information was now available for the searching and the isolated, and bisexuality received a kind of legitimization in popular culture. While Presbyterian bisexuals were "starving for language" in the churches, it was increasingly easy to feed the hunger outside our congregations. This is also the period when most major university campuses began including bisexuals explicitly in their lesbian and gay groups and bi groups became common in large cities. Many newsletters and periodicals were also established.

On the ecumenical Christian front, the United Methodist Church is arguably the mainline denomination closest to the Presbyterian Church (U.S.A.) in liturgical practice and religious culture, as well as in its relatively antique attitudes toward sexuality and spirituality. Nonetheless, Methodists are ahead on the subject of bisexuality. Early in 1991 Affirmation, the Methodist action and support group for "gay men and lesbians," voted to change its language to the more inclusive "gay men, lesbians and bisexuals."

At the same time Katalyst, the newsletter for the Methodist Reconciling Congregation Program, which welcomes members of all orientations, became inclusive. And in the fall of 1991, the magazine of the Reconciling Congregation Program, *Open Hands*, published an entire issue entitled "Bisexuality: Perceptions and Realities."[10] This magazine is well received and routinely subscribed to by United Methodist congregations and campus ministries. It serves as education for the questioning and information for all. This particular issue was groundbreaking in that it gave voice to bisexual Christians and discussed the intersection between sexuality and spirituality. The bisexuality issue of *Open Hands* became a mainstay in campus ministry and college bisexuality education and training and, now that the magazine has become ecumenical, is still available.

As for Presbyterians, in 1993 Lisa Bove, then comoderator of Presbyterians for Lesbian and Gay Concerns (analogous to United Methodists' Affirmation), presented a motion to change its name to incorporate bisexuals.[11] The body chose instead to study the issue and to include occasional articles and letters on the topic in its newsletter, the *More Light Update*.[12]

---

well as to mainline chain bookstores. *Closer to Home: Bisexuality and Feminism*, ed. Elizabeth Reba Weise (Seattle: Seal Press, 1992) brought women and feminists firmly into the picture, and the constellation was complete.

[10] *Open Hands* 7, no. 2 (fall 1991).

[11] *More Light Update* (May 1993): 10.

[12] Gaylesbitrans activist groups in the Presbyterian Church have used the name "More

In May 1994, however, PLGC voted against a name change. In 1998 PLGC merged with the Presbyterian More Light Churches Network, which affirms ordaining to church office all qualified persons, gay or straight. A new generic name was chosen for the group: More Light Presbyterians.

In sum, while there is no naming of bisexuality in official Presbyterian documents or in the names of advocacy groups devoted to changing denominational policy, in the 1990s the word appears in the "unofficial" Presbyterian social activist press, most notably in the *More Light Update*. For those with eyes to see and ears to hear, there is now at least mention being made in gaylesbi Presbyterian circles.

The Power of the Spoken Word

It is a truism that institutional church policies and papers on "sensitive" social issues follow rather than lead cultural movements. Likewise, the spoken word usually precedes written language. In this context it is the job of advocacy groups in denominations to educate and inform, to be in dialogue and to offer "real experiences," to lobby and to "act up" and to refuse to go away, in order to bring about desired ecclesiastical change. During the mid-1990s that has been the chosen method by which gay men, lesbian women, and their heterosexual allies worked, in an increasingly hostile environment, for full inclusion and participation in the Presbyterian Church (U.S.A.). Alongside this effort for gay-lesbian inclusion in a heterosexist church was a tiny group working toward bisexual inclusion in the gay-lesbian movement—and therefore in the heterosexist church. Early on, the response from gay male and lesbian leaders was that the word "bisexual" should still remain unspoken. But for some, that began to change.

As the newsletter *More Light Update* became inclusive in the early 1990s, we suffered a dearth of open bisexual writers and surfaced the dilemma of gay and lesbian authors not wanting to "speak for us." The dilemma served as a double bind. On the one hand, not to mention us perpetuated invisibility and silencing; not to give information to those questioning or ignorant maintained the closet. On the other, and in the same manner that women claim the right to name their experience, bisexual men and

Light" after Protestant Reformer John Robinson, who left England in 1620 seeking religious freedom in this country and stated that God had "yet more light" to shed on biblical interpretation.

women themselves must name, shape, and define our own reality. It is an ethical bind of the closet's making. In the end, most of us prefer that education and information be available, and agree that it is helpful when respectful allies use the language.

In the last ten years, however, the most open milieus for folks of all orientations have been campus ministries, university programs, and courses, conferences, and retreats: here bisexuals have found our voices. Outside the Sunday morning sanctuary, individual progressive people of faith, professors in colleges and seminaries, administrators and student deans, pastors and programmers have been speaking and teaching inclusively in courses in church history, Christian ethics, sexuality and spirituality, queer hermeneutics, women's and gender studies, sociology and psychology. There are still many who oppose us and who may in the end prevail. But the liberals among us document increasing openness in school-age populations, as well as the presence of out bisexual students and groups engaging the issue. With the advent of e-mail, networks grow and bisexual bibliographies proliferate. Individual Presbyterians, queer and allies, are doing faithful educational, pastoral, and advocacy work outside of denominational structures, participating in bringing about change for all of us.

When in 1992 the Permanent Judicial Commission of the General Assembly refused Jane Adams Spahr's call as co-pastor to the Downtown United Presbyterian Church of Rochester, New York, she and her colleagues began a cooperative ministry "That All May Freely Serve." She and others since enlisted have become "evangelists" for full inclusiveness in the denomination. Janie has criss-crossed the nation, preaching, teaching, listening, encouraging, grieving, and lifting up faithful nonheterosexual Christians, their families, and friends. Especially during the listening in her peripatetic ministry, she encountered many who were bisexual and transgender, and she became one of the first to make an intentional spoken language shift to "lesbian, gay, bisexual, and transgender" persons. In her frequent open discussions, panels, and forums, she educates around these words and answers again and again questions such as What's a bisexual person? Why do you include bisexuals? This kind of patient persistence and dedication change hearts and minds, and over the years have changed the language of most movement friends as well. Formulations like "GLBT" or "gaylesbitrans" are now probably more common than not.

Called Out

The 1995 publication of *Called Out: The Voices and Gifts of Lesbian, Gay, Bisexual, and Transgendered Presbyterians,* edited by Janie Spahr, Kathryn Poethig, Selisse Berry, and Melinda McLain represented another step forward.[13] Not only did the book include the stories of two Presbyterian bisexual women, Kathleen Buckley and Diana Vezmar-Bailey; not only did it include the words "Presbyterian" and "bisexual" in the title; but it also included us in all the introductory essays and analyses. It set a new tone for the movement, and its publication in time for the 1995 General Assembly in Cincinnati was a real cause for celebration. Funds were raised to mail copies to General Assembly commissioners the following year, and readings were held to get the stories "out." In 1997 its sequel, *Called Out With,* was published, composed of stories of heterosexual allies whose hearts and minds were transformed by the witness of gay, lesbian, bisexual and transgender persons in their lives.

It is a testimony to good political organization and to the use of media in conservative camps that the general populace still believes that "the church" unilaterally condemns gay, lesbian, bisexual, and transgender folk. While this is often true at the institutional level, and is lived out painfully in many congregations, there are also now many fully inclusive congregations, Presbyterian and otherwise, in Protestant denominations. Nonetheless, I am heartened by the fact that books like *Called Out* and *Called Out With,* together with those by Chris Glaser, are now routinely available in large chain bookstores, not only in the gaylesbi but also the spirituality sections. It is good to know that those "inquiring" can find an inclusive Christian message. And it is good to know that bisexuals are now "part of the family" for the written record. Paraphrasing an old question, for those asking, Can you be Presbyterian and bisexual? the answer is "You bet!" Nonetheless, we have a long way to go before our mere existence is translated into a full and honored place at the institutional table, as our struggle with Amendment B highlights.

Amendment B

With all this activity, there was still no mention of the word bisexuality in official Presbyterian documents—but a new tone was set in activist

[13] See n. 1 above.

groups. As the 1996 General Assembly in Albuquerque approached, social change organizations outside official denominational structures included bisexual concerns for the first time: a fact sheet was prepared for distribution, and later a coordinator, Kathleen Buckley, was chosen. And lesbian, gay, bisexual, transgender, and heterosexual activists readied themselves to make a faithful witness at the assembly.

A special Assembly Committee on Ordination and Human Sexuality was created to examine the results of national sexuality dialogues and overtures to the Assembly, to hold hearings, and to debate action. The result of this committee's deliberations was the proposal, and the eventual successful inclusion, of Amendment B in the constitution of the Presbyterian Church (U.S.A.).

The amendment's text reads:

> Those who are called to office in the church are to lead a life in obedience to Scripture and in conformity to the historic confessional standards of the church. Among these standards is the requirement to live either in fidelity within the covenant of marriage between a man and a woman (W-4.9001), or chastity in singleness. Persons refusing to repent of any self-acknowledged practice which the confessions call sin shall not be ordained and/or installed as deacons, elders, or ministers of the Word and Sacrament.

This amendment, so theologically flawed and so disastrous for the queer church community, spent a year in discussion and ratification in presbyteries. It was confirmed in sufficient numbers, following our polity, to return in 1997 for constitutional incorporation. It survived an attempt to rewrite it, and by March of 1998 was "the law of Presbyterian land." It stands now as an embarrassment to the denomination, flying in the face of long-standing commitments to inclusivity and setting the stage for judicial action.

And interestingly, it nowhere mentions its target group—gay and lesbian Presbyterians—by name. Early on, it was widely thought that the amendment's backers didn't wish to appear to be singling out gay men and lesbians for attack, although homosexuality had been almost the sole topic of discussion during the amendment's formulation.

The effect of not naming gay men and lesbians up front is, of course, to imply that *all* persons who unrepentantly transgress any "practice the confessions call sin" are liable to judicial action. Humorous discussion about "self accusing for the sin of usury" and the like occurred for a time, but it was clear that the brunt of accusations would be against individuals like ecclesiastically disobedient More Light church pastors, More Light congregations, and presbyteries validating "irregular" calls and installing to such ministries.

A movement based on individual conscience and on the extant Presbyterian constitution has arisen, to call actions such as gay elder ordinations once named "disobedient" (as in civil disobedience) *obedient*. In addition, "covenants of dissent," in which governing bodies state that they cannot abide by Amendment B without violating standards of conscience or faith, proliferate; other calls to inclusive community abound. And punitive legal cases based on Amendment B are beginning, as predicted.

In the midst of denominational spite and repression, something very interesting has happened. Bisexuality is still "a word the institutional church cannot speak," but suddenly bisexuals are included in the mean spirit of Amendment B. By virtue of not naming gay men and lesbians in the amendment, a "fill-in-the-blank space" is de facto created for all sexual (and perhaps other) minorities to be added for the purpose of discrimination. While this may not have been the intent of all writers of the amendment, it's too clever not to have been deliberate on the part of some. Any past query about whether or not bisexuals, transgenders, or transsexuals are intended in the word "homosexual" is now beside the point. To be included in the Constitution of the Presbyterian Church (U.S.A) by virtue of Amendment B's loose language is at best a Pyrrhic victory for bisexuals. Now we're here (and queer), without even speaking the word!

A Word We Must Now Speak

In the 1990s we faced an explosion of learning about human sexualities, gender socialization and acculturation, sex role development, identity politics, racial and ethnic difference, genetic engineering, and psychological development theory. In the midst of this, our language shifts uncomfortably, and we change. We are committed not to name others, but to use the names they choose for themselves, that we choose for ourselves.

For naming is a spiritual issue. The Hebrew people taught us that to name others is reductionist and represents an exercise of power over them. "I AM" taught us that our identity is "of God," and that we live into it from the inside out, changing and growing and "becoming who we are becoming" over time. A history full of epithets, changing from one period of fear or prejudice to the next, teaches us that names can become weapons filled with hate. And developing liberation movements teach us that silence and silencing others by not naming them can be as power-filled and imperializing as prejudicial naming.

While names used in the arena of sexual orientation can be fluid, this is probably no more true here than it is for racial and ethnic identities. Bi- and tri-racial persons in particular often struggle with identity, self-naming, and communities of belonging, and they represent perhaps the best analogy to bisexual persons. I believe that the bi- and tri- among us, with regard to any characteristic, possess possibilities for healthy bridging and healing in communities riven by discord with regard to racism, sexism, heterosexism, and ethno-centrism.

Many now recognize how imprecise our namings of sexuality, orientation, affinity, and preference are, and we try to speak carefully and with integrity. Names themselves can be problematic—certainly bisexuality, with its implied dualism or "two-ness," is. And names evolve over time, varying across community lines. In the end, we seek a balance somewhere between jettisoning all labels and calling ourselves simply "sexual"; and celebrating the real and exciting diversities our various sexualities present.

It is important that bisexuals affirm the choice of the term lesbian by women who sometimes choose opposite-sex partners; of the name gay by men who sometimes sleep with women; of heterosexual by those who have occasional same-sex relationships, although these same people might also be called bisexual. Self-naming has as much to do with politics, community of choice, even expediency or timing as it does with the sex of our partners.

These "variations on a theme" demonstrate the Spirit's good gift of sexuality freely experienced, while not necessarily using the language of bisexuality. It reflects just how much more work we need to do, however, when self-named gay men, lesbians, and heterosexuals come out privately as bisexual to the publicly out bisexual among us. Fearful of any number of things, these friends choose to hide their bisexuality. Rather than criticizing each other, it is important to name the sin here as heterosexism, and to take action to refuse the closets heterosexism requires—obviously for gay men and lesbians, often for "nonexclusive heterosexuals," and particularly for bisexuals. And it is important that the queer community refuse horizontal violence, acknowledging the heterosexist society that encourages it.

Speaking the Truth in Love

To speak of bisexuality at all is obviously to move beyond two dualistic frames: gay and straight, and gay and lesbian. By its very simplicity, such "twoness" offers opposing views that sway the uneducated, the fearful, the absolutists, and becomes the stuff of demagoguery and tyranny when used to cheer one group over and against the other.

It is often argued by gay men, lesbians, and allies that such simple, dualistic thought is what will be most politically expedient in "the battle of the sexualities." Some deeply believe that to introduce bisexuality and other orientations into the dialogue adds ethical or spiritual complexities requiring too much time for education. Such argumentation assumes that full inclusion should—or perhaps can only—be won first for gay men and lesbians ("homosexuals"); and that justice for other queer groups will follow in a second wave. It's my own opinion that to follow this tack embeds "doing to ourselves what others do to us," by becoming the oppressors' agents and ourselves acting out discrimination against some of the members of our community.

It's impossible to know now whether full incorporation into the Presbyterian Church (U.S.A.) can be won for gay men and lesbian women at all—without first splitting into two streams, liberal and conservative. Absent such information, it seems inauthentic to ask bisexuals and transgenders to wait until those in power are ready to include us too: to do so seems perilously close to arguments advanced by those opposed to women's ordination or racial desegregation and civil rights for all persons in the past. How long, O Lord!

Perhaps more importantly, I have great respect for the Spirit and for her gifts to persons of all sexual expressions. It seems likely to me that full transformation around the celebration of all sexualities will come when we are *all* named and present, rather than through a strategy that excludes some of us. To suppose otherwise may risk shortchanging the Spirit or "playing God." In addition to the gifts of heterosexual, gay male and lesbian Presbyterians, the gifts of bisexuals and others may ultimately be required for the whole church truly to become one body.

A Word Whose Time Has Come

It took twenty-five years for the word bisexual to appear on the T-shirts for the San Francisco Pride March in 1995. The years between the dream and the reality were filled with organizing, educating, and advocating on the part of the bisexual community and our allies, and for this I am grateful. It is my fervent hope, since that job has been done and campus and church activist and ally work continues, that it won't take the queer Presbyterian community that long again to add bisexuals to our symbolic denominational T-shirts, logos and names, mastheads and e-mail addresses. We bisexuals are ready!

The time has come for queer Presbyterians to speak the word "bisexuality," to write it, to define it unapologetically, and to take pride in it and in our full inclusivity in the beautiful panorama of human sexualities. I believe that the education many require before using "the B-word" is actually education around all queer sexualities; that this can be done briefly, positively, and simply; and indeed that it is already off and running. We need only to join in. God knows it is healing and healthy work for us all.

I do believe that the day is coming, though it's not yet here, when inclusive language for sexualities in Presbyterian curricula and polity, documents and theology, living and loving will be the norm. The Reverend Howard Warren (the gay male Presbyterian pastor for pastoral care at Damian House ministries for People with Aids in Indianapolis) speaks of the "wildly inclusive God" of love. May we who are in God's image, every one of us, grow to be wildly inclusive, too.

From Minister to Sex Radical: Further (Mis)Adventures of a Lesbian-Identified Bisexual Fag Hag

ELLEN TERRIS BRENNER

IN 1991 I WAS DELIGHTED to have an essay of mine, entitled "My life as a lesbian-identified bisexual fag hag," appear in the groundbreaking anthology *Bi Any Other Name: Bisexual People Speak Out.*[1] The piece was a lighthearted-but-serious look at my multilayered coming-out journey—first as a fag hag, then as a lesbian, and finally as a bisexual—amidst the often-skirmishing queer communities of Boston during the 1980s. "In the privacy of my own heart," I wrote, "I knew that the way I really wanted to be was wild and free, happily nonmonogamous, or even kinky (if I felt like it) . . . with both women and men."[2] Though barriers were plentiful, I expressed a conviction that having discovered the bisexual community, this freedom was at last within sight.

Despite this confidence, two significant omissions from that piece revealed how far beyond my grasp that freedom still lay. First, I did not publish the piece using my full and correct name. Next, I did not reveal the fact that I was then a candidate for the Unitarian Universalist (UU) ministry.

To be sure, I was hardly hiding my bisexuality in the closet at that point in my ministerial career, or at any point before or since. I had stood up and mouthed off about bisexuality at my seminary, being one of the few queers in my largely Methodist seminary who could afford to speak out on queer issues without instantly torpedoing her chances of ordination. I had stood up and mouthed off about it at General Assembly, our denom-

[1] Ellen Terris, "My life as a lesbian-identified bisexual fag hag," in *Bi Any Other Name: Bisexual People Speak Out,* ed. Loraine Hutchins and Lani Kaahumanu (Boston: Alyson Publications, 1991), 56–59.

[2] Ibid., 58.

ination's annual convention, as part of team efforts to pass resolutions for queer rights and against far-right hate legislation. My ministerial search packet (the hefty notebook of vitae, sermons, photos, and other examples of the budding minister in action assembled by every UU minister seeking a parish call) was rife with mentions of my sexual orientation and activism. I had just the year before published a "Bisexuality 101"-style consciousness-raising piece, with my full name and candidacy status on it, in the official newsletter of the UU Women's Federation (UUWF).[3]

However, it's illuminating to compare that UUWF article and the one from *Bi Any Other Name.* The former was the epitome of sober-sided, responsible, politically correct minister-speak. The "My Life As . . ." piece, on the other hand, could never be mistaken for minister-speak, even among the relatively free-wheeling ranks of the UU ministry. Certainly, in terms of provocativeness, it was not out there with the likes of Susie Bright and Pat Califia, for whom I admitted an admiration therein. But I did dare to drop the terms "nonmonogamy" and "kink" and even "S/M" (sadomasochism), in a tone which was in no way disparaging.[4]

At the point that *Bi Any Other Name* was heading to press, and editors Lani Kaahumanu and Loraine Hutchins were trying to get contributors to fish or cut bait on the issue of pseudonyms or real names, I was heading for the first time into the ministerial search process. The year past had been a hard one for openly queer UU ministerial candidates. UU leadership in recent years had taken admirably huge strides in policy, affirming

[3] The Rev. Ellen T. Brenner, "Some Complex Truths About Bisexuality," *The Communicator* (newsletter of the Unitarian Universalist Women's Federation, June/July 1990): 1.

[4] I want to stress here that when I talk about nonmonogamy, kink, S/M, and other such terms that have sometimes been gathered under the umbrella term "radical sexuality," I am exclusively referring to safe, sane, and mutually consensual acts shared between willing and fully informed adults.

Among those practices, "polyamory" has been most often defined as maintaining faithful sexual relationships between more than two people; nonmonogamy connotes a more open set of relationships, but still mutually consensual among all involved parties. "Kink" is an affectionate slang term loosely referring to practices such as sado-masochism (S/M), bondage and discipline (B/D), and a host of other assorted acronyms, connoting various types of sexual play involving intense physical and emotional stimulation.

To go into the depth required to explain more fully all the definitions, mores, and ethics of these admittedly controversial sexualities would fill many books besides this one. Fortunately, many such books have been written, a number of which are excellent. Among these, I'd recommend Dossie Easton and Catherine Liszt, *The Ethical Slut: A Guide to Infinite Sexual Possibilities* (San Francisco: Greenery Press, 1998); and Jay Wiseman, *SM 101: A Realistic Introduction* (San Francisco: Greenery Press, 1998). In particular, I draw the reader's attention to Wiseman's clear and concise discussion of how consensual BDSM is most definitely not sexual abuse (pp. 41–44).

the rights of queer people to occupy the pulpit as well as the pew. However, the rank and file were, as is often the case, lagging behind. A number of my queer colleagues lost calls to churches for which they were eminently qualified, purely from congregational homophobia, and the whole lot of us were getting jumpy. It seemed like a really bad moment to have my true name appear on an article that even many of my queer colleagues might find controversial, just waiting for a jittery search committee to stumble upon.

So, trying my damnedest to convince myself that I had already taken more than my share of risks, and that it was perfectly acceptable in a potentially hostile environment to pick and choose my battles, I told Lani and Loraine to sign me "Ellen Terris."[5] As I did so I knew I was selling out the whole point of the piece—and that this sellout symbolized with devilish exactitude the compromise I was making at that time regarding my aspirations for sexual freedom. But I did it nonetheless.

The Contradictions of the Liberal Ministry for People of "Fringe" Identities

I had been seeing this fundamental contradiction coming for some years. On the one hand, many of the studies and experiences I had participated in from the time I entered seminary had actually helped to fuel my sexual self-discovery. Feminist thealogies gave me permission to seek wholeness, tear down the boundary between body and mind/spirit instilled in me by society, and celebrate my embodied woman-self as the incarnation of God/ess herself. Liberation theologies empowered me to use the praxis of my own real life as the foundation for my theological truth.

Yet the feminists and liberationists whose writings encouraged my explorations in those days often turned a blind eye to their remaining conservative assumptions—especially on matters of sex. Only a few included queer people at all in their vision of liberation. If we were included, we would often be quickly mentioned as one of several oppressed groups; or else completely desexualized, as if the only way to

[5] Terris was my late mother's maiden name. Using her name was another way of mollifying myself for having copped out on using my real name. Since then, I've started using Terris in place of the middle name my mother gave me, which was Therese. It has occurred to me that my mother's choice of a middle name so close to the one she gave up may have been her unconscious way of preserving that piece of her identity. And isn't preservation of identity part of what this is all about?

affirm us as more than our sexual activity was to gloss over the realities of our sexual selves.

Two examples of this obliteration, both from books I otherwise loved, are found in *Sexism and God-Talk,* by Rosemary Radford Ruether and *Original Blessing: A Primer in Creation Spirituality,* by Matthew Fox.[6] In *Sexism and God-Talk,* Ms. Ruether mentions lesbians just a bare handful of times, mainly brief references to their presence in the liberal and radical feminist movements. And in *Original Blessing,* Fox resoundingly declared the importance of founding a liberating theology upon the experience of oppressed peoples such as homosexuals, but gave no details of what the real-life content of that experience might be. Especially when the recovery of the sensual into religion is such a central and admirable part of Fox's Creation Spirituality, this is an unfortunate omission.

Few liberationists bothered to mention bisexuals—in fact, if they were gay or lesbian themselves they often demonstrated active biphobia. Transgendered people weren't even on their political maps. And as for more radical sexualities such as SM, I could at that time find no theologian so daring as to condone such goings-on. In fact, the topic could provoke some of these supposedly radical theologians into a flurry of condemnation that would have done Jerry Falwell proud.

Examples abound, but some of the works that rankle me the most include James B. Nelson's generally sex-positive and groundbreaking book *Embodiment: An Approach to Sexuality and Christian Theology,* whose refreshingly thorough and affirming chapter on gay people, the church, and the roots of homophobia is preceded by a section dismissing sadomasochism as "pathological" practices, "highly suspect as paths to fulfillment, even when both partners are willing and both are receiving pleasure, as apparently is usually the case."[7]

Another example: In her ironically titled *Pure Lust,* Mary Daly takes the classic radical-feminist tack of conflating all of patriarchal society with what she calls "masosadism" and thereupon condemns those lesbian sex radicals of the 1980s who were exploring consensual S/M as "pseudofeminists" and "tools of the sadosociety in its continuing effort to destroy female consciousness."[8]

[6] Rosemary Radford Ruether, *Sexism and God-Talk* (Boston: Beacon Press, 1983); Matthew Fox, *Original Blessing: A Primer in Creation Spirituality* (Santa Fe: Bear & Co., 1983), 268–69.

[7] James B. Nelson, *Embodiment: An Approach to Sexuality and Christian Theology* (Minneapolis: Augsburg, 1978), 177.

[8] Mary Daly, *Pure Lust* (Boston: Beacon Press, 1984), 66.

And in the otherwise excellent *Touching Our Strength: The Erotic as Power and the Love of God,* Carter Heyward goes along with Mary Daly in conflating sadomasochism with the power-over structures of patriarchal society. She then insists:

> My concern is not basically with sexual sadomasochistic (s/m) cultures among heterosexual people, gay men, or lesbians, but rather with the broader sense in which sadomasochism has deformed us all as a people.

She erroneously opines, "that the larger social context of sadomasochism has helped create the sexual s/m cultures, infusing many women and men with an embodied confusion of violence and ecstasy."[9] Even though she urges that S/M people not be judged wrong or bad on account of their sexualities, it is apparent to me that she has already done just that.

Meanwhile, the UU congregation in which I had first found a home welcomed me with loads of queer and goddess/pagan presence, including sessions of the groundbreaking "Cakes for the Queen of Heaven" goddess-spirituality curriculum, plus some of the first meetings of the Covenant of UU Pagans. There I also met some members of Boston's thriving bisexual activist community, beginning the personal blossoming I went on to describe in the "Lesbian-identified Bisexual Fag Hag" piece. Yet even within that liberal-even-for-UUism congregation there were some members who were uncomfortable with, for instance, open relationships, triadic relationships, anything that did not exactly ape the model of the monogamous heterosexual dyad.

Gradually I came to notice the glass ceiling to one's acceptability as a sexual minority in the UU movement, based on how closely one was assimilated to heterosexual norms. You could be out, and they'd be proud to accept you. You could even be dykey or faggy—within certain unspoken but clear limits. But forget about drag, forget about leather, and your relationship had damn well better look like the same-sex version of Ozzie and Harriet—updated for the egalitarian 1980s, of course—or else folks would start getting nervous.

To be fair to my religious movement, which I do genuinely love, I have to point out that this phenomenon is not unique to Unitarian Universalism—nor, for that matter, unique to the issue of sexual orientation and identity. I have seen this same ambivalence toward all sorts of minorities

[9] Carter Heyward, *Touching Our Strength: The Erotic as Power and the Love of God* (San Francisco: Harper & Row, 1989), 105–9.

afflict liberal institutions of every stripe, both religious and secular, including many liberal queer institutions. There are, unfortunately, a lot of liberals out there who may embrace oppressed minorities with all good intention, but still have not dealt with their remaining internalized oppressions, let alone the basic fear of anything challenging to status-quo majority norms. All too often this results in conditional acceptance of minority peoples to the extent that they can pass as something familiar and nonthreatening to the majority.

I am far from alone in noticing this blind spot in the vision of many liberals. For example, in *Being Liberal in an Illiberal Age: Why I Am a Unitarian Universalist,* Jack Mendelsohn writes:

> The trouble with too many liberals, according to radicalized blacks, women, youth, gays, and peace activists, is their complacent spirit. Yes, they have a decent concern for social change. But where is the passion? Where is the sense of their own oppression? Buried in middle-class standards. That's where it is. Tucked into the benefits that infuriatingly unjust social structures have bestowed upon them. Yes, they would like to share these benefits with the less fortunate, those who have been locked out and denied access, but at little or no cost to themselves and their children.[10]

Now, there are many levels to the purgatory of passing, and sometimes, when one finds a place that will accept you about 75 percent of the way, sticking the remaining 25 percent back in the closet seems a small price to pay for 100 percent acceptance. But that price also includes a loss of authenticity, and that's a critical loss in the liberal ministry, in which authenticity of self is just about the only theological/philosophical touchstone on which our entire eclectic movement can agree. "The true preacher," said our Unitarian forebear Ralph Waldo Emerson, "can be known by this, that he [*sic*] deals out to the people his life"[11]—that is, the true preacher ministers honestly and wholeheartedly from one's personal experience. But how can one deal out to people one's life as Emerson urges, when one has agreed to remove from one's life-deck a couple of one's strongest trumps?

As my relationship with the ministry deepened, I had the same sort of foreboding I'd felt at the start of certain lover relationships. I knew these

[10] Jack Mendelsohn, *Being Liberal in an Illiberal Age: Why I Am a Unitarian Universalist* (Boston: Beacon Press, 1985), 4.

[11] Ralph Waldo Emerson, "The Divinity School Address," as reprinted in *Three Prophets of Religious Liberalism: Channing, Emerson, Parker,* ed. Conrad Wright (Boston: Unitarian Universalist Association, 1986), 91.

key issues I was trying so hard to ignore were inevitably going to come back to haunt me and would ultimately be the relationship's undoing. But just as in every one of those other relationships, my passion for the object was too strong for me to turn back. And so, despite all the lessons about the dangers of suppressing pieces of myself I had documented so enthusiastically in the Fag Hag essay, I prepared to do so yet again.

Five years serving a white middle-class congregation in the suburbs of Seattle and I'd had it. It wasn't a bad congregation—far from it; it was a gathering of interesting and lively people, with deep concerns and inquiring minds. But within a few weeks of arriving, they made it clear to me, in a thousand subtle, often unconscious ways, that they needed me to be as much like them as possible. I could be out, but it had to be an assimilated, well-mannered outness, indistinguishable from their lives as quiet, suburban, vanilla, monogamous couples. I went as far as I could go with ministering to them at the place they were in—after all, they had every right to their lives, as much as I did to mine. But that was exactly the point. I had to live their life rather than mine, for the life I wanted to live would have blown their minds so thoroughly that they could never have opened up to my ministry. And the strain of this most peculiar out-but-not-out closet eventually wore me out.

So I resigned from the full-time parish ministry in 1995 and went back to pick up where I left off in my journey toward sexual freedom.

Reclaiming the Seat of My Spiritual Power

Things had progressed in the queer communities in the years I had been so deeply occupied elsewhere. Despite the continuing objections of certain ideologues and assimilationist types, there had been a resurgence in the popularity and acceptance of such traditional queer mores as drag, butch/femme, and kink/leather/SM.

Seattle had developed an especially thriving leather/kink community, including a sizable polyamorous pansexual contingent. The pansexual subcommunity was especially fascinating to me as a bisexual person because of its diversity. Within it were individuals who identified as straight and as gay or lesbian as well as numerous bisexuals. A number of these folks also happened to be transgendered persons, male-to-female and female-to-male. Further, many of these people were happy to share BDSM "play" with each other regardless of the gender or sexual orientations of the persons involved. This is not to say there weren't problems and misunderstandings—no community is immune to those. Yet I could think of few other sectors of the queer community where that broad a range of sexualities and genders got along with that high a level of equanimity. I was impressed.

With great fear and trembling, terrified that word would somehow get back to my UU communities and I'd see all those bridges upon which I'd labored go up in smoke, I began to venture into this heady new social territory. And I made a discovery.

It wasn't just that these people offered me a level of sexual acceptance that I'd been dreaming of for years—such that my bisexuality and polyamory were commonplace. It wasn't just that they demonstrated an ethical consideration for each other's persons and desires that revealed the lie of the old radical-feminist denunciations of BDSM as "patriarchal violence." It wasn't even just that I got off—though I did indeed, and more often and exultantly than I had in all my years of "vanilla" sex.

It was that at last, I was getting to experience for myself this "erotic as power" concept about which I'd heard all the feminist theorists go on.[12] Others said they found it in nice, gentle, soothing, vanilla sex, and in activities sensual but completely nonsexual. Yet as hard as I had tried by those means, I caught only glimmers of whatever power they were talking about. But then I experienced radical sex—wild, fierce, funny, bawdy, boundaries-pushing, label-defying sensation-expanding sex, sex that ushered me into altered states of mind, sex that was primal, sex that was majickal, sex that roared with the divine serpent fire of the Goddess. And by means of these rituals of sex I opened up my person to the power of the erotic in its full shamanistic intensity.

At last. This was a spiritual/sexual power that I recognized as home.

What makes this radical sex spiritual? Partly, that aspect it has in common with vanilla sex (for those who are wired to best get off on that), and for that matter with any number of nonsexual techniques for opening to wider consciousness through physical disciplines. Regardless of the spiritual practice by which we reach out to the Transcendent, and regardless of

[12] Audre Lorde, *Uses of the Erotic: The Erotic as Power* (Trumansburg, N.Y.: Crossing Press, 1981); reprinted in *Sister Outsider: Essays and Speeches* (Trumansburg, N.Y.: Crossing Press, 1984). I have nothing but the utmost respect for Ms. Lorde, who originated this concept. In fact, every word of this historic essay of hers rings true for me. My point is that I just had to go a bit further in my sexuality to connect with it in my own life and body.

one's thea/ology of what Deities/Beings/Consciousnesses/Processes are reaching back, there is a common base within us as embodied fleshly beings. We have certain biochemical pathways within our bodies, certain interplays of neurotransmitters and hormones and blood sugars, that when played just right vault our minds into the altered states of consciousness in which we can open to the Divine. Radical sex, for those to whom it calls, is just one of many ways of triggering that altered state.

But there is also something unique to BDSM sexuality when used as a spiritual practice. In it are faint echoes of shamanistic spiritual practices from many other and older cultures, such as the *okeepah* (Sun Dance) performed by certain Native American tribes, and the *kavadi* of Malaysia and India. In it also are elements that resonate with my own mystical/pagan/Jungian thealogy, in which death-and-rebirth myths such as Inanna's journey to the underworld play a key role. There is simply something big and ancient and archetypal about the act of achieving altered states by means of consensually giving and receiving extreme body/mind sensation. I'm a little too new at it all to name it more exactly. It is something about which I, and many other modern participants for that matter, are just beginning to learn. But I am not alone in feeling there's something special and important about this path, something worth following.

Part of me regrets all the detours I had to take before I could free myself enough to take this path. Another part of me realizes that my decade preparing for and then participating in the parish ministry also enriched me in many ways—not least of which was grounding me in the studies I needed to fully appreciate my radical rediscovery. Still another part of me is frankly nervous about what my UU friends, lay and clergy, will make of all this. Now that I'll no longer be keeping my sexuality safely nonthreatening, I worry that some will never want to speak to me again, and others will conclude I've gone round the bend. Though I am dead certain there will be at least a few others who will be quietly cheering me on.

Mostly, though, the fears and regrets are far outweighed by the pleasure, the freedom, the inspiration—and the sense of adventure. Pat Califia has written:

> Being a sex radical means being defiant as well as deviant. It means being aware that there is something dissatisfying and dishonest about the way sex is talked about (or hidden) in daily life. It also means questioning the way our society assigns privilege based on adherence to its moral codes, and in fact makes every sexual choice a matter of morality. If you believe that these inequities can be addressed only through extreme social change, then you

> qualify as a sex radical, even if you prefer to get off in the missionary position and still believe there are only two genders.[13]

By that definition, then, I've been something of a sex radical the whole time I was a full-time parish minister and for decades before that. I'm just being a little more radical—and obvious—about it now. And it feels very, very, good.

[13] Pat Califia, *Public Sex: The Culture of Radical Sex* (Pittsburgh: Cleis Press, 1994).

The Fear of Growing Things

Elizabeth Andrew

In early June, a party from my small Methodist congregation carpools from the Sunday service into downtown Minneapolis for the Pride Parade. The city park is jubilant. Thousands mill around in brightly colored T-shirts, carrying water bottles, balloons, condoms, placards, candy to toss into the crowd. . . . Our group's banner bears the flame, cross, and rainbow flag. The kids who fight over carrying it are sometimes the children of heterosexual couples and sometimes of gay couples.

My choice to walk with the church and not with the bi women or with the educators is a conscious one.

Compared with other groups, our contingent—even the whole section of religious-affiliated organizations—is quite small. It saddens me that Christians, made passive by their presumption of salvation, are historically the last to risk their necks by championing issues of civil rights. Marching becomes for me a witness to a God who yearns for justice.

The dykes on bikes roar up the length of the parade, the politicians throw buttons, the Parents and Friends of Lesbians and Gays cause a thunder of applause, the queens wave their gloved hands from the backs of convertibles, the AIDS hospice workers march solemnly. We move in the midst of it all, testifying that the Creator relishes such diversity.

It is a joyful revolution that my congregation is waging. Despite the refusal of the Methodist Church to ordain "self-avowed practicing homosexuals," we know that when a church, the body of Christ, loves the bodies of its members, what miracles *can't* happen within its walls? We wink at our lesbian pastor and bless any union where health and happiness are found. We are living proof of how truths work their transformation: What is possible for one person is possible for a congregation, and what is possible for a congregation is possible even for a backward, bigoted institution.

As I march, I think of Marianne Williamson's words:

> We were born to make manifest the Glory of God that is within us. When we let our own light shine, we unconsciously give other people permission to do the same. As we are liberated from our own fear, our presence automatically liberates others.[1]

This is liberation, this colorful conglomeration of marchers. Perhaps each of us individually is afraid, with good reason. But the crowd frees us from private fears, so what we make manifest is a tremendous amount of glory and a lot of noise. For now, the Methodist conference pretends not to see the inclusivity of this joyful witness. But we are patient. Our ministry is as much to the church as it is to its members.

We believe in change.

When prayer is radical, it sheds its illusion of privacy. What we think is an intimate encounter with God swiftly has ramifications in the broader world, as our prayer transforms itself into words and actions.

Similarly, radical faith leaves the charming whitewashed walls of a church and breaks into the political realm. The manner in which we manifest the sacred is more fundamental than any conscious belief about God. There is the God we profess and the one we live, day in and day out—the one who determines our practice of that ignominious word "lifestyle." No matter what our heads or hearts tell us, the God we live is the one we believe in. This is where we invest our time, energy, and money; this is where our creativity and passion go; this is the object of our love and longing.

For a number of years, I taught public school seventh grade English in a wealthy suburb of Minneapolis. Despite the prestige, good pay, and bright students, I found myself growing increasingly unhappy, until it occurred to me to look at the spiritual geography of my day. My resources were flung far into the suburbs, away from the heart of the city where my church was located, where I was out, where, in fragments of stolen time, I wrote. What I held sacred in practice was security and an obligation to be socially responsible. I thought this meant holding down a job and making a difference in children's lives.

But the silence I kept within the school walls was also a submission to the God of conservative suburbia. This God had a two-car garage and

[1] Marianne Williamson, originally in *A Return to Love* (New York: HarperCollins, 1993), quoted in "Let Your Light Shine," *Utne Reader* (January/February 1996): 128.

boundaries about sexuality as clear as the locked gates of a walled community. There was no forum for deviation. What was not outright sin regarding sexual identity was at least a violation of lunchroom social mores, which dictated that "coming out" unnecessarily exposed privacies. A wedding ring, however, revealed nothing indiscreet. So much was invested in the constructs of normalcy—the money and energy of lifetimes—that the stakes were high. This God was a moral judge, unwavering in his consistency, with a will as clear as night and day.

For the year and a half after I came out to myself, I walked through the halls of the middle school carrying in me a word that, when mouthed, would cost me my job or, worse, prohibit me from putting my hand on a child's shoulder. At the beginning of the school year I told my classes that I would not tolerate put-downs and specifically listed gender, race, religion, height, looks, money, and sexual orientation ("that means gay, lesbian and bi jokes, kids"). A week passed and the hate-mail began arriving in my mail slot, cc'ed to the principal. Typed unevenly on flimsy paper, unsigned with no return address, full of misspellings, its contents were so unoriginal they almost made me laugh. But still, my hands shook when I folded that paper back into thirds. On my way down to lunch, the principal snatched me into her office. "Remember," she said, "you are always accountable to the parents of your students." For the next thirty days, a crank caller rang my home at eight o'clock at night and hung up when I answered. Not long afterward, a colleague of mine recommended to a student a novel whose main character has a gay uncle. The student's parent, without having read the book, stood up during a school board meeting and thrust the paperback toward the superintendent, who also had never read the book, and demanded that the teacher be fired. The superintendent agreed. For a year and a half, I tried to silence the ticking bomb of my own secret, but knew precisely how powerful its inevitable explosion would be.

What is it about me that could possibly be threatening? It seems that if the single, female seventh grade teacher in room 164—the one who is binding books with her rowdy classes today—if she names herself as bisexual, then she must be the wild card that's ripping up the moral fabric. She defies everything that is intended to bind this loose construct together. She's an insult to committed, monogamous relationships. She is sexually insatiable. Is there a rule regarding gender behavior that she doesn't break? More than half of her students come from divorced families; they suffer from shuttling between two homes; they lose their homework and toothbrushes and don't know what to give for an address. Someone—surely the bisexual—is to blame. It's easier to condemn those who live outside the rules than to question whether the standards we have for moral behavior, which we hold so dear, are destroying us.

It is for this reason that coming out of the closet, in every context, is political. "The Other is in me," I say, first to myself, then to family and friends, and finally to the broader world. That which I've tried to push to the periphery of my identity—this comprehensive, commensurate attraction to one gender or the other, alien to my culture and most frightening to me—is in me. It is this Other that is threatening. It wreaks havoc on the safe assumptions people make for survival. It might mean that the Other is in anyone, or everyone, and at the bottom of things we are each alone and different. It might mean that God is the Ultimate Other rather than the familiar, kindly face that looks an awful lot like our own.

Those of us who embody ambiguity invite alarm equitably to hetero- and homosexuals alike. We can't be pinned down. To the gay community, the bisexual is a waffler, someone who can't decide between the sexes and who has an easy out if the social stigmas grow unbearable. She stands in the way of civil rights because popular opinion associates her immorality with the Movement. What difference does it make to anyone if the bisexual is celibate in her singleness, valuing faithfulness in relationship above sexual freedom? If she understands bisexuality to be physical attraction to the individual rather than to the gender? What difference does it make that her students love to write poetry and fill notebook after notebook of increasingly articulate prose? What about when she leaves her career for the contemplative life of a Christian faith community? Christian? The contradictions are too many to resolve satisfactorily. She is one of them. She is the Other.

Quizzical looks come from every direction. It's generally puzzling that I named myself bisexual while single and uninvolved. Why bother? What seems natural to me when I'm attracted to a beautiful person of one gender or another becomes heavy with lewd connotations in the language of my society: bisexual, a word understood by a moral judgment on the actions it implies rather than its subtleties of lived potential.

At city gatherings of bi women, I worry when someone gets too excited about the book I am writing. "Finally," they say, "a bi woman's story will be told." Already I sense their disappointment when the climax is not made of luscious, tongue-twisting descriptions of diverse intimate moments. I worry that this absence will be misinterpreted as a condemnation, an aloof moral superiority, when it is not. The old-fashioned "values" I adhere to (sexual conservatism, monogamy, long-term commitment, the responsibility to, in some manner or another, raise children) apply very well to myself, but I don't presuppose that they apply to everyone.

Who am I, then, to claim this word "bisexual"? I reach into the center of my identity where creative energy resides like the gaseous light particles inside a birthing star, and I release it, a swift chain reaction until everything burns, the core's substance brilliantly exposed to the vastness of space. Deep in my most intimate, internal movements, this is who I am. Why not let it shine? Why not tell my story, which has a foot in the body and a foot in the spirit, instead of feet in the warm beds of both men and women, as everyone would expect? Bisexuality gives a name to the physical attraction I feel randomly, recklessly. It's my contribution to diversity, even on the margins. I claim it and lift it up in gratitude for the expanse of inclusive space within a word.

The challenge of claiming my Christianity in the queer community is equally strenuous. During introductions at a workshop on sexuality and spirituality, I introduce myself as a member of an ecumenical Christian community. A transgendered woman in the room stands up and shakes her fist at me. "How dare you say I'm sinful?" she demands. "How dare you say that Christ is the only answer?" I sit at the front of the room, my heart sinking. I know the real question to be, "How dare I profess a religion that's caused this much hurt?" "Not all Christians believe those things," I respond. "It's possible to be a Christian and accept the validity of other faiths. It is possible to understand sin as that which separates us from what is uplifting, healing, and what leads to justice." After the workshop she and I hash out explanations and are able to touch one another's hands in the end.

The story of how we are each embodied spirit is a story of liberation, radical in its theology, political in its transformative power, and always a personal struggle. "Who do you say I am?" Jesus asked the disciples. It's a deceptively simple question, with horrific consequences. Name me, prods the God incarnate. What you name divine walks among you. I name my experience simply, honestly, then watch the repercussions ripple outward until my little word takes on the world. As within every piece of creation, the sacred resides at my essence. It is brilliant, and profoundly bisexual. With all its power, it works to transform me into its true image, the same way it works to transform the world: from the inside out.

This, then, is what calls me to question, How could I ever leave the church? My witness from inside its ranks is to divinity embracing diversity. Someone must stick around to hold the institution accountable to its original ministry. Someone must heal the wounds it has inflicted in the name of love. Someone must march jubilantly in the Pride Parade, throwing chocolate kisses toward the bystanders and shouting, "Hugs and kisses from the Methodist Church!" Perhaps it is my gift, to embody complexity and stand firm in the knowledge that we are all loved.

Where God resides is any place that creation is at work and truth is spoken. This is how we become instruments for change in the world. In the midst of crowds, I claim my body and I claim my God—the Ultimate Other, a creator with equanimity and multifarious taste.

Full Circle

CHERYL SORIANO

I WAS TWENTY-TWO YEARS OLD, fresh out of college, and although I did not know it at the time, I was about to be rejected for who I was. She called me into her room and opened her well-worn Bible to Romans 1:26–27. She began reading aloud:

> For this cause God gave them up unto vile affections: for even their women did change the natural use into that which is against nature. And likewise also the men, leaving the natural use of the woman, burned in their lust one toward another; men with men working that which is unseemly, and receiving in themselves that recompense of their error which was meet.

My heart sank, deep as it could possibly go. She was telling me in no uncertain terms that my relationship with my new girlfriend, Grace, was a personal affront to her, to the family, and to God Himself. My mother was concerned for my soul, advising me to take the "normal" path— my afterlife insurance policy. She reminded me of a televangelist when she used phrases such as, "Hate the sin. Love the sinner." These verses and her words haunted me, and I began to curse my religious upbringing.

I grew up with fundamentalist Christian parents and Catholic aunts and uncles. I went to church twice on Sunday, in addition to attending Sunday school. I also went to mass when I stayed with my aunts and uncles. I alternated between holy water and kneelers on the road and fire and brimstone at home. When I came of age, I decided to pursue Catholicism. I felt more spiritually nourished in the Catholic Church, appreciating the beauty of the mass and the ritual.

I had a very strong faith when I was younger. I could feel God's presence around me. I knew He would be there whenever I needed Him. I talked to Him daily, even though I resented going to church twice on

Sunday. The sermons never really changed. They were about the need to be saved and the consequences of not being saved. I felt like I "got it" the first time, and I did not feel the need to go that often. My parents felt differently, and they forced me to go. I was turned off by church and religion when I started college. Going to church, particularly the fundamentalist Christian churches, seemed pointless to me because I was not getting anything out of it. When I was feeling depressed, I would attend mass, but that was very infrequently. I focused most of my attention on academics. My spirituality was an intrinsic part of who I was, and even though I was not growing in my faith, it was still there. I did not attend services, but I knew my relationship with God remained the same.

It surprises me that a woman coming from such a conservative background would ever identify as bisexual. I had always had feelings for men, although I felt I did not relate to them as well as I did to women. I felt more emotionally connected to women, which made it easier to become closer to them. Men were my friends, lovers, and sexual partners, but I gave my heart more easily to women because I understood them as much as they understood me. When I started to notice that I had feelings for women, I did not suppress them. I was very experimental, and I felt the need to try almost anything once. This liberal attitude was coupled with fear. I was raised with the notion that homosexuality was disgusting and a sin, and I knew that my family would never approve. Yet I did not let my fear and these teachings stop me. I was twenty-one years old at the time, and I was happy to be exploring my attractions to women. However, I was also afraid of what my family would think. The first time I was with a woman sexually, it felt very natural. Ever since that day, I have identified as bisexual—as being able to be in loving relationships where gender is not an issue.

Considering my religious background, to be bisexual and proud of who I was proved difficult. In the fundamentalist Christian churches I attended, I heard their dogma incessantly—that homosexuality was a sin. I began to realize that some "Christians," viewed my sexuality as disgusting and "gross," to quote a family member. Because I identified as bisexual, my struggle was difficult. It became infinitely more difficult when I "came out."

I came out to the world because I fell in love with an amazing woman—Grace. I remember that day clearly. It was the day before my college graduation, and I had invited Grace, my new girlfriend, to the commencement ceremonies in San Diego. My mother, father, and aunt asked me why I invited her. They were wary of her because she was a very masculine-looking woman. I said, "This is an important day for me, and I want her here." My aunt verbally backed me into a corner, asking, "Are you some kind of lesbian?" Despite the fear of rejection from my family, I could never live with myself if I lied about who I was. I replied, "No, I am bisexual." My mother and my aunt started to cry. My father walked out of the room.

My graduation was bittersweet. Even though I had accomplished something important, I felt as though I had let everyone down, just because I was in love with a woman. They hugged and kissed me, telling me how proud they were of me, but I could feel their disappointment. One of my cousins told me that those in my family who attended my graduation talked about me and my new girlfriend, Grace, in a big family meeting at my aunt's house in San Clemente. I remember vividly that my younger sister did not talk to me very much at all. When I would say or ask something, her answers were very curt. The day after the graduation, she had a severe anxiety attack. She had difficulty breathing, and I drove her, at top-speed, to the nearest emergency room. My girlfriend and my cousin were also in the car, and my parents and aunts followed. She was given oxygen, and she was hooked up to different monitors. While we were all in the emergency waiting room, my mother complained of shooting pain in her back and legs. She was also seen in the emergency room that day. No one verbally conveyed their feelings to me, but I felt that it was all my fault. My aunts chose to blame my girlfriend. They confronted her and told her that she was the cause of all of this. They asked her to go home. I was angry that she was the one being blamed for my coming out. That day was a nightmare. Since then everything in my life, including my spirituality, has changed.

I talked to my cousin, a Methodist minister, shortly after. He was there to feel the aftershock of my earth-shaking coming out. I will never forget the love he showed me and the words he used to comfort me. He told me, "If that's who you are, you were created by God and loved by Him." Those words made my soul wail with gratitude and pain. I was eternally thankful for his unconditional love, but I was not at the point where I could totally accept myself, as he did me.

I cursed my existence and sank into a deep depression that lasted about six months. My girlfriend and I returned to the San Francisco Bay Area briefly, only to collect our personal belongings. I took the money I had received as graduation gifts, cashed out a CD, and we moved to Hollywood. We loved each other so much, but we had a miserable experience there financially. I was severely depressed. I lost nearly thirty pounds by the time our stay in Hollywood ended and we moved back to the Bay Area.

During this depressing time, which I refer to as "the dark night of my soul," I read something that challenged my despair. "It is better to be hated for who you are, than loved for who you are not." That made me feel somewhat stronger, but it did not appease my spirit. I wanted God to love me, but I could not feel that He did. What if I was wrong? What if I really was offending Him? These questions changed how I worshiped Him. For the next three years, I didn't feel comfortable hearing mass, even if it healed my soul. I decided to get my spiritual nourishment from the ocean, and I would drive to the coast on Sundays. I would sit and watch the waves, overwhelmed by the beauty of His creation. My heart would ache, and sometimes I would just cry. I wanted to feel peaceful in church again, but I could not. I wanted to meet God in His house, but because of my fear and sadness, I met Him where I felt most comfortable and closest to Him.

During this time, I delved into metaphysical subjects as a way to connect with my spiritual side. I started practicing divination by reading Tarot cards and Runes. I also began practicing my own form of ritual candle burning. These rituals combined Catholic prayers and novenas with aspects of Wiccan and Hoodoo magick (i.e., using appropriate candle colors, paying attention to lunar cycles, and using special anointing oils). I was always told that doing these things was dabbling with the occult. However, I felt closer to God and my spirit when I practiced them, so I never viewed it as "wrong." This was very healing for me, but I also realized that focusing on that work kept me from dealing directly with my spiritual struggle. I knew that doing these things could monopolize my time, so I would not have to face my fear of worshiping God in a church.

For three years, I spent a lot of free time reading for people, and performing candle ritual for myself and others. It made me feel good that I was able to help people. Then, one Sunday evening, I watched a rerun of the television show *Touched by an Angel.* I had never seen that episode before. It was about a gay man who was dying of AIDS. He went back home for Christmas to reconcile with his father. In the story, the father rejected him because he was gay. The angel, Monica, appeared and told the father that he needed to mend his relationship with his son. The father asked why an angel from God would ever support "queers." I will never forget how the angel answered that question.

She said that none of God's creation is queer. By the time the credits rolled, I was crying. I could not believe a television show could evoke such emotion in me, but this episode did. I cried for an hour after that. I kept asking God why my parents could not love me for who I was. Why was I destined to live such a miserable life?

After watching that episode, I felt the need to go to mass, even though I was still very afraid. I felt as if God was nudging at my soul. For a week, I tried to talk myself out of it, but by the following Sunday I went. I remember walking into the church, blessing myself with holy water. I took a deep breath and opened the doors. I walked nervously to the back pew, respectfully bowing before the crucifix before kneeling. My heart was beating fast. As I prayed to God to ease my fear, I could feel the peace that had eluded me for the past three years. I had an epiphany that Sunday. I believe God was really there, communicating to my spirit, reassuring me that He loved me and that my life was a gift, not destined to be miserable. I felt stronger in my faith than I ever had before in my life.

I made a vow that I would grow in my faith. My faith in God had been the only thing that kept me going at times in the past, and I was elated to have it back. I went to mass more often, and my comfort level about attending church grew.

I started to explore the possibility that my bisexuality and spirituality did not contradict each other. Since both of them were part of who I was, I wanted to be comfortable that both existed. I looked for websites online that dealt with gay, lesbian, bisexual, and transgendered people and Christianity.

I found the online news journal *Whosoever,* which dealt with these issues. I read stories about people who were Christian and still lived an "alternative" lifestyle. The name *Whosoever* came from verse John 3:16: "For God so loved the world that He gave His only begotten Son that WHOSOEVER believeth in Him, would not perish but have everlasting life."

I had never really noticed the word "whosoever" in that verse until that moment. I searched the site further and found a story written by the editor of the journal, Candace Chellew. It was called, "Coming Out to God." Her words were so poignant. One thing she wrote resonated in my mind. "That night I discovered that I may have turned my back on God, but He had never turned His back on me." I kept reading that sentence over and over again. I felt that God drew me to that website, the story, and her words. Nothing could have been more healing for me.

I realized then that He loved me for who I was, because I was part of His creation. My bisexuality was just another thread in the tapestry of my identity, and He decided to include that in me. I felt His unconditional love strongly again. I finally began accepting myself because I knew again that God loved and accepted me.

From that day forward, I have grown stronger in my faith. This faith has been tested in nearly insurmountable ways. I have passed and failed. Even though doubted, God remained steadfast.

In January 1999 I nearly died from complications from a routine appendectomy. I had a fever of 108 and a 75/50 blood pressure. I did not take the time to recuperate because of my financial situation. Two weeks out of surgery, I was back to work. I pushed my body to the limit, working as much as I could. I then took a "vacation" to Hawaii, a family reunion that was even more hellish than my graduation. I confronted aspects of my childhood I did not want to deal with, and it was excruciatingly painful. My fight-or-flight reaction kicked in, and I flew fast and free from the problem. I should have known by then that running only makes the situation worsen. I mentally broke down and was hospitalized. Thankfully, psychiatrists correctly diagnosed me as Bipolar I, rapid cycling.

I did some of the hardest work I have ever done in my life in the past eight months. I dealt with both physical and mental illness and the stigma that surrounds the latter. I cursed God, and I praised Him.

This struggle continues, and God proves Himself daily. When I do not want to get out of bed in the morning the sun is there to awaken me. When I am terrified to go to sleep at night, the moon and stars lull me. Hearing mass comforts me. The homilies are relevant, and seeing the number of devoted men and women reminds me that I am not alone.

I tell those who believe my fate is sealed about my certainty. I had only kept silent before because I was not secure in my relationship with God. Many fundamentalist Christians believe and communicate to me that I will go to hell because I love both men and women. They often quote verses such as Romans 1:26–27, as my mother had. When others charge in with fire and brimstone, I tell them that I never want to see my spirituality in the context of where I might spend eternity. I am living now. My focus is on how I can make my stay on earth the best it can be, on how I can become closer to God, and on cherishing the people that come into my life.

I also read that many biblical scholars believe that the homosexual activity referred to in the Bible is different from the modern gay, lesbian, and bisexual relationships of today. It no longer matters to me. The bottom line is that I love the people I am with, and "love" is the operative word. How can God see my loving people as wrong? Did God really support the bigotry and hatred that certain people felt toward people like me? I realize that loving people is something for which I cannot be condemned.

My faith is secure because it is tested daily. I hear mass without reservation or fear. I still practice divination and candle ritual for people, and I am on the road to becoming a practicing Catholic again. My bisexuality and spirituality are important parts of who I am, and they now peacefully coexist in my life. It took me five years, but now I can say with confidence that I have come full circle to sit comfortably atop this divinely sanctioned fence. Verses such as Romans 1:26–27, which used to haunt me, do not bother me anymore. I remind myself of John 3:16, the basic tenet of Christianity. "Whosoever" includes me.

As Emily Saliers of the Indigo Girls wrote: "A lesson learned, a loving God, and things in their own time. In nothing more do I trust."

My Proclivities: Buddhism, Bisexuality, Theory, Action

P. S. NELLHAUS

It's not enough that there are no differences among people. Rather, it's that the Buddha, while fully recognizing people's differences, does not discriminate among them. The Buddha respects people's individuality and desires that they may freely manifest their unique qualities. He is neither partial nor adverse towards people on account of their individual proclivities. The Buddha loves, rejoices at and tries to bring out each person's uniqueness; this is his compassion and his wisdom.[1]

BUDDHISM IS, FOR THOSE UNFAMILIAR, somewhat complex to explain. What has been called Buddhism within most of Western culture is not clearly defined or qualified. What is commonly called Buddhism is often Zen or Tibetan beliefs and practices or some kind of generic mishmash that makes no distinction between different sects (as opposed to bisexuality, which is sometimes looked upon as a mishmash of different sex).

What I call Buddhism is more formally known as the Buddhism of Nichiren Daishonin. Nichiren was a thirteenth-century Japanese priest who taught that all people, regardless of gender or status, could attain enlightenment by reciting the words *Nam-Myoho-Renge-Kyo,* the title of the Lotus Sutra. The formal part of the practice includes the repetitive chanting of *Nam-Myoho-Renge-Kyo* and reading aloud excerpts from the Lotus Sutra. *Nam-Myoho-Renge-Kyo* is defined as the law of simultaneous cause and effect through sound. Because of the importance of sound, one

[1] Daisaku Ikeda, in Daisaku Ikeda, Katsuiji Saito, Takanori Endo, Haruo Suda, "Dialogue on the Lotus Sutra," Part 12, *Seikyo Times,* Number 422 (SGI-USA; September 1996): 22.

chants aloud rather than silently reading or meditating as part of the formal practice. Why recite words in an archaic Asian language? This particular Buddhism proves its validity to those who chant, as we experience the movement toward manifesting a wiser, happier, and more fulfilled state of being. Studying the writings of Nichiren and Buddhist scholars, and sharing information about this Buddhism are also part of this practice.

Most practitioners of this particular form of Buddhism are members of a lay organization, SGI (Soka Gakkai International). The United States branch is known as SGI-USA. This organization, founded in Japan in 1930, literally translates as The Society for the Creation of Value. The current leader is Daisaku Ikeda, the third president of the SGI. Using the concept of mentor and disciple as the foundation, President Ikeda offers himself as an example of how to correctly present and manifest Buddhism. His role is to emphasize the correct practice of Buddhism. He is not an object of cultlike veneration. In fact, he publicly questions the motives of those who imitate him, especially for the wrong reasons. President Ikeda has provided me with the most clues to reconciling my identities of bisexuality and Buddhism.

> Because it is such a powerful force in the world today, the Western Judeo-Christian tradition is often accepted as the arbiter of natural behavior of humans. If Europeans and their descendant nations of North America accept something as normal, then anything different is seen as abnormal. Such a view ignores the great diversity of human existence.[2]

In the writings of Nichiren Daishonin, collectively known as *Goshos* (letters), there is nothing specifically referring to alternative sexuality. The couple of references to sex are in what could be termed a procreative context, essentially saying that sex, like any other human activity, is not separate from Buddhism. As Nichiren Daishonin wrote:

> Even during the physical union of man and woman, when one chants Nam-Myoho-Renge-Kyo, then earthly desires are enlightenment and the sufferings of birth and death are nirvana.[3]

The other *Gosho* reference to sex states:

> You may question how it is that the Buddha can reside within us when our

[2] Walter L. Williams, *The Spirit and the Flesh* (Boston: Beacon Press, 1986), 1.

[3] Nichiren Daishonin, "Earthly Desires Are Enlightenment," in *The Major Writings of Nichiren Daishonin, Volume 2* (Tokyo: Nichiren Shoshu International Center, 1981), 229.

> bodies, originating from our parents' sperm and blood are the source of the three poisons (greed, anger, and stupidity) and the seat of carnal desires.[4]

While at this time there is nothing available in the letters of Nichiren Daishonin that addresses sex beyond the two passages quoted, one can make some of these connections using other passages from the *Gosho*, parts of the Lotus Sutra, and the writings of President Ikeda.

First, I looked at ethical notions of sexuality, and I found that President Ikeda said:

> Desire cannot really be extinguished; it can either be suppressed from the conscious to the sub-conscious level of the psyche . . . or alternatively it can be oriented deliberately to objectives that are right for oneself and are good for one's fellow human beings and for the universe as a whole.[5]

I know that the only rules in Buddhism concern not slandering oneself, others, and the law of *Nam-Myoho-Renge-Kyo.* There are no strict prohibitions concerning behavior as may be found in other faiths. Instead of emphasizing sin and punishment, Buddhism is self-directed. From both what is said and what is left unsaid, I conclude that sex and sexuality are subject to one's individual needs and desires, and that what is important is that action be based on respect for oneself and for others. Ideally the goal of any relationship is of creating value.[6]

> Oranges are not the only fruit.
>
> —Nell Gwynne[7]

Next, I explored the question of whether Buddhism would consider bisexuality to be naturally occurring. In the Nichiren Buddhist view; "All phenomena are contained within one's life, down to the last particle of dust. The nine mountains and the eight seas are encompassed by one's body. . . ."[8]

If "all phenomena" encompasses variations in gender and sexuality, then it should be a given that there are people who embody these varia-

[4] Nichiren Daishonin, "New Year's Gosho," in *The Major Writings of Nichiren Daishonin, Volume 1* (Tokyo: Nichiren Shoshu International Center, 1979), 271–72.

[5] Arnold J. Toynbee and Daisaku Ikeda, *Choose Life: A Dialogue* (Oxford: Oxford University Press, 1976), 335.

[6] Win Hunter and John Delveno, "Sex, Sexuality and Gender," *UK Express,* no. 296 (SGI-UK, February 1996): 4–13. This groundbreaking essay gives the first overview in English from a Buddhist perspective.

[7] Jeanette Winterson, *Oranges Are Not the Only Fruit* (London: Pandora Press, 1985).

[8] Nichiren Daishonin, *Nichiren Daishonin Gosho Zenshu* (Tokyo: Soka Gakkai, 1952), 1473.

tions. And, if we believe that what occurs elsewhere in nature is also natural for humans, this principle is further reinforced. In his book *Biological Exuberance: Animal Homosexuality and Natural Diversity,* Bruce Bagemihl presents documented evidence that various forms of sexual behavior and expression assumed to be strictly human have reasonably similar equivalents among certain species of birds and mammals. This includes not only expressions of bisexuality or exclusive homosexuality but also forms of transgendered expression ranging from one gender having the physical appearance of another gender to the actual ability to change gender.[9]

While several species of animals display bisexual behavior in some form, the bonobo, an ape somewhat similar to the chimpanzee, has attracted the most attention. Only classified in 1929 as a separate ape species, and relatively unknown compared to the chimpanzee, the bonobo's DNA is 98 percent similar to human DNA.[10] If there is no separation between natural phenomena and Buddhism, using what is implied but not stated, this too validates bisexuality within a Buddhist perspective.

I then explored another principle of bisexuality . . . that gender and gender roles may be fluid, rather than fixed. I found support for this in President Ikeda's interpretation of the Vimalakirti Sutra.[11] At an assembly of disciples, a "goddess" appears spreading flowers from above. The flowers that do not land on the ground stick to the robes of the disciples. Shariputra (Foremost in Wisdom) and the other disciples attempt to remove the flowers from their robes based on the belief that the flowers are inappropriate for monks. Also, the "goddess," being a woman, is considered incapable of enlightenment according to earlier Buddhist teachings. As Shariputra can only conceive of men being enlightened, he challenges the "goddess" to change out of her female form because no enlightened being would choose to be a woman. The "goddess" uses her magic to change Shariputra into a woman, while she takes on Shariputra's form. She then quotes from Shakyamuni, the historical, first Buddha, "In the equality of all beings, there is neither man nor woman."[12] While not

[9] See Bruce Bagemihl, *Biological Exuberance—Animal Homosexuality and Natural Diversity* (New York: St. Martin's Press, 1999).

[10] Frans De Waal and Frans Lanting, *Bonobo—The Forgotten Ape* (Berkeley: University of California Press, 1997), 5.

[11] Lisa Jones, "Equality of All Beings," *World Tribune,* no. 3222 (SGI-USA, December 18 and 25, 1998): 2.

[12] Daisaku Ikeda, *Buddhism: The First Millennium* (New York: Kodansha International, 1977), 106–7.

specifically addressing bisexuality, what this story suggests is that gender and gender roles, even when codified in society, are viewed as transient from a Buddhist perspective. If they are transient, then why would sexual orientation toward one or the other be fixed?

The parable of the dragon girl is similar to the Vimalakirti Sutra. In that parable, the eight-year-old daughter of the Dragon King attained enlightenment immediately after hearing the Lotus Sutra. When some of Shakyamuni's disciples are still unconvinced, the dragon girl transforms herself into a man with the thirty-two features and eighty characteristics of a Buddha. This story tells us that one can become a Buddha regardless of gender, age, or (metaphorically) species; and that one can attain enlightenment quickly with the Lotus Sutra.

President Ikeda points out that because the dragon girl has already attained Buddhahood, her transformation to a man is an expedient means of convincing the other disciples of her enlightenment. He further explains: "The dragon girl has the form of an animal and naturally the world of Buddhahood is also inherent in the world of Animality. Her Buddhahood is invisible, however, to an eye that is colored by prejudice."[13]

In statements that could be alluding to bisexuality, President Ikeda also says of this parable: "From the standpoint of life's eternity, distinctions of male and female are not set in stone. Rather, we may be born as a man in one life, and as a woman in another. Moreover, all people have both male and female sides."[14] And, "In any society, certain qualities will be sought in men and in women according to the standards of that society. And the more closely people try to match those stereotypes, the more other traits within them will tend to be repressed."[15]

> Cherry, plum, peach or apricot blossom all, just as they are, are entities possessing their own unique qualities.[16]

How does Buddhist theory, which is indirect or open to interpretation, impact on how Buddhist organizations view bisexuality? To date, the organizational response has been on the broader issues that impact all lesbians, gays, bisexuals, and transgender peoples. SGI-USA has made a radical step by officially performing same-sex marriages based on the

[13] Daisaku Ikeda, Katsuji Saito, Takanori Endo, Haruo Suda, "Dialogue on the Lotus Sutra," Part 20, *Living Buddhism* 1, no. 7 (SGI-USA, July 1997): 36.

[14] Ibid., 45

[15] Ibid., 46.

[16] Nichiren Daishonin, *Nichiren Daishonin Gosho Senshu* (Tokyo: Soka Gakkai, 1952), 784.

traditional wedding ceremony. It is understood that there is no legal or civil weight to these ceremonies, but within the framework of Buddhism, all committed relationships and the people within them can be validated.

Beginning in 1998, members in San Francisco participated in the Pride Parade as an official SGI activity. In recent years SGI-USA has gotten more involved with community and civic activities, but this was the first time that members were involved with the GLBT community in a very public way as Buddhists. Before this march the organization had conducted AIDS-related fundraising events while keeping a distance from the GLBT community. Boston members marched in the 1999 parade.

That these activities are happening at all is due to the grassroots efforts of members who struggled to close the gap between theory and action expressed in the writings of Nichiren Daishonin and President Ikeda. Leadership from the lay membership of a Buddhist organization is not unusual.

The SGI membership may be making the most impact on the local level. In some larger cities, GLBT members meet, sometimes under formal auspices at their respective SGI centers, or at informal gatherings in a member's home. In 1996, when diversity was being discussed by organization leaders, members began to organize meetings based on that theme.

In Denver, I helped organize the first meeting in SGI-USA devoted to the theme of sexual diversity. The gay and lesbian planners fully supported making the presentation inclusive of bisexual and transgender issues. Some of the straight membership put up resistance and suggested having spokespersons only for the straight, gay, and lesbian points of view. We ultimately prevailed, and the meeting was fully inclusive. This was particularly important because there was a male-to-female transsexual member who felt she could no longer practice Buddhism with other Denver members.

On January 19, 1999, we presented, "Sexual Diversity from a Buddhist Perspective," featuring a gay man, a lesbian, a bisexual, and a transsexual, two Buddhists, two non-Buddhists. Over one hundred members and guests attended, more than some people had anticipated. More striking than the number of members there was that the top leaders of SGI in Denver, some of whom expressed reservations about the meeting in advance, also attended. The consensus was that we accomplished what was intended: to put a human face on sexual diversity.

In Buddhism, we speak of *shoten zenjin,* or those elements from the universe that appear to support us in some way. In organizing this presentation it seemed that *shoten zenjin* was operating.

On the more specific front of bisexual organizing, it has only been in the past few months that bisexual SGI members have begun connecting with each other through the internet. As with most bisexuals, there are differing degrees of being out to other SGI members, and of being part of the GLBT community. As we explore connecting with one another, I find that the practical intersection of Buddhism and bisexuality is in the concept of diversity. Bisexuality emphasizes diversity within diversity. The ideal we model to our lesbian, gay, and straight colleagues is an environment of mutual respect where people can express the full range of their complex identities. This goal is expressed by President Ikeda:

> It is a fact that the images of masculinity and femininity we have in our consciousness are deeply influenced by cultural traditions that have developed over a long period of time. And the influence of these traditions thoroughly pervades every aspect of the social ethos, including language, religion, systems of organization, education and scholarship. Therefore, it seems to me that the important thing is not that society come up with a particular model for how men and women ought to behave, but that people first and foremost make tenacious effort to live as decent human beings, and allow others to do the same.[17]

[17] Daisaku Ikeda, Katsuji Saito, Takanori Endo, Haruo Suda, "Dialogue on the Lotus Sutra," Part 20, *Living Buddhism* 1, no. 7 (SGI-USA, July 1997): 45.

The Goddess Blesses All Forms of Love

STARHAWK

Circle round, and I'll tell you a story about how the Maypole came to be . . . .

Once upon a time, a long time ago—or maybe in a time not yet come—there came a springtime when no flowers bloomed.

The plum trees and cherry trees showed no white or pink or red blossoms. No daffodils pushed up from the cold ground; no buds formed on the roses. No lilacs perfumed the air, and no poppies opened their bright petals to the wind. And the worst thing of all was that nobody seemed to notice.

Except for one young girl, named Vivian.

"Where are all the flowers?" Vivian asked everyone she met, and everyone looked at her strangely.

"Flowers? What flowers?" asked the woman who delivered their mail. "I don't have time to worry about flowers—I've got a route to cover."

"Maybe she means flour," said the man who ran the corner shop. "Maybe she wants to bake a cake."

"I've heard of flowers," said the woman at the library. "I know I've seen a reference to them somewhere."

"I've got a great computer game with flowers," said her brother. "Who needs to dig in the dirt when you can grow your own virtual garden?"

"Maybe she needs to go to bed early," said her mother. "Perhaps she is coming down with something."

"Doesn't anyone miss the flowers?" Vivian cried.

"She's confused," said her teacher. "We must be kind to her."

"She's ill," said the doctor. "We must cure her."

"She's loony!" said the other boys and girls, and they made fun of her until Vivian got so mad she ran out of her schoolyard into the deep woods.

She ran and ran until she couldn't run any more. She flung herself down in a patch of grass and began to cry.

"Nobody loves me!" she cried. "Nobody cares about the flowers! Nobody cares about me!"

"That's exactly how I feel," said a small voice by her ear. Vivian lifted her head and saw a tiny, scruffy, shabby little dandelion. Its petals were tattered, its stem was bent, and it looked like it might collapse at any moment. But it was the only flower she had seen all spring, and she was thrilled down to her toes.

"Oh, dandelion!" she cried. "I'm so happy to see you. You are so beautiful!"

"Not really," the dandelion said modestly, but it perked up.

"Why aren't there any flowers this spring? Why doesn't anybody miss them?" Vivian asked.

"Exactly," the dandelion said. "Nobody misses the flowers, so why should we bloom? Some kind of love has gone out of the world, and so the earth spirits are sick and the flowers have disappeared. But with the right kind of love, you can call them back again."

"What kind of love?" Vivian asked.

But the dandelion only said, "Do you really think I am beautiful? After all, I'm the most common of flowers."

"I think you are gorgeous!" Vivian said.

The dandelion sighed. "Then I can die happy!" It collapsed on the ground, and one by one its petals shriveled and faded.

"Poor flower!" Vivian mourned. "You really were beautiful!" But she sat up and dried her tears. For now she knew that if she could only find the right kind of love, she could bring the flowers back.

Vivian dried her eyes and went home.

"Oh, Vivian! I was so worried about you!" cried her mother.

"I was looking for you everywhere!" said her father.

"I was surfing the Web, trying to locate you," said her brother.

"Do you love me?" Vivian asked.

"Of course," said her parents.

"I guess," said her brother.

"Then help me bring the flowers back! Help me find the right kind of love."

Her parents shrugged and raised their eyebrows, but they followed Vivian down into the town. Her brother rolled his eyes, but he came, too.

"Vivian! Where did you go?" cried all the girls and boys.

"I went to find the flowers. And now I know that if we can find the right kind of love, we can bring them back!"

"Flowers, always flowers!" said one of the girls. "You've got flowers on the brain!"

"She's distressed," said the teacher. "We must be patient with her."

"She's disturbed," said the doctor. "We must humor her."

And so they let Vivian form them all into a circle in the center of town. They held hands and closed their eyes, but nothing happened.

"The circle isn't big enough," Vivian cried. "We need more kinds of love!"

"I'll go get my Uncle Donald and Uncle Rick!" cried one of the girls. "They love each other."

"Do you think their kind of love can bring the flowers back?" hooted one of the boys.

"We need all kinds of love," Vivian said. "We don't know what kind of love is the right kind of love."

"I'll go get my boyfriend!" cried the older sister of one of Vivian's friends.

"I'll get my mothers," said one of the boys. "They love each other, and they love me, too."

"I love my job," said the woman who carried the mail, stepping into the circle. "I love bringing letters to people."

"I love my neighborhood," said the grocer, taking her hand.

"I love the trees," said an old woman who lived in the woods.

"I love to read," said the librarian.

"I love my garden," said a tall man carrying a spade.

"I love my dog!" said a very small boy.

"Your dog!" All the children laughed. "You think your dog will bring back the flowers?"

"My dog loves me better than any of you!" the boy said, and he ran to get him.

The circle grew larger and larger.

"It's still not big enough!" Vivian cried.

"No circle of love can ever be big enough to hold all forms of love," she heard a voice say. Holding her hand was a beautiful woman, her hair crowned with all the flowers of spring, her eyes deep as wells and dancing with light like the sparkling surface of a laughing stream. Her face was old and young at the same time, and it seemed to change before Vivian's eyes. One moment she was dark as a velvet pansy, in the next she was pale as a white lily. She was young and fresh and smooth as a newly opened rose, and then ancient and wrinkled as a walnut.

"Who are you?" Vivian asked.

"I am the Goddess," the woman said. "The Queen of the May. You have called me back from the Otherworld with your circle of love."

"Then we did find the right kind of love after all!" Vivian cried joyfully.

The May Queen smiled. "There is no right kind of love," she said. "The Goddess blesses all forms of love. Whenever you join together in a circle with love and trust, you call me."

"Then how do we bring the flowers back?" Vivian asked.

"Here's what you must do," the May Queen said. She pointed to the center of the circle, where a tall pole stood. "My tree of life has become a dead stick—but you can bring it to life again. Make a circle of your arms, as if you were trying to hug the air." Vivian did, and found herself hugging a big silver ring. "That is my circle of rebirth—tie it to the top of the tree and set the pole in the ground." She tossed her head, and from her hair shining ribbons of a hundred colors fell to the ground. "And here are the ribbons of love. Tie each one to the ring of life—for each ribbon stands for a different kind of love, and without all of them, the circle is not whole.

"Here is the love parents have for children . . .

"And here is the love you have for your best friend . . .

"And here is the passionate love two women can have for each other . . .

"And here is the love you have for your grandparents . . .

"And here is the love you have for a pet . . .

"And here is the love and passion a woman and a man may have between them . . .

"And here is the love you have for a friend that you fought with and then made up with . . .

"And here is wild, devoted love between men . . .

"And here is the love you have for a really great teacher . . .

"And here is the love you have for your sisters and brothers . . .

"And here is the love you have for your sisters and brothers when they're driving you crazy . . .

"And here is the love you have for your aunties and uncles . . .

"And here is love for music and art . . .

"And here is the love that generates children and calls new souls . . .

"And here is the love people have for each other when they work hard together . . .

"And here is the love that generates new ideas . . .

"Take hold of my ribbons, dance around my tree, wrap the tree of life in love, and the flowers will bloom again."

And so the people built a Maypole and danced the Maypole dance all through the day. And as they danced, white and pink blossoms popped out on the plum trees and cherry trees. Daffodils pushed up from the ground, and buds formed on the roses. Lilacs perfumed the air, and poppies opened their bright petals to the wind.

When the dance was over, the May Queen gathered all the children close to her. "I must leave you now," she said, "but the flowers will remain in all their different shapes and scents and colors, to remind you to honor all forms of love. And because it was a child whose love brought me back, I will give you children three gifts: that many kinds of love will come to you, each in the right time; that you will be able to say yes to the love that is right for you; that you will be free to say no to the love that is not right for you. For while all love is blessed, only you can know what kinds of love are right for you. And now I must leave, but every year, when you dance the Maypole, I will be with you, whether you can see me or not. For in that way, I am just like love." And at that she disappeared.

But the flowers remained through the whole summer. And ever after, when the spring came, the people danced the Maypole with bright ribbons in honor of the flowers and all the colors of love.

Contributors

ELIZABETH ANDREW is a writer, teacher, and spiritual director living in Minneapolis. She earned her M.F.A. in creative writing from Hamline University and has published essays in *The Christian Century, Open Hands,* and *Re-Imagining,* as well as literary journals. She teaches classes on spiritual memoir and writing as a spiritual discipline at the Loft, a literary center in Minneapolis. For three years she lived in community at the ARC Retreat Center. She continues her work in retreat ministry at the Carondelet Center with the Sisters of St. Joseph in St. Paul.

GARY "BEAU" BOWEN is a Native American of mixed Creek Indian and Scotch-Irish descent. He is a traditional dancer, a bisexual transsexual man, and founder and coordinator-in-chief of the American Boyz organization for female-to-male transgender people (ftm) and their significant others, friends, families, and allies (soffas).

ELLEN TERRIS BRENNER was born in 1956 in New York City, the granddaughter of four Eastern European Jewish socialists. She earned a B.A. in psychology and social relations from Harvard/Radcliffe in 1979, and an M.Div. from Boston University School of Theology in 1989. Ordained a Unitarian Universalist minister in 1990, she served as a parish minister until she chose to resign in 1995. Ellen currently lives, plays, and writes in Seattle, Washington; her essays and short fiction have appeared in on-line and small-press venues, and she is at work on a novel.

SUSAN HALCOMB CRAIG is an out bisexual pastor in the Presbyterian Church (U.S.A.) serving a "More Light" congregation (which may call, ordain, install qualified gay, lesbian, bisexual persons to church office) on the

University of Southern California campus. She is an activist for justice causes and is writing her thesis for a Doctor of Ministry degree in bisexuality and spirituality.

KELLY M. CRESAP, PH.D., is a scholar, activist, and performance artist currently teaching drama and cultural studies at the University of Tennessee-Knoxville. He has written for *Seattle Gay News, Seattle Weekly,* the *Japan Times, Postmodern Culture,* and the anthology *The Queer Sixties.* He leads the bisexual support group of Asheville, North Carolina. His partner, Michael, has persuaded him, after years of abstinence, to try popcorn at the movies.

MARCIA DEIHL has been a musician, writer, and activist in the Cambridge area for twenty-five years. She played music in The New Harmony Sisterhood Band (1973–1980) and the Oxymorons (1987–1993). She co-edited *All Our Lives: A Women's Songbook* (Diana Press, 1976), co-wrote a chapter (with Robyn Ochs) in *Homophobia: How We All Pay the Price* (Beacon Press, 1992), and has contributed several music and theater reviews to *Sojourner: A Women's Forum.* Along with Robyn Ochs, she was a co-founder of the Boston Bisexual Women's Network (1983). Currently, she's a member of the Cambridge Lavender Alliance and a book reviewer for the *Harvard Review.*

LYNN DOBBS is a full-time social-justice activist. He and his partner founded Partners for Peace and in that name they create opportunities for furthering personal and social transformation. He is on the board of directors of the Lambda Letters Project, the Peace Resource Center of San Diego, and a volunteer with Project YANO (Youth and Non-military Opportunities). He is also an intern with the Human Awareness Institute.

GANAPATI SHIVANANDA DURGADAS is a fifty-one-year-old mystic and fringe-culture aficionado. He has a master's degree in psychology, concentrated in East/West psychotherapy and counseling. A former substance abuse counselor who is returning to community activism and organizing, he is a critic of the professional human services system for its continued virulent racism, sexism, and classism.

LAUREL DYKSTRA has lived in community most of her adult life. She is an itinerant biblical scholar and activist, currently living on the West Coast between the Tacoma, Vancouver, and Victoria Catholic Worker Communities. Laurel has studied biology, feminism, and theology and is currently working on some writing on Exodus, a feminist theological comic strip and the Campaign to Close the US Army School of the Americas. She supplements her lifestyle through the fine art of dumpster diving.

GRETA EHRIG's poetry and translations have appeared in *Southern Poetry Review, Delos,* and *Problem Child.* She was selected as a semifinalist in Louisiana Literature's 1999 Poetry Contest for "Owl Lover," a piece with bisexual spirituality themes. Her writing has been supported by the Lannan Foundation, the National League of American Pen Women, and American University, where she obtained an MFA in Creative Writing and edited *Folio* literary journal.

BARBARA GIBSON is a retired college teacher and mental health counselor, now devoting full time to writing and learning. She will receive her D.Min. degree from Matthew Fox's University of Creation Spirituality in the year 2000, which is also the year of her seventieth birthday. Her dissertation consists of several short plays written for her faith community, which is an alternative, interfaith congregation in Olympia, Washington. She has two daughters, two grandchildren, and a great-grandson.

AYAL HAUSFELD, creator the the jacket art, is an artist and graduate student in art therapy living in Washington, D.C.

MARY E. HUNT is a Catholic feminist theologian. She is the co-founder and co-director of the Women's Alliance for Theology, Ethics and Ritual (WATER) in Silver Spring, Maryland, a nonprofit educational center. She is an adjunct professor of women's studies at Georgetown University. Mary writes and lectures widely on ethical issues based on her social activism.

LORAINE HUTCHINS is a Washington, D.C., sex educator and sexual healer researching sacred sexual traditions in the United States today. She is co-editor of *Bi Any Other Name: Bisexual People Speak Out,* a book that helped to catalyze the bisexual movement. She starred in Betty Dodson's popular first video *Selfloving: Portrait of a Women's Sexuality Seminar,* along with nine other orgasming women. She has been a multi-issue activist and organizer for almost thirty years, co-founding AMBi, the Alliance of Multicultural Bisexuals, and BiNet USA: The National Bisexual Network in the early 1990s. Most recently she founded EroSpirit Sacred Sexualities Seminar series, a free, experiential public seminar series in Washington D.C.

RAVEN KALDERA is a minister of the newly forming neo-pagan Hearthgrove Church, a parent, a writer, a farmer, a shaman, an intersex FTM activist, and a troublemaker. 'Tis an ill wind that blows no minds.

DANNY KLOPOVIC lives in Melbourne, Australia, with his partner of five years, D J Paris, and their cat, Dylan. His passions are his partner; his friends; theological studies; social-justice, environmental, and peace activism; and chatting on the Internet.

DEBRA KOLODNY has been an activist in the faith and social-justice movements for over twenty years. She served two terms as a National Coordinator for BiNet USA, the National Bisexual Network, founded several local bisexual groups, published over a dozen articles and trained hundreds on bisexuality. She is currently the facilitator of the National Religious Leadership Roundtable and is one of many lay leaders in her *chavura* (independent Jewish community). Debra is a Jew who practices tai chi, a bisexual feminist partnered with a non-Jewish man, a professional consultant creating labor management partnerships, and a bisexual faith activist; her life and work serve as a bridge between worlds.

PASHTA MARYMOON is a witch, priestess, and founder of the Kairosean tradition of Wicca. She has been a practicing Quaker for twenty-five years and is a member of Subud (Indonesian spiritual practice) and a Wiccan lay minister in a metaphysical Christian church. She has an honors degree in world religions and is a graduate of the lay division of Unity (church) School of Metaphysics. Pashta has been active in several social-change movements and currently works as visiting clergy for prisons for the Temple of the Lady and is active in interfaith work. Pashta has been married twice, once to a man, once to a womyn, but is presently divorced and celibate by choice. She has two grown children and one grandson. She and her cat, Cerridwen, live in Victoria, B.C., Canada.

SHERRY MARTS is a feminist witch, ritualist, writer, healer, Reiki master, warrior woman, and aspiring sex radical with more than ten years of study and experience in feminist witchcraft, healing, and ritual. She has facilitated workshops and taught classes in sacred sex, Wiccan ritual, energy healing, and a variety of topics related to witchcraft and feminist spirituality. She is a Consecret in the Cella Training Program of the Women's Thealogical Institute of the Re-Formed Congregation of the Goddess-International. Her interests include exploring the mystery of "You are Goddess" through deep friendship, fabulous sex, and rock climbing.

P. S. NELLHAUS lives in Denver, Colorado, also known as the "Plain City of the Queens." While human objects of affection are subject to change, constant passions include cheesy horror films from the late 50s and early 60s, McDonald's cheeseburgers, and a fulfilling relationship with amazon.com. E-mail lensdarkly@yahoo.com for more information. Just don't expect a straight response.

SOROR OCHO has been studying, practicing, teaching, and writing on magick, mysticism, and spirituality since 1977. As a former member of the Ordo Templis Orientis (O.T.O), or the Order of the Temple of the East, she studied under the tutelage of internationally renowned British author and occultist Kenneth Grant. She has authored numerous books and articles on spirituality and is a practicing magickian and tantrica. She resides in the greater New York area, where she continues to explore her spirituality, sexuality, and the mysteries of the universe.

DIANE PASTA is a member of Salmon Bay Meeting of the Religious Society of Friends in Seattle, Washington. She divides her time between being a middle school math teacher and studying, writing, and speaking about faith. Her devotional writing emphasizes the practical integration of faith into busy lives, using queries to assist the reader in spiritual self-direction. Her family consists of a wife, a fifteen-year-old daughter, and four dogs.

ROBIN RENEE is a singer/songwriter who lives in New Brunswick, New Jersey. Her poetry has appeared in publications including *The New York Quarterly, OUT/LOOK, Northeast Corridor,* and *Inciting Desire.* She is the lead vocalist of the alternative pop band The Loved Ones. Their latest release is *15 Minutes with The Loved Ones,* on Hedgehog Records.

ROSEFIRE lives in a brick and stucco farmhouse in Michigan, with her husband, two children, and a dog. She is on the faculty of the University of Michigan and has published and won awards for both her technical and research articles as well as for her poetry.

GILLY ROSENTHOL is a World Wide Web designer in Somerville, Massachusetts. She is active in Keshet, the Jewish GLBT activist group; Kolot, the Jewish GLBT speakers bureau; and is on the board of SpeakOut, the speakers bureau on sexual orientation and gender identity issues.

CANYON SAM, a writer, performance artist, and activist from San Francisco, won acclaim across the United States and Canada for her first solo show, *THE DISSIDENT,* about her travels in China and Tibet and her human rights work with Tibetan nuns. She has performed at the Walker Art Center, the Asia Society, the Solo Mio festival, Highways, and Women in View, Vancouver. Ms. Sam's fiction and nonfiction appear in the *Shambhala Sun,* the

Seattle Review, and *Lesbian Love Stories.* Her forthcoming book is entitled *One Hundred Voices of Tara: Spiritual Journey Among Tibetan Women.*

ANN SCHRANZ was raised Missouri Synod Lutheran in Wisconsin. She has degrees in journalism and business administration. Ann identifies as a polyamorous bisexual and is a member of the Unitarian Universalist Church in Tampa, Florida. She is currently interested in explorations of the landscape of sexual desire as related to cultural and social evolution, in a transpersonal context.

CHERYL SORIANO is a "wanna-be" writer, living in the San Francisco Bay Area. She graduated from the University of California, San Diego, in 1993 with a B.A. in ethnic studies. Pursuing her graduate school education is a dream she will make a reality before she leaves this earthly plane. She earns her "filthy lucre" by being a technical writer in the Silicon Valley, a job she still believes is too grown-up for her.

STARHAWK, author of *The Spiral Dance, The Fifth Sacred Thing,* and *Walking to Mercury,* is one of the foremost voices of the women's spirituality movement. She lives with her husband, stepchildren, and Goddess children in San Francisco, where she works with the Reclaiming Collective.

ANGEL THREATT is a second-year student in the M.F.A. program in creative writing, fiction, at the University of Maryland. A lesbian-identified bisexual, she uses writing to heal and to transform images of self and of the communities of which she is a part. Her bisexuality is a part of a worldview that envisions people as spirit incarnated in socially gendered bodies. Her work has been published in *Early Embraces: True-Life Stories of Women Describing Their First Lesbian Experience,* edited by Lindsey Elder. She is at work on her first novel.

VALERIE TOBIN is a bisexual activist and writer. She has been working, studying and advocating within the field of women's health for several years and expects to be for many more.

AMANDA UDIS-KESSLER is a writer, musician, sociologist, and educator in the Boston area. Her essays on bisexuality, feminism, homophobia, and religion have appeared in more than ten books and a number of journals. Amanda is an award-winning hymn writer and composer, is currently working on a doctoral dissertation on the sociology of privilege, and hopes to get to seminary at some point. Of the many blessings in her life, she is currently most grateful for the presence and love of her fabulous partner, Phoebe Lostroh.

AURORA ROSE WOLF is a mental health professional and spirit medium who lives on the East Coast. She keeps herself grounded by involving herself deeply in political activism for two different causes. Living on the edge of the forest, she makes time daily to seek out and appreciate the spirits of nature. She plans to devote herself to metaphysical writing in the future.

Cover Art
by Ayal Hausfeld

The cover art is a product of a partnership between the artist and the editor, working to create an image that captures many of the themes of this book: yearning toward wholeness and balance, living in a both/and posture, finding the intersections of multiple paths, integrating body and spirit, and experiencing relationships and spirit beyond gender roles and identities. The four elements are represented: earth (the lotus), water (beneath the lotus), fire (the flame), and air (the tongues of flame above the primary image). Female, male, and androgynous imagery also appear: the gynocentric lotus, the phallic flame, and the androgynous figures in the flame. Finally, there is the intimation of ascension and of the connection between the earth and the heavens (immanence and transcendence) in the figures reaching skyward in the flames and also of the possibility for wholeness and integration among seemingly disconnected elements (flame and flower).